A CHILD'S DAY

Sociology of Children and Families series

Series editors: **Esther Dermott**, University of Bristol, UK and **Debbie Watson**, University of Huddersfield, UK

The Sociology of Children and Families monograph series brings together the latest international research on children, childhood and families and pushes forward theory in the sociology of childhood and family life. Books in the series cover major global issues affecting children and families.

Forthcoming in the series:

Black Mothers and Attachment Parenting
A Black Feminist Analysis of Intensive Mothering in Britain and Canada
Patricia Hamilton, November 2020

Out now in the series:

Social Research Matters
A Life in Family Social Science
Julia Brannen, Dec 2019

Designing Parental Leave Policy:
The Norway Model and the Changing Face of Fatherhood
Elin Kvande and **Berit Brandth**, July 2020

Sharing Care:
Equal and Primary Caregiver Fathers and Early Years Parenting
Paul Hodkinson and **Rachel Brooks**, July 2020

Find out more at

bristoluniversitypress.co.uk

A CHILD'S DAY

A Comprehensive Analysis of Change in Children's Time Use in the UK

Killian Mullan

BRISTOL
UNIVERSITY
PRESS

First published in Great Britain in 2022 by

Bristol University Press
University of Bristol
1-9 Old Park Hill
Bristol
BS2 8BB
UK
t: +44 (0)117 954 5940
e: bup-info@bristol.ac.uk

Details of international sales and distribution partners are available at bristoluniversitypress.co.uk

British Library Cataloguing in Publication Data
A catalogue record for this book is available from the British Library

ISBN 978-1-5292-0170-3 paperback
ISBN 978-1-5292-0169-7 hardcover
ISBN 978-1-5292-5292-7 ePub
ISBN 978-1-5292-5292-0 ePdf

The right of Killian Mullan to be identified as author of this work has been asserted by him in accordance with the Copyright, Designs and Patents Act 1988.

Cover design: blu inc, Bristol
Front cover image: 'Boy with stick at beach' Thomas Hawk / Stocksy

Contents

List of Figures and Tables   vi
Acknowledgements   xi

1   Introduction   1

2   Time for Education and Culture   27

3   Time for Health   59

4   Time for Family   87

5   Time for Technology   117

6   How Children Feel About How They Spend Time   145

7   Conclusion   165

References   179
Index   195

List of Figures and Tables

Figures

1.1 An overview of a child's day: average time in bed,   19
eating/personal care, education-related activities,
housework, paid work and free time on school and
non-school days in 1975, 2000 and 2015

2.1 The school day in 1975, 2000 and 2015   34

2.2 Average minutes children 8–16 years spend doing   36
homework on school and non-school days in 1975,
2000 and 2015: parental education and child gender

2.3 Average minutes children 8–16 years spend reading in   39
1975, 2000 and 2015: parental education
and gender

2.4 Average minutes children 8–16 years spend doing   41
homework, study or reading in 1975, 2000 and
2015: parental education and child gender

2.5 Association between parent and child reading in 1975,   44
2000 and 2015

2.6 Parental education and children's predicted monthly   47
participation in cultural activities

2.7 Association between parent and child participation in   50
cultural activities during the month in 2000 and 2015

3.1 Average minutes children 8–16 years spend in screen   65
time on school and non-school days in 1975, 2000
and 2015: parental education and child gender

3.2 Average minutes children 8–16 years spend doing sport   68
on school and non-school days in 1975, 2000 and
2015: parental education and child gender

3.3 Average minutes children 8–16 years spend in out-of-   71
home play on school and non-school days in 1975,
2000 and 2015: parental education and child gender

3.4 Average minutes in sport and out-of-home play 73
combined on school and non-school days in 1975,
2000 and 2015: children 8–11 and 12–16 years

3.5 Association between parent and child monthly 81
engagement in sporting activities

4.1 Average minutes children 8–16 years spend at home 93
with parents on school and non-school days in 1975,
2000 and 2015: parental education and child gender

4.2 Average minutes children 8–16 years spend at 94
home when parents are not home on school and
non-school days in 1975, 2000 and 2015: parental
education and child gender

4.3 Average minutes at home with mothers, fathers, both 95
parents and neither parent on school days and non-
school days in 1975, 2000 and 2015: children 8–11
and 12–16 years

4.4 Average minutes children 8–16 years spend at home 96
with mothers, fathers, both parents and neither parent
on school days and non-school days in 1975, 2000 and
2015 by mothers' employment status

4.5 Trends in screen time in context 99
4.6 Trends in homework, study and reading in context 102
4.7 Trends in domestic activities in context 104
4.8 Trends in total non-screen leisure in context 105
4.9 Average minutes children 8–16 years spend in shared 109
eating on school and non-school days in 1975, 2000
and 2015: maternal employment and parental education

4.10 Daily participation rate (%) in shared eating on school 110
and non-school days in 1975, 2000 and 2015: children
8–11 and 12–16 years

4.11 Average minutes children 8–16 years spend in shared 112
TV on school and non-school days in 1975, 2000 and
2015: maternal employment and parental education

5.1 Average minutes children 8–16 years spend watching 121
TV, using computers and playing video games on
school and non-school days in 2000 and 2015

5.2 Average minutes boys' and girls' spend watching TV, 122
using computers and playing video games on school
and non-school days in 2000 and 2015

5.3 Average screen time incorporating time using devices 127
for boys and girls 8–16 years on school and non-school
days in 2015

5.4   Boys' and girls' average time using a device and not   128
       using a device when doing different activities outside
       school on school and non-school days in 2015
5.5   Average minutes co-present with parents, others   134
       (siblings/friends) and alone when at the same location
       as parents on school and non-school days in 2000 and
       2015: children 8–11 and 12–16 years
5.6   Proportion of time spent with parents, others (siblings/   137
       friends) and alone not using a device and using a
       device in 2015 on school days and non-school days:
       children 8–11 and 12–16 years
5.7   Average minutes parents are using devices when they   138
       are near their children and children's reports of whom
       they are co-present with, on school and non-school
       days in 2015
6.1   Distribution of relative levels of enjoyment for different   150
       activities: children 8–16 years in 2015
6.2   Distribution of relative levels of enjoyment for different   154
       modes of travel: children 8–16 years in 2015
6.3   Enjoyment of activities in different social contexts   155
6.4   Enjoyment of time in different activities when using   157
       and not using a device

Tables

2.1   Average minutes in homework and study on school and   35
       non-school days in 1975, 2000 and 2015: children 8–11
       and 12–16 years
2.2   Average minutes reading on school and non-school days   38
       in 1975, 2000 and 2015: children 8–11 and 12–16 years
2.3   Percentage of children 8–16 years with a parent who   43
       reads on a diary day in 1975, 2000 and 2015 in families
       where parents have compulsory only or post-
       compulsory education
2.4   Children's monthly participation in different cultural   46
       activities in 2000 and 2015: children 8–11 and 12–16 years
2.5   Percentage of children 8–16 years whose parents   48
       participate in different cultural activities in 2000 and
       2015 in families where parents have compulsory only or
       post-compulsory education

2.6	Association between children's monthly engagement in cultural activities and daily time in reading and homework in 2000 and 2015	52
2.7	Association between parent monthly engagement in cultural activities and children's daily time in reading and homework in 2000 and 2015	52
3.1	Average minutes screen time on school and non-school days in 1975, 2000 and 2015: children 8–11 and 12–16 years	64
3.2	Average minutes spent doing sport and exercise on school and non-school days in 1975, 2000 and 2015: children 8–11 and 12–16 years	67
3.3	Average minutes in out-of-home play on school and non-school days in 1975, 2000 and 2015: children 8–11 and 12–16 years	70
3.4	Average minutes in different modes of travel on school and non-school days in 2000 and 2015: children 8–11 and 12–16 years	74
3.5	Distribution of the number of times children 8–16 years engage in different sporting activities: boys and girls in 2000 and 2015	76
3.6	Association between monthly engagement in sport and daily average minutes in sport, screen time, non-screen leisure and active travel: boys and girls in 2000 and 2015	78
3.7	The number of times parents engage in different sporting activities: 2000 and 2015	79
3.8	Association between mothers' and fathers' monthly engagement in sport and children's average minutes in sport, screen time and non-screen leisure: boys and girls in 2000 and 2015	82
4.1	Average minutes at home with and without parents on school and non-school days in 1975, 2000 and 2015: children 8–11 and 12–16 years	91
4.2	Trends in screen time in context: parental education	100
4.3	Trends in screen time in context: maternal employment	101
4.4	Trends in homework and reading in context: parental education	102
4.5	Trends in homework and reading in context: maternal employment	103
4.6	Average minutes in shared eating on school and non-school days in 1975, 2000 and 2015: children 8–11 and 12–16 years	107

4.7	Average minutes shared TV on school and non-school days in 1975, 2000 and 2015: children 8–11 and 12–16 years	111
5.1	Children's access to computers and the internet at home in 2000 and 2015: child age and parental education	118
5.2	Children's access to tablets, smartphones and mobile phones on school and non-school days in 2015: children 8–11 and 12–16 years	119
5.3	Average minutes using devices (smartphones, tablets, computers) on school and non-school days in 2015: children 8–11 and 12–16 years	124
5.4	Average minutes screen time when not using a device, using a device and other time using a device on school and non-school days in 2015: children 8–11 and 12–16 years	126
5.5	Association between monthly engagement in sport and daily average minutes in screen time with and without devices, other time using devices and total time using devices: boys and girls in 2015	130
5.6	Average minutes at the same location as parents on school and non-school days in 2000 and 2015: children 8–11 and 12–16 years	132
5.7	Average minutes with others (siblings/friends) and alone when not at the same location as parents or at school, on school and non-school days in 2000 and 2015: children 8–11 and 12–16 years	134
5.8	Average minutes using devices with parents, others (siblings/friends) and alone on school and non-school days in 2015: children 8–11 and 12–16 years	136
5.9	Average minutes using device during time in parent-child shared activities on school and non-school days in 2015	140
6.1	Association between feeling rushed and time in homework, screen time, non-screen leisure and work activities in 2000 and 2015	160

Acknowledgements

Most of the work on this book was completed when I worked at the Centre for Time Use Research (then at the University of Oxford). I am deeply grateful to Jonathan Gershuny and Oriel Sullivan for supporting me in getting this book off the ground, and for giving me the time to work on it. I would like also to thank Sandra Hofferth and Series Editors Esther Dermott and Debbie Watson for providing me with thoughtful and encouraging comments on an earlier draft of the manuscript, which certainly helped to improve the book. Thanks finally to Victoria Pittman and Shannon Kneis at Policy Press/Bristol University Press for patiently (and persistently) walking me through the process of publishing this book.

1

Introduction

In response to an earlier research paper of mine analysing change in children's time use in the UK (Mullan, 2019), which bore the same title as this book, the following tweet was posted on the social media platform Twitter:[1]

> In case you needed convincing. "A child's day: trends" "between 1975 and 2015 children increased their time at home, and spent more time in screen-based activities and doing homework."

Most of the tweet is a direct quote from the paper's abstract, but the first five words struck me immediately as going to the very heart of something I was tackling in my research on change in children's time use. Take the example of homework. Few would argue that children are not spending more time doing homework today than in previous decades, but in the course of my research I could find no published data or research that showed clearly that children's time doing homework had increased in the UK. In fact, there was scarcely data at all on the time children in the UK spent doing homework. To take another example, it has surely reached the status of truism to state that children today spend less time playing outdoors than in the past. There is comparatively more evidence to support this, but it would fail to meet standards applied to any serious question about adult time use. Mayer Hillman and colleagues' famous study of change in children's independent mobility has a good claim to have had a deep influence in supporting the view that children's time outdoors decreased from the 1970s onwards (Hillman et al, 1990). This study, however, makes no direct reference to any measure of how much time children spend outdoors. In fact, they are explicit in stating, for example, that there exists no survey evidence 'about the amount of time children spend playing in the streets'. (Hillman et al, 1990: 78) The key indicators they use to infer change in the time children spend outdoors are *licences* granted to children, such as being allowed to come home from school alone or go to places other than school alone. The authors conclude that the increases they found in restrictions placed on children's independent mobility 'suggests that the geographical scope of [children's] play territory has been much reduced, along with the amount of unsupervised time they spend outside the home'. (Hillman et al, 1990: 78) While most likely broadly correct it is nonetheless the case that this research, along with the few other limited studies available, provides little more than a vague assertion about change in this key aspect of children's time use.

Empirical research may produce results that overturn widely held convictions about some social question or issue, or shift thinking in completely new directions. It could easily be said that this is the raison d'être of any research. Yet the issue here is that many of the basic convictions widely held about changes in children's time use are broadly correct. Does it matter then that the evidence base is so limited if the conclusions are correct? Does this mean that there is little call for further research into changes in children's time use? This book stands as a testament to my view that this is not the case. I do not seek here to address questions around how commonplace understandings about change in children's time use come to be secured, and I do not suggest that quantitative survey data are the only valid sources of knowledge about the social world. I do argue, however, that what we know about change in children's daily time use is incredibly stunted because of the sparse evidence base. Beyond relatively vague free-floating assertions about children spending more or less time in this or that activity, we do not have good answers to numerous further questions. By how much actually has children's time in any given activity changed? Do any changes found apply for all children, or vary by factors such as age, gender, or socio-economic status? Is change concentrated in particular periods or is it persistent over time? How do supposed changes in children's time use intersect with structural features of time use, such as time in school or parents' time in paid work? What are the relationships between children's time in different activities, and how does change in any one activity intersect with time in other activities that fit together to form a child's day? And how does change in children's time use connect with changes in time use in the wider family setting, including in relation to parents' time use? In approaching this book, I ask readers in effect to *de*-convince themselves of what they know about change in children's time use. In many cases no doubt, you will arrive back where you started but hopefully with a richer understanding of the many contingencies attached to change in children's daily lives and perhaps encountering some surprises along the way.

Childhood scholars in the social sciences have mapped out a number of distinct research terrains emphasising different aspects of children and childhood in society (James et al, 1998), two of which are of particular relevance to this study. The first is referred to as the 'structural' perspective on children in society and draws attention to children as a permanent group in society. This perspective has examined changes in children's roles in society, through changes in their time spent in paid work and education, as well as calling for more data on, and from, children as a group in society. The second theoretical perspective focuses on the social construction of childhood and seeks to highlight children's active role in this process, often through analysis of children's everyday lives drawing directly on children as informants. This book adds to our understanding of children as a fixed social group in society through studying change in their daily time use patterns using data from nationally representative time use surveys, collected from children themselves at different points in time (1975, 2000, 2015). The data provide information about the different activities that children engage in throughout the day, which are deeply integrated with processes of social construction. Although this book does not examine directly processes of social construction, studying changing patterns of time use for different groups of children (for example, based on age and gender) can inform us about change and stability in one of the key foundations for social constructions of childhood. Children's time use, moreover, can act as a link between everyday processes of social construction and the structural perspective on children as a permanent but changing group in our society.

In the remainder of this introduction, I first trace out some of the major strands of social change thought to have had an impact on different areas of children's daily time use. The relationship between children's time use and outcomes relating to their health, development, and well-being is considered in a critical discussion drawing together strands of thought from the sociology of childhood and research on child well-being. The data, measures and methods of the empirical analysis are then set out, followed by a first outline of change in a child's day over four decades between 1975 and 2015. The introduction finishes with an overview of the content of the rest of the book.

Children's time use in a changing society

The past several decades have witnessed rapid social, economic, and technological change, widely thought to have affected many aspects of children's daily lives. Technological change potentially has had the most direct impact on children's lives, and certainly has garnered the most attention, through changes affecting screen-based activities. In 1975, TV was the only screen that children paid any attention to, but it was competing with an array of videogame consoles and personal computers for children's attention by the turn of the millennium. Since then, gathering pace from around 2010 onwards, the widespread diffusion of powerful mobile devices combined with enhanced internet connections has reshaped the ways we consume various media, shop, learn, and interact with others. Children's access to and use of the internet and mobile devices has attracted much attention, with some arguing that their daily lives are now excessively oriented toward screen-based activities and life online (for example, Palmer, 2007).

Technological change is not the only factor potentially influencing children's daily lives in this respect, however. There is a longstanding sense that children's local environments have become increasingly unsafe for them to play in or spend time outdoors (Hillman et al, 1990; Valentine, 1997). Some have gone so far as to suggest that there has developed in our society over the past several decades a culture of fear and paranoia surrounding children's safety that is disproportionate to the level of risk children face in daily life (Furedi, 2002; Furedi, 2005). Public reactions to parents who seemingly ignore social norms around child safety give some indication of the strength of this culture. Note, for example, the critical response when the columnist Lenore Skenazy wrote that she let her 9-year-old son ride the New York subway alone and was subsequently dubbed 'America's worst mom' (Skenazy, 2009). Although this is a single case, amplified through social media, it is indicative of a generalised concern for children's safety that arguably has had a direct impact on children's daily lives in reducing the time they spend outdoors, away from direct parental supervision, with a shift towards spending more time indoors or in structured activities like organised sport.

Education is a further major domain in children's lives where there has been persistent change over many decades. The economic crises of the mid-1970s heralded the emergence and subsequent entrenchment of neoliberal economic and social policies. These developments affected children most directly through changes in education consistently viewed by successive governments as needing radical reform, with an emphasis on raising 'standards' and increasing educational attainment (Chitty, 2009). As success in education has become more important for more children, for employment and related outcomes, children are under increasing pressure to devote time to succeed in education (Ennew, 1994; Prout, 2005).

Taken together, there is a prevailing sense that children are increasingly spending more time in screen-based activities and online, more time indoors and in organised or structured leisure activities, and more time devoted to activities associated with their education. The extent to which this is in fact the case is one of the principal questions running throughout this book, which presents the results of a major study of change in how children in the UK spend time across a range of daily activities spanning four decades from the mid-1970s up to 2015. Understanding more about how children's time use has changed can tell us much about the extent to which changes in our society may have altered children's daily lives over the past four decades.

Children are not, however, a homogenous group in our society and time use varies depending on factors such as age, gender and socio-economic status. Therefore, as well as looking at overall change in children's time use, the book examines differences in trends associated with these key characteristics. Age has a profound, though changeable, influence on how children spend their time (James and Prout, 1997). This ranges from laws in our society governing the ages at which children must be in school and determining how much time children can spend in paid work, to social norms about what is appropriate or suitable for children at different ages with respect to the time they spend in different activities. There are questions about, for example, how old a child should be before it is appropriate for them to supervise younger siblings, or the appropriate age for a child to own or use a mobile phone. Over time, social norms around the age-appropriateness of time spent in different activities are subject to change. It is possible to observe this through studying changes in the extent to which age is associated with time in other activities, as well as changes in the social dimensions of time use such as time spent with parents or away from parents. Throughout, this book analyses the relationship between children's time use and age, investigating the extent to which there has been change in this relationship over time and revealing that in many areas of time use children's age has become less salient.

Gender also exerts a strong influence on children's time use (Maudlin and Meeks, 1990), and this book closely examines gender differences in children's time use over the past four decades. There is some basis to suppose that gender may have become less salient in shaping how children spend their time. Social norms and attitudes surrounding gender equality are changing, with more traditional views around gender, such as thinking that 'a woman's job is to look after the home', becoming less prevalent over time (Taylor and Scott, 2018). Whether this is consequential for the daily lives and time use patterns of children is an open question, however. Gender essentialism in education and employment stubbornly persists, and women still confront profound inequality in the division of labour and related areas (England, 2010). Time use is a core mode through which gender roles are learned and enacted (Oakley, 2015), and this book will show throughout that gender differences in how children spend time have persisted over many decades, even widening in some areas.

Turning to children's socio-economic background, over the period we are studying the general standard of living has increased with steadily declining rates of absolute poverty (McGuinness, 2018). However, in tandem, society has become more unequal over the past several decades (Cribb et al, 2018), and many argue that the influence of children's socio-economic background has become more pronounced during this period against this backdrop of increasing income inequality (McLanahan, 2004; Richards et al, 2016; Putnam, 2015). It is well established (typically with reference to parental education) that there are significant differences in children's time use associated with socio-economic background in activities such as homework and reading (Bianchi and Robinson, 1997; Mullan, 2010), screen-based activities (Hofferth, 2010), and extracurricular activities (Lareau, 2003). The analysis presented here suggests that differences in children's time use associated with socio-economic background (based on parental education level) are persistent and in some cases widening.

Through the use of nationally representative data, collected at three points in time spanning four decades (1975, 2000, 2015), provided by children themselves, this book emphasises children's status as a fixed group in our society, whose daily lives are impacted by long-term social trends and thereby fits within a structural perspective on childhood (Qvortrup, 2011). Prior research from this perspective has drawn attention to long-term changes in the status and contribution of children to society, identifying a long-term shift whereby children have moved from spending a significant amount of time in paid work to spending a substantial amount of time in formal schooling, the so-called 'scholarisation' of childhood (Qvortrup, 2012). This area in the sociology of childhood, however, has had an overly narrow focus on the macro-economic contribution of children to the continuance society, with limited empirical research stemming from it. Empirical interest in changes in how children spend their time, however, need not be restricted to time allocated to paid work or education. Broadly understood as having a focus on studying children as a permanent group in society, and with an interest in how social change affects children's daily lives, there is considerable potential for further research in this area of the sociology of childhood; this book represents a major effort in this regard. In moving forward, however, it is important to recognise that children are not merely passively reacting to 'external' changes in society; they play an active part in constructing their social worlds in an ever-changing society. This is brought more clearly into view in the next section through a consideration of children's time use in relation to their health and well-being.

Children's time use and 'outcomes'

Changing patterns of time use may not warrant much concern or interest on their own but for the fact that how children spend their time very often sits at the centre of explanations for worsening trends in certain outcomes relating to children's health and well-being. There is a strong intuitive basis for this. We would reasonably expect that children who spend plenty of time in physical activity and exercise would have generally good health, and that children who devote time to activities like homework and reading will tend to benefit in terms of improved educational outcomes. Conversely, rising levels of being overweight and of obesity among children are commonly associated with their spending too much time in sedentary screen-based activities, with the view in some quarters that worsening mental health outcomes are in part associated with children spending too much time online (Palmer, 2007).

This book will highlight numerous studies linking different aspects of children's time use to various outcomes relating to their health, development, and well-being. It does not, however, set out to argue that studying children's time use is worthwhile only to the extent that this may link, positively or negatively, to future outcomes. To do so risks lapsing into an unsustainable, though still deeply engrained, perspective that sees childhood primarily as a time of life spent getting ready for adulthood. This perspective runs through different branches of the social sciences, perhaps seen most starkly in relation to the time children spend in activities devoted to their education. In economics, for example, the time children devote to their education is theorised as an investment in human capital, which children accumulate over time, and from which they in later years yield a return in the form of employment and income (Becker, 1993). In sociology, the classical view of education is that it serves primarily to further socialise children, beyond the family, thereby enabling them to function 'normally' as adults in society (Durkheim, 1961). At the extreme, children here are empty vessels or blank slates, passively formed and informed through processes of learning and socialisation to become fully functioning (adult) members of society.

Childhood sociologists have been at the forefront in challenging this conventional perspective of children and children's present lives. They refute the view of childhood as time spent preparing (effectively waiting) for adulthood – of children as somehow being incomplete, unfinished, or a work in progress – emphasising rather that children are complete human *beings* and not simply human *becomings*, and that they are active creative agents fully involved in their daily lives and social worlds (James et al, 1998). Emerging from this has been a proliferation of studies probing the everyday lives and social worlds of children, without reference to their futures, where the voices and perspectives of children themselves have priority (for example, Mayall, 1994; Holloway and Valentine, 2000; Mayall, 2002; Hedegaard et al, 2012; Thompson et al, 2018). Reflecting the importance of children's time use as a basis for social construction, this research typically takes children's time use as a starting or entry point for probing further into processes of social construction.

Empirical studies of children's everyday lives have employed various methods to collect information about how children spend time. Alanen's (2001) study of the daily lives of children in a town in central Finland collected '*inventories*' containing information about their daily activities, the people they were with, and their reflections on the purpose and personal significance of time in different activities. Christensen and James (2001), in a study of children's time at school in Northern England, asked children to draw '*My Week*' charts, visually documenting how much time they spent in different activities during the week (see also Christensen and James, 2000). Other studies have drawn data on children's time use from detailed interviews with children (Mayall, 2002), participant observation (Hedegaard, 2012), video ethnography (Aronsson, 2012), mobile phone diaries (Plowman and Stevenson, 2012), and 'day in the life of' approaches describing the sequence of children's activities and interactions throughout an entire day (Katz, 2004; Thompson et al, 2018).

These varied approaches to collecting data on how children spend time provide a rich source of information about the daily lives and interactions of children, but they generally ignore or abstract from

time as a measurable quantity. The focus rather is on trying to understand more about children's daily lives as they occur *in* time, where
quantitative measures of time use place emphasis on daily life as being
composed *of* time (Adam, 1994; Gershuny, 2000). The study of
children's daily lives *in* time, or 'time *in* childhood' (James and Prout,
1997: 231), foregrounds the qualitative dimensions of time and daily
life, addressing various questions about children's experiences of
time in different activities and as a structuring constraint, and about
children's negotiations with parents and others about how they spend
time. This body of research on children's everyday lives demonstrates
clearly how children engage critically and creatively in constructing
their daily lives and social worlds (James and Prout, 1997). A second
way in which questions about time enter discussions about childhood
is through references to it as a period of time. Here, in what James
and Prout (1997: 230) refer to as the 'time *of* childhood', emphasis is
placed on the social construction of the ageing process. Yet this time
of childhood, seen at the level of the everyday lives of children, also
connects with questions concerning how much time children spend
in different activities throughout each day.

A separate strand of research also centred on the present lives of
children, and which has to some extent incorporated quantitative
measures of children's time use, relates to efforts to measure and monitor
child well-being. Child well-being is multi-dimensional, captured in
both objective and subjective indicators across a number of present-
life domains such as health, happiness, safety and security. Concerns
about child well-being came to national prominence in the early 2000s
following the publication of international data on subjective well-being
revealing that children in the United Kingdom (UK) compared particularly badly with children in other developed economies (UNICEF,
2007). This hit a nerve. At a national level, the UK had ratified the
United Nations Convention on the Rights of the Child in 1991,
thus committing to protecting the rights and well-being of children.
Stemming from this, the role of Children's Commissioner for England[2]
was established in 2004 to serve as an advocate for children's rights and
well-being. The proposition then, that the well-being of children in
the UK was substantially worse than in comparable countries (possibly even the worst), sparked a national debate stimulating efforts to
monitor and improve child well-being (Bradshaw et al, 2016; Layard
and Dunn, 2009; The Children's Society, 2013), and the UK now
publishes national statistics on child well-being (ONS, 2014a).

The emergence of child well-being as a national concern has brought
renewed attention to child outcomes, but at the same time this concern

emphasises the status of children as a permanent structural component of our society. Work in this area has gone some distance to broach the gap between public displays of concern about children's well-being and the availability of public data relating to children (Qvortrup, 1997). It has achieved this in part by extending our understanding of an outcome to include both future and contemporaneous indicators of child well-being, with children's time use representing a key contemporaneous indicator (Ben-Arieh and Frønes, 2011). Children's time use thus has featured in studies of child well-being both as a distinct well-being domain (The Children's Society, 2013; Keung, 2016), and as indicators of a specific well-being domain such as health, education, or subjective well-being (ONS, 2014a). While welcoming the inclusion of children's time use into studies of child well-being, a risk remains, with a focus solely on 'outcomes' even if contemporaneous, that only those areas of children's time use deemed to offer a clear indicator of a defined area of well-being are considered at the expense of a comprehensive survey of a child's day. Such a survey would encompass the full range of different activities children spend time in, explore the relationships between these varied activities comprising a child's day, and examine features of the daily social context in which these activities occur.

Taking the connection between time use and well-being as a starting point, the study of change in children's time use presented in this book is organised into themes touching on different aspects of child well-being. Chapters 2 and 3 address areas of time use linked to education and health, two major domains of children's well-being. These chapters examine change over time in how long children spend in key activities such as screen use and sport (health), and homework and reading (education), and study the extent and nature of correlations between activities within these distinct areas of child well-being. Going further, these chapters explore change and stability in the relationship between child and parent time in key activities in these domains, addressing questions about the manner and extent to which parents may influence children's time use. Chapter 4 studies children's daily time use connected to family, in particular change in the time children spend with and away from parents and change in time in shared activities with parents. This chapter treats family as a major element of the social context of daily life, shaping the character of time spent in daily activities. Chapter 5 looks at children's time use in connection with technology. Technology is not usually construed as a distinct area of well-being, nor an outcome as such, and there is a case to be made that technology could be incorporated into areas of well-being already covered (such as health and family). Given the prominence of technology in debates about child well-being, however, it merits separate attention, although the chapter also addresses connections to related themes through analysis of the relationship between time using technology and children's activities and the social contexts of time use. In this sense, this book views children's use of technology, not unlike their relationship with family, as a composing layer of the context of their daily lives. Chapter 6 takes up the theme of subjective well-being, addressing subjective dimensions of time use including enjoyment of time and experiences of time pressure.

This study does not test for causal links between children's time use and particular outcomes. As will be highlighted at various points throughout this book, there is a wealth of research showing robust correlations between children's time use and outcomes relating to the health, development, and well-being. Very few studies however, have sought, or been able, to identify any direct causal links. This is in no small part an empirical problem, but a cause/effect model where time use (the cause) is logically prior to an outcome (effect) may not be appropriate when using time use data collected on a single day. There are, moreover, critical theoretical difficulties with the view that children's time use is primarily worth studying only in connection with future outcomes. Research in child well-being has effectively reconfigured the problem of the relationship between time use and outcomes into one of measurement. Here, child well-being is defined conceptually across various domains, and indicators linked to these domains are identified. Children's time use features in studies of child well-being both in connection with specific outcomes (such as physical activity and health), and as a key domain of well-being itself. In both cases, children's time use is not of interest only because of possible links to future outcomes, but because it is informative in connection with children's contemporaneous well-*being*. Drawing on both approaches, this book treats children's time use as a complete and distinct area of their present lives and studies change in children's time use organised along major themes connected to child well-being. Each of these themes touches on different areas of children's time use that, taken together, make up a child's day.

This book goes further than previous research looking at children's time use in connection with well-being in several key respects. First, it is the most comprehensive study of change in children's time use encompassing a range of different activities connected to each theme. Second, relationships between time in different activities, particularly in education, health and technology, are examined. In this way, the book situates trends in children's time in specific activities within the general context of time they spend in other activities through the day, thereby building up a more complete picture of change in children's daily time use. Third, in addition to studying children's activities, the book foregrounds the family and social context within which children spend time. Specifically, the book examines trends in children's time with parents, with others, and time spent alone, when at home and at other locations. It furthermore looks at changes in the relationship between parents' time use and children's time use, particularly in areas relating to education, health and technology.

The analysis varies across chapters in accordance with the types of measures analysed and the data available (a detailed outline of the content of the book is provided later in this introduction). Across most chapters, however, three broad questions are addressed. The first is, simply, how has children's time use changed? This incorporates analysis of change in activities, change in the social context of time use, change in shared activities with parents, and change in time related to using technology. Trends over all children and for children in key sub-groups, such as age, gender and socio-economic background, are considered throughout. The second broad question posed is: what is the relationship between different elements of children's time use? Here the analysis examines associations between activities within the areas of education and health, and it studies the overlap between children's activities and the social context of daily life, and their time using technology. Finally, the third broad question addressed is: what is the relationship between parents' and children's time use? This includes studying the relationship between parents' and children's time in the same activities (as in the chapters on health and education) as well as studying the influence of the presence of parents on children's time use in the chapter on the family.

Capturing daily life: measuring time use

There are numerous ways to collect information about how much time we spend in different activities throughout the day. The simplest, and often most feasible, approach is to ask people to recall how much time they spent in a given activity. For example, to measure time watching TV we might ask questions in a survey like the following:

- How much time did you spend watching TV yesterday?
- How much time do you usually spend watching TV on a typical weekday/school day or weekend/non-school day?

Responses to these questions yield recall-based measures of time use (watching TV in this example). Respondents may be allowed to freely give an answer in hours and minutes, or they might be asked to select from a pre-coded list of duration ranges (for example, none, up to one hour, 1–2 hours, 3–4 hours, and so on). Responses to these types of questions are often the main source of information we have about children's time in different activities. The problem with these types of questions is that our ability to recall accurately how much time we spend in different activities may not be very reliable, and responses may be vulnerable to a social desirability bias (Robinson, 1985; Gershuny, 2000). These problems are exacerbated when, which sometimes occurs, parents are asked to recall how much time their children spend in different activities (Lauricella et al, 2016).

A further limitation of recall-based measures of time use is that it is not possible to combine responses to questions about different activities in order to build up a picture of daily life that reliably captures time spent in various different activities throughout the day. Broad activity groups such as screen time and physical activity are each composed of time spent in many different activities. For example, screen time includes watching TV, using computers or playing video games, and physical activity comprises time spent in sport, active travel and play, among other activities. Constructing a full picture of patterns in children's daily activities over time requires understanding trends in the various components within broad activity classifications. It is also vital to be able to make valid comparisons of trends in time spent across different activity domains relating to children's education, health, and well-being.

Time use surveys are a superior method for collecting reliable data about how we spend our time throughout the day (further detail about the surveys used in this study is provided in the following section). Time use surveys do not ask respondents directly about how much time they spend in different activities. Respondents instead provide information in a time diary about the full sequence of activities they engaged in throughout the day, which is less subject to recall bias. Time use surveys, therefore, collect information about all the activities a person engages in throughout the day, allowing for a comprehensive analysis of time spent in a range of different activities. The diary format, moreover, emphasises the timing and sequence of activities throughout the day rather than the duration of time spent in activities, thereby guarding against social desirability bias. The total time in any activity is then computed by summing the durations for all episodes of that activity recorded in the diary throughout the day. Measures of children's time use constructed in this way form the core of the analysis in this book.

Another common way of measuring the extent to which children engage in certain activities is to ask them whether and how often they do so. For example, we can ask children whether over the past week/month/year they did any sporting activity, and if so the number of times they engaged in sporting activities during a specified time period (typically a week or a month). These are not strictly time use measures, though they are commonly used to support statements concerning children's time use. Although a poor substitute for measures of daily time use in many activities, they are useful when studying children's engagement in activities that occur relatively infrequently, such as visiting museums or art galleries. The analysis at certain points in the book draws on information about children's participation in cultural and sporting activities over a period of one month to supplement data on children's time in related activities during the day.

The data

This book uses data from three nationally representative time use surveys carried out in 1974–5, 2000–01, and 2014–15. The British Broadcasting Corporation (BBC) Audience Research Department carried out the earliest survey in the mid-1970s. The Office for National Statistics (ONS) carried out the 2000–01 survey, and Jonathan Gershuny and Oriel Sullivan of the Centre for Time Use Research conducted the latest survey in collaboration with the National Centre for Social Research. Each of these surveys obtained representative samples of the population of UK residential households using a multi-stage cluster stratified sample design. The 1974–5 BBC survey did not sample from Northern Ireland.

At the core of a time use survey is a time diary instrument used by respondents to provide details about their time use throughout the day. Typically (and this is the case for all three surveys used in this book) respondents complete the time diary by reporting in their own words the sequence of main activities they engaged in throughout the day. In addition, they can include information about any other secondary activity they engaged in, such as listening to music while travelling. Giving respondents the option to report any secondary activity is preferable, as this does not force them to omit one activity when they are engaging in two activities simultaneously. Data on secondary activities were not collected consistently across the three surveys used here, as only information about media use (TV and radio) was collected in the earlier survey. This book therefore concentrates on children's time in primary activities, covering time in a broad range of activities making up a child's day.

The UK Time Use Surveys in 2000–01 and 2014–15 used an almost identical activity code frame based on Harmonised European Time Use Survey (HETUS) guidelines (Eurostat, 2009), specifically designed to ensure comparability of time-use measures both across countries and over time. Therefore, the basic harmonisation task involved converting the activity code frame in the BBC 1974–5 survey to correspond with the HETUS activity codes. The BBC code frame is simpler than the HETUS code frame. For example, the BBC code frame contains a single code for 'sport', where the HETUS code frame contains specific codes for different types of sport. Therefore, detailed codes in the later surveys are collapsed into broader activity categories to be comparable with activity codes in the BBC survey.

In addition to information about daily activities, respondents may provide information about the wider context, namely where the activity occurred (location) and who else was present during the activity (co-presence). In this respect the latter two surveys (2000–01 and 2014–15) differ substantially from the earliest survey (1974–5) which collected limited information about location (activity occurred at home or elsewhere) and no co-presence information. The time diaries in later UK surveys collected more detailed information about the respondent's location and mode of travel, and about time respondents were with family members including parents, others they know, and time when they were alone. This information, along with information about children's activities, is used to construct a rich set of measures of children's time use combining data on children's activities with data on the social context of those activities. As well as using information provided by children, time use data provided by parents are used to construct measures of parents' time use referenced at different points throughout the book.

In the 1974–5 survey, respondents completed a diary for seven consecutive days, and respondents in the later surveys completed a diary for one weekday and one weekend day within the same seven-day period. The later surveys collected diaries throughout the year, whereas the 1974–5 survey collected data in February, August and September, which provides a reasonable coverage of days across seasons. The unit of analysis is referred to technically as a *person-day* reflecting the fact that the surveys sample both individuals and days. The analysis in this book focuses on time use by children aged 8–16 years and includes at certain points analysis of data from their parents. Data were used from around 3,100 children providing just under 8,000 diary days (person-days). Although it would be possible to include older adolescents (aged 17–19 years) living at home, there have been substantial changes in both post–16 education and the transitions young people make from education to work over the past several decades which would require careful attention and take the book in a substantially different direction.

The statistical analysis

The results presented in this book come from a series of multivariate regression models where the outcomes of interest are measures of different areas of children's daily time use. Most of these measures relate to the different activities that children engage in (for example, screen time, homework, sport), but measures relating to the social context of daily life (such as time at home and time with parents) are also analysed. Multivariate regression analysis is used to estimate change in different measures of time use in 2000 and 2015 compared with the reference year of 1975, together with post-hoc tests to compare differences in time use between 2000 and 2015. Differences in trends associated with factors such as child age groups (8–11 years and 12–16 years), gender (female/male) and family socio-economic background are estimated by including interactions between survey year and the relevant factor. Descriptive results are reported in tables and graphs throughout the book in the form of predicted average minutes in activities derived from these regression models along with estimates of 95% confidence intervals (CI).

The influence of socio-economic background on children's time use forms a major component of the analysis in this book. There are a number of closely related ways of capturing information about children's socio-economic background, including using parental education, social class or family income. The analysis in this book utilises information about parental education, as there are some critical limitations in the data available in the surveys on income and social class. Unfortunately, there is no measure of income in the BBC 1975 survey, and income variables in later surveys suffer from relatively high levels of non-response. Income matters for children's lives and well-being (Cooper and Stewart, 2017), but has not featured heavily in research on children's time use. Given the lack of comparable data on income across all surveys, data on income are not included in the analysis.

Income aside, there are several different measures of social class in the three surveys, but it is unlikely that these are comparable over time. In the BBC 1975 survey there is a variable called 'Family Occupational Status' (FOC) corresponding to the head of household on a five-point scale (A, B, C1, C2, D) with a further category for unemployed (E).[3] This appears similar to the Register General Social

Class (RGSC), widely used as the standard measure of social class up to the 1980s, but it is not clear from the survey documentation whether the FOC and RGSC measures are validly comparable. The later surveys contain information about the National Statistics Socio-Economic Classification (NS-SEC) for adults in employment, which is the current standard occupation-based measure of social class for the UK. Although it is possible to convert this measure into the older RGSC measure of social class, with some loss of information, there is no certainty that this is comparable with the FOC measure in the BBC 1975 survey. A further issue with social class measures in all surveys is that they relate only to those who are in employment (and in the earlier survey only to the head of household who was in most cases a man). Using these measures effectively excludes children with no parent in paid work from the analysis, which will disproportionately affect children in lone-mother families.

This leaves education as a key indicator of socio-economic background about which there is information in all surveys for all parents irrespective of employment status. Educational attainment by parents has increased dramatically, adding some complications in terms of comparing measures of education over time. In the mid-1970s, very few parents would have held a degree, but this has increased dramatically following the expansion in higher education of the past several decades. As parents increasingly obtain higher education qualifications, the composition of this group may change, possibly affecting the validity of comparisons over time.

The approach taken in this book uses information about the age parents left full-time education and adjusts for increases over time in modal age of leaving full-time education. In the mid-1970s, most parents finished full-time education at age 16 years, increasing to age 17 around 2000 and to age 18 by 2015. The official age marking the end of compulsory schooling for parents did not change over this period (set at 16 years from the mid-1970s onwards), but the expansion in further and higher education effectively shifted the age of leaving full-time education upwards. It is worth noting in connection with this that, from 2008, young people aged 16–18 years who were not in full-time employment, must be in full-time education or training, effectively formalising the modal age for leaving full-time education that had emerged.

The empirical analysis thus differentiates between households where at least one parent remained in school beyond compulsory education, as defined here in relation to the modal age of leaving full-time education, and those where neither parent remained in school beyond compulsory education (that is, both parents have compulsory schooling only). Information about mothers' and fathers' education is therefore combined and is supplemented with information from the later surveys (2000 and 2015) about the highest qualification parents received to account for the acquisition of tertiary qualifications by parents later in life. There is no information about qualifications in the BBC 1975 survey. There is no completely satisfactory measure of socio-economic background and the approach adopted in this book is far from perfect. It has the advantage, however, of drawing on information about school-leaving age that is comparable across time and which gives equal weight to information from mothers and fathers.

The multivariate analysis furthermore controls for maternal employment, whether the child lives in a lone-mother or two-parent household, the number of children aged 0–17 years in the household, and the age of the youngest child in the household. Long-term demographic shifts have altered the composition of children's families, with more children living in smaller families with fewer siblings, and more children growing up in lone-parent (primarily lone-mother) families (ONS, 2009; ONS 2016), and more children living in dual-earner households (ONS, 2015). Finally, in addition to these factors, at various points the book studies connections between child and parent time use by including information about parents' time use in the regression models. Details of this will be set out in the relevant sections of the book.

A first overview of a child's day

Each chapter of this book focuses on a different area of children's daily time use relating to themes including education, health, and family (an outline of the content of the book is set out in the subsequent section). In advance of that, Figure 1.1 shows, for school and non-school days, the average time children spent in bed,[4] in personal activities (eating and personal care), in education-related activities (school and study), doing housework, paid work, and their total free time (which is mostly leisure activities) in 1975, 2000 and 2015. Time in these activities together comprises the entire 1,440 minutes of a single day.

As shown in Figure 1.1, children aged 8–16 years spent on average 581 minutes (9.7 hours) in bed on school days in 1975. This decreased slightly by 6 minutes in 2000 and by a further 2 minutes in 2015, and these small changes were not statistically significant. Children aged 8–16 years spend more time in bed on non-school days, and this increased by 14 minutes between 1975 and 2000 and by around

Figure 1.1: An overview of a child's day: average time in bed, eating/ personal care, education-related activities, housework, paid work and free time on school and non-school days in 1975, 2000 and 2015

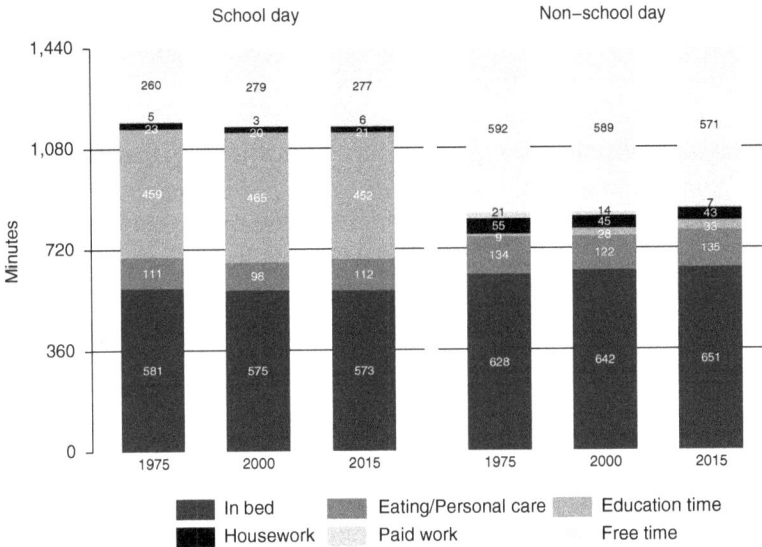

School day   Non–school day

Minutes

1,440

260   279   277

5   3   6
23   20   21

592   589   571

1,080

459   465   452

21   14   7
55   45   43
9   28   33
134   122   135

720

111   98   112

360

581   575   573

628   642   651

0

1975   2000   2015   1975   2000   2015

In bed   Eating/Personal care   Education time
Housework   Paid work   Free time

23 minutes between 1975 and 2015, in both cases significantly. This increase in time in bed is perhaps surprising given results from a large body of research showing that time in screen-based activities, which has increased over the study period (see Chapter 3), is negatively associated with sleep time (for reviews see Cain and Gradisar, 2010; Hale and Guan, 2015). Yet this increase among children aged 8–16 years in the UK mirrors increases found among adults over the same period, counteracting a common narrative that adults are spending less time sleeping (Lamote de Grignon Pérez et al, 2018).

Children aged 8–16 years spent less time in personal activities in 2000 than in 1975, on both school and non-school days. Note that this change was concentrated in personal care activities as there was no change in time eating. This decrease in time in personal care activities between 1975 and 2000 may be connected to increases in showering over the past several decades, which is generally considered a quicker, more time efficient, way of washing oneself than taking baths (Hand et al, 2005). Yet this change reversed following an increase in time in personal care activities between 2000 and 2015, with children now spending a similar amount of time in personal care in 2015 and in 1975. Although practices in relation to showering and bathing have not much changed since 2000, social standards and conventions relating to personal care and appearance are far from static (Shove, 2003). The emergence of social media, which children routinely use to post images of themselves ('selfies'), has increased pressures on children in relation to their appearance (Fardouly and Vartanian, 2016), which might explain the increase in time children spend in personal care activities between 2000 and 2015. Unfortunately, the coding of this particular activity is ambiguous, and there is no information on the different motivations for spending time in this activity; this book does not pursue this question further.

Time in education-related activities (predominantly time at school) consumes much of the school day. As shown in Figure 1.1, children spend around 7.5 hours in education-related activities with very little change in this over time. Not surprisingly, time in education-related activities is much lower on non-school days, but there has been a substantial increase in this time between 1975 and both 2000 and 2015. The following chapter delves further into this time looking at changes in time at school and time doing homework and study on both school and non-school days.

The time children spend in education-related activities is only one component of the time they dedicated to non-leisure activities. Two further work-related parts of a child's day are time they spend doing housework and paid work (Mayall, 1994). Children aged 8–16 years in the UK spend more time in the former than the latter across all years. They spent around 20 minutes per day doing housework on school days and this has not changed over four decades between 1975 and 2015. On non-school days, their time doing housework is greater, but it decreased by just over 10 minutes between 1975 and 2000. Chapter 4 looks further at children's time in housework.

Time use data can also inform us about children's engagement in paid work. There are no official statistics on children's labour force participation, but studies show that children in the UK do engage in paid work (Morrow, 1994; Jones, 2002). Information about time in paid work reported by children in time diaries in 1975, 2000, and 2015, reveals that close to 13 per cent of children aged 8–16 years spent some time in paid work in 1975, which decreased to around 8 per cent in both 2000 and 2015. It is not surprising, therefore, to observe that the average time children spend in paid work is relatively low and that it is decreasing over time particularly on non-school days (see Figure 1.1). This trend over the past several decades is arguably the extreme tail end of a much longer-term transition by children, noted earlier, away from spending time in paid work towards spending more time focused on education (Qvortrup, 2012).

Children spend a substantial remainder of their day in 'free' time activities comprised mostly of leisure time. Total free time increased slightly between 1975 and 2000 on school days rising from 260 minutes in 1975 to 279 minutes in 2000, with little change between 2000 and 2015. There was little change in total free time between 1975 and 2000 on non-school days, but free time decreased by close to 20 minutes between 2000 and 2015, offset primarily by increases in time in bed and in personal care. Much of the remainder of this book is devoted to a detailed analysis of change in children free time, an outline of which is now set out.

Outline of the book

This book is organised across five chapters each focusing on a specific theme relating to different aspects of a child's day, starting in Chapter 2 with an examination of trends in children's time in education-related activities. The chapter begins by outlining major changes in education over the past several decades, charting trends in children's attainment, and exploring the extent to which these changes have influenced how children spend their time in activities associated with education over four decades between 1975 and 2015. The analysis starts with an overview of children's time at school in 1975, 2000 and 2015, showing that there has been very little change in the total time children spend at school. Trends in the time children spend in activities linked to education, such as doing homework and personal study, are then presented. As well as looking at overall trends, the analysis unpacks differences in time in these activities between girls and boys and between children with parents who have different levels of education. Socio-economic and gender differences in school attainment have persisted over time alongside increasing attainment for all children. Whether these inequalities reverberate in the amount of time children devote to their education outside school is a major subject of the analysis in this chapter.

The time children spend reading, and participating in cultural activities, may also impact on their education through the acquisition of cultural capital. According to ideas developed by Pierre Bourdieu (Bourdieu, 2010 [1984]), engagement with cultural activities such as reading and visiting galleries helps to develop cultural capital, which in turn is valued and rewarded in formal education and ultimately deployed to maintain/contest positions within and across different fields of activity. Therefore, in addition to the analysis of trends in homework and study, Chapter 2 studies trends in children's time reading and their participation in a wide range of cultural activities, such as going to galleries and museums or the cinema and sporting events. Middle-class parents typically possess relatively high levels of cultural capital, evidenced in their relatively higher qualification and participation in different cultural practices, which may in turn help sustain socio-economic differences in educational outcomes for children. Although this book does not consider educational outcomes directly, Chapter 2 investigates the relationship between children's engagement in cultural activities and both parental education and parents' engagement in those same activities.

Chapter 3 takes up the analysis of children's time use relating to their health. Concerns about the prevalence of obesity and being overweight among children, and associated health problems, have drawn attention to questions around whether children are spending too much time in sedentary screen-based activities on the one hand and not enough time in active physical activities on the other. Technological change has greatly enhanced the capacity for children to spend time in a wide variety of screen-based activities, and persistent concerns about children's safety outdoors have led to increasing restrictions on the time children spend outside. These factors have likely coalesced over recent decades, resulting in children leading lives that are less active and spent indoors focused on screens. The widespread view is that this is indeed the case. Considering the evidence for this, Chapter 3 analyses long-term trends in screen time (comprised of time watching TV, using computers and playing video games) alongside trends in physical activities such as sport and exercise, play outside the home, and active travel (walking and cycling).

Broadly, the analysis in Chapter 3 confirms that children are spending more time in screen-based activities but with certain qualifications. They are also spending less time in play outside the home and less time in active travel. Time in sport and exercise increased up to 2000 but remained unchanged thereafter. This suggests that time in relatively informal physical activity is declining, which has only partially been replaced by time in relatively more structured time in sport and exercise. The results hint that there might be a degree of substitution between screen time and certain types of physical activity. Chapter 3 probes further into this question through an innovative analysis of the relationship between children's engagement in sporting activities and their daily time use using data on children's monthly engagement in sporting activities (from the 2000 and 2015 surveys only); it reveals a negative relationship between engagement in sporting activities and daily screen time, but only among boys. Placing children's engagement in sporting activities in the wider family context, Chapter 3 ends by bringing into view parents' participation in sporting activities captured in the later surveys (2000 and 2015), studying the relationship between this and children's monthly engagement in sport and daily time use patterns, including screen time.

Chapter 4 marks a departure from the previous two chapters by focusing less on what children are doing and more on whom they are with, particularly on the time they spend with their parents. Chapter 3 referred to a rising concern for children's safety in society over the past several decades, showing that children were spending more time in screen-based activities (as well as increases in homework and study noted in Chapter 2), and less time in activities outside the home (play and active travel). Chapter 4 foregrounds information about the time children spend at home in order to study trends in the time children aged 8–16 years in the UK spend at home, both with and without their parents, over four decades between 1975 and 2015. Overall trends in the time children are at home with and without parents are disaggregated by child age and gender, and parental education. Associations between mothers' employment and children's time with mothers and fathers between 1975 and 2015 are also examined, providing a new perspective on changes in the gender division of labour from the perspective of children aged 8–16 years in terms of the time they spend with mothers and fathers.

Combining information on children's daily activities with information on the social context of children's time use, Chapter 4 delves further into the analysis of trends in children's activities in context. The objective here is to make explicit the link between activities and the family context and to highlight how changes in activity patterns intertwine with changes in *where* children spend time and *with whom* they spend time. It demonstrates clearly how trends in screen time overlap with trends in spending more time at home, primarily when with parents. As well as screen time, Chapter 4 examines overlapping trends in social context and in children's time in non-screen leisure, housework and shopping, and homework and reading. Combining data on activities and social context also sheds further light on the influence of factors such as parental education and mother's employment on children's daily activities. Lastly, this chapter on the family sets out, for the first time, the results of a study of change over four decades between 1975 and 2015 in the time children and parents spend in shared activities. The analysis here focuses on shared time eating and watching TV at home, which are the most common shared activities and the most straightforwardly comparable across the study period, and again explores changing associations between time in these shared family activities and children's age and gender, parental education and maternal employment.

The influence of technological change has featured heavily in the background to the analysis of trends in children's activities linked to health (in Chapter 3), and changes in the social context of children's daily activities (in Chapter 4). Chapter 5 brings children's time using technology to the centre of the analysis. Given the focus on relatively recent technological change (from 2000 onwards), this chapter focuses on data in the two later UK Time Use Surveys (2000–01 and 2014–15). The chapter begins, by way of introduction, with an overview of change between 2000 and 2015 in children's access to different computers, the internet, and mobile devices. It then revisits trends in screen-based activities, differentiating between time watching TV, using computers, and playing video games. Following this, using the data collected in 2015 only about the time children spend using devices (smartphones, tablets, or computers) irrespective of what their main activity is, we examine the total time children spend using devices throughout the day. The chapter then merges information about children's time in screen-based activities (when this is their main activity) with information about the time children spend using devices to construct and analyse a broader, perhaps more comprehensive, measure of screen time.

The second major section of Chapter 5 focuses on the intersection of time using devices and time spent with others such as family and friends or time alone. Building directly on the analysis of children's time at home with and without parents, this chapter brings in additional information about who children report being co-present with in the later surveys (2000 and 2015), incorporating time at home and at other locations. It examines change in the time children spend with parents, with others they know (siblings, friends), and time they spend alone between 2000 and 2015, when they report being at the same location as their parents and during time when they are away from their parents. It then brings together information about children's time using devices and social context to examine the distribution of time using devices across different social contexts. As well as studying children's time using devices, Chapter 5 also examines the time parents spend using devices thereby providing key insights on time using devices in the wider family context.

Attention turns in Chapter 6 to the subjective dimensions of children's experience of time use. Subjective well-being is a major element of children's overall well-being concerning, among other things, children's general happiness with life or happiness in relation to specific life domains, including time use. Research on the subjective experience of time use, on *feelings* about time use, is an emerging interest in the study of time use. Although there is a growing literature on this topic in relation to adults, we know little about children's subjective experience of time use. Recent developments in the measurement of the subjective experience of time spent in different activities argue that it is best to assess this as far as possible *during* time in those activities rather than retrospectively. In the latest UK Time Use Survey respondents could indicate how much they enjoyed spending time in different activities throughout the day. With this novel data, Chapter 6 presents an analysis of how much children enjoy their time use; it covers their activities, how much they enjoy different modes of travel, and their enjoyment of time in different social contexts such as time with parents, others they know, and time alone. This chapter also examines the rarely studied experience of time pressure among children, presenting new data for children in the UK and looking at the relationship between time pressure among children and time use patterns.

Notes

[1] https://twitter.com/Greg_Mannion/status/986689783740157959
[2] Other countries in the UK have each also established a Children's Commissioner.
[3] The BBC 1975 survey also contains a three-point measure of social class (A, B, C) based on the interviewers' perceptions.
[4] Strictly, this is a measure of time in bed including time children are either sleeping or awake.

Time for Education and Culture

Doing well in school has become increasingly important in shaping the pathways children can take through further and higher education, onto outcomes linked to employment and earnings. At the mid-point of the 20th century, only a relatively small proportion of children progressed from compulsory education onto higher education, and these were pre-dominantly from more advantaged families (Smith, 2000). Many young people finished compulsory schooling with few or no qualifications and joined the labour force, with limited opportunities to pursue fur-ther education and training. The economic shocks of the early 1970s led to high rates of youth unemployment, and eventually to a major restructuring of the economy away from manufacturing towards a service-dominated, knowledge-based economy. In response to these shifts, successive governments have sought to extend participation in further and higher education, and increase educational attainment at all levels (Machin and Vignoles, 2006).

As Smith (2000) remarks, by the turn of the 20th century examinations at age 16 no longer marked the end of education, but a ticket for admission into the next stage. And, as continuing in educa-tion beyond age 16 has become the norm, more children in secondary school have been taking final exams in more subjects, obtaining ever higher levels of educational attainment. The proportion leaving school with no qualifications steadily declined over the decades leading up to 2000 (Smith, 2000). In England, 44.5 per cent of pupils obtained A★-C grades in five or more GCSEs in 1995/6. This increased to 50 per cent in 2000/01, 70 per cent in 2008/09, and reached 82 per cent in 2012/13.[1] There are similar trends in other parts of the UK. In Northern Ireland, for example, 61 per cent of pupils achieved A★-C grades five or more GSCEs in 2004/05, rising to 83 per cent in 2014/2015.[2]

The increasingly intense focus on success in education in recent years has affected children in primary schools too. Children in primary schools throughout the UK must now take national tests for numeracy and literacy, and the teaching and learning in primary schools are increasingly oriented towards attaining high scores on these tests. This is a relatively recent development. In the mid-1970s, most children in the UK progressed through primary school into secondary school without any formal testing. The widely discredited 11+ exam, which children took at the end of primary school to determine selection into more academically oriented grammar schools or more practically focused secondary modern schools, was phased out in most parts of the UK by the mid-1970s with the majority of children attending non-selective comprehensive schools.

Although testing in primary school to determine selection into secondary education is still not widespread in the UK, it has become the norm for children to be subject to repeated testing and continual assessment in order to measure attainment and monitor progress throughout primary school. Attainment in primary schools, as measured at Key Stage 2 at around age 11, has been rising too. Looking at the results for mathematics, 67 per cent of pupils in England achieved Level 4 or above in 1997, rising to 83 per cent in 2006 and 89 per cent in 2015.[3] Other parts of the UK reporting these figures[4] show a similar trend over the past several years. In Wales for example, again in mathematics, 79 per cent of pupils attained Level 4 or above at Key Stage 2 in 2006, rising to 90 per cent in 2015.[5]

The most dominant area of children's time use linked to education is the time they spend in school. Outside school, however, children can engage in a number of other activities that might support positive outcomes in education. The first of these, and most obvious, is time doing homework and study outside school. Research shows a small positive link between the time children spend doing homework and educational outcomes for older secondary school pupils, but with little clear effect on attainment in primary school (Sharp et al, 2001; Cooper et al, 2006). Nevertheless, there can be little doubt that homework is widely seen as an essential component of children's education throughout school. Indeed, as part of a concerted move to involve parents in helping to raise children's school attainment in the late 1990s, the New Labour government set recommendations for the amount of time children should spend doing homework (DfEE, 1998).

Despite supposed interest in the time children spend doing homework and study, remarkably little is actually known about precisely how much time children spend in these activities daily and how this has changed. Increases in children's time in homework are expected given the increased importance of education for children's outcomes, but data on children's daily homework time in the UK are extremely limited (see Weston, 1999). Mullis et al (2004; 2015), using recall-based measures, report that the proportion of children aged 13–14 years in England engaging in maths homework for around 1–3 hours per week fell from 37 per cent in 2003 to 26 per cent in 2015 (a similar decrease was found for science homework). However, no previous study has presented reliable data on long-term trends in children's time in homework across all subjects. Addressing this directly, against a backdrop of rising school attainment over the past several decades, this chapter studies trends in children's time doing homework between 1975 and 2015, differentiating between those in primary school (8–11 years) and those in secondary school (12–16 years).

As well as examining overall trends in children's time doing homework and study, this chapter analyses differences in trends associated with parental education to explore the extent to which trends in time doing homework and study reflect socio-economic differences in educational outcomes. Despite increasing levels of school attainment, children from lower socio-economic backgrounds overall persistently obtain fewer qualifications from school than those from relatively more advantaged families. For example, a substantially lower proportion of pupils in England eligible for free school meals, a well-established marker of socio-economic disadvantage, obtained five or more GCSE grades A★-C in any subject between 2005 and 2014.[6] Grade C or higher in English and mathematics is a minimum standard for entry for many further and higher education courses and the socio-economic attainment gap is higher and most persistent when results for these subjects are included in the data. Education departments in Scotland,[7] Wales,[8] and Northern Ireland[9] report comparable socio-economic gaps in secondary school attainment.

The renewed onus on testing and assessment in primary school has revealed how socio-economic differences in attainment emerge early. In Wales for example, 64.1 per cent of children eligible for free school meals achieved the expected level in Key Stage 2 maths (according to teacher assessment) compared with 84 per cent for children not eligible for free school meals. The corresponding figures for 2014 were 77.3 per cent and 91.8 per cent respectively.[10] In England in 2015, two thirds of children eligible for free school meals achieved Level 4 or above in tests for reading, writing and mathematics combined, compared with 82.7 per cent of children not eligible for free school meals.[11] Northern Ireland reports similar, though narrower, gaps at Key Stage 2 based on measures of disadvantage at the school level.[12]

Echoing socio-economic disparities in school attainment, children in higher socio-economic groups spend more time doing homework and study. Middle-class families in both the US and the UK have been shown to prioritise children's engagement in homework and study (Devine, 2004), and time-use research shows that children in families with highly educated parents spend more time studying than those with parents with lower education (Bianchi and Robinson, 1997; Hofferth and Sandberg, 2001; Mullan, 2019). This chapter examines differences in children's time doing homework and study associated with parental education over three decades between 1975 and 2015. The chapter also presents a breakdown of trends in time doing homework for boys and girls to examine gender differences over time. In addition to socio-economic differences in school attainment, there are persistent gender differences with girls outperforming boys in GCSE attainment (DfES, 2007; DfE, 2012[13]), and time use research highlights a consistent gender difference in homework time (Gershenson and Holt, 2015).

As well as the time children spend doing homework and study, reading is a further daily activity linked to education. Learning to read is a major function of the primary stage of education and developing competence and appreciation of reading is a core objective running throughout compulsory education. In the UK, reaching a minimum standard of grade C in English is a requirement for progression onto further and higher education and reading is central to this. Compared to time spent doing homework and study, which is strictly tied to education and has a strong compulsory element, children may spend time reading as a discretionary leisure activity. Indeed, highlighting reading as a leisure activity is central to efforts to promote reading among children by encouraging, and demonstrating the benefits of, reading for pleasure (Clark and Rumbold, 2006). This touches on a further ambiguity surrounding reading as an activity: though it may directly influence educational outcomes, and it is in fact a major component of formal assessment in education, it is also closely related to the acquisition of *cultural capital*.

Pierre Bourdieu (see, for example, Bourdieu, 2010 [1984]) has argued that socio-economic differences in educational attainment can be linked to differences in cultural capital acquired and deployed in different socio-economic settings. This so-called cultural capital theory of social reproduction implies that levels of cultural capital will vary according to socio-economic background, and that cultural capital is positively associated with educational outcomes (Jæger and Breen, 2016). Cultural capital has been defined as 'institutionalized, i.e., widely shared, high status cultural signals (attitudes, preferences, formal knowledge, behaviors, goods and credentials) used for social and cultural exclusion' (Lamont and Lareau, 1988: 156). Empirical research measures children's cultural capital with reference to reading and the home literacy environment, and through children's engagement in other cultural activities such as going to the theatre, museums or art galleries. Prior research has established robust correlations between cultural capital, socio-economic status and children's educational outcomes (DiMaggio, 1982; DeGraaf et al, 2000; Sullivan 2001; Jæger, 2011).

As well as examining trends in daily time doing homework and study, this chapter sets out an analysis of trends in children's time reading between 1975 and 2015, together with a study of trends in children's engagement in a range of cultural activities including visiting art galleries and museums, and other forms of cultural participation. Data on engagement in various cultural activities is available only in the later surveys (2000 and 2015) and the analysis of trends here will thus be restricted to those years. The analysis gives particular attention to differences over time associated with parental education (an indicator of socio-economic status) in children's engagement in these cultural activities. The analysis will also examine differences associated with gender: significant differences between boys and girls have emerged in educational outcomes, but prior research on the influence of cultural capital in relation to educational outcomes has ignored gender differences, with socio-economic background being the dominant factor in consideration.

A core tenet of Bourdieu's thinking on the reproduction of social inequalities is that middle-class parents can transmit cultural capital to their children, who in turn exploit it to their educational advantage in a school environment attuned to receive and reward 'high status cultural signals', thereby perpetuating socio-economic differences in educational attainment (Jæger and Breen, 2016). According to Sullivan (2001), positive associations between parent and child engagement in cultural activities can be an indication of the transmission of cultural capital from parents to children, and she finds a strong positive association between parent and child cultural capital. Children in advantaged families typically have parents with relatively high levels of cultural capital, evidenced in part by their possession of higher education qualifications and by their relatively high propensity to engage in cultural activities such as visiting museums, galleries, and theatres (Sullivan, 2001). As well as analysing trends in children's engagement in cultural activities linked to education (daily reading, monthly visits to art galleries, libraries, and so on), the chapter examines the relationship between children's and parents' engagement in different cultural activities through time.

The relationship between different cultural activities is a further topic necessitating closer inspection. Studies linking cultural capital to children's educational attainment highlight reading as especially important (DeGraaf et al, 2000; Sullivan, 2001; Jæger, 2011). Learning to read is a core part of the curriculum in primary school and being able to read competently and confidently is fundamental to success throughout compulsory schooling across a range of subjects. It is perhaps not surprising, therefore, that a number of studies show that reading and the home literacy environment are more strongly associated with educational outcomes than cultural activities like visiting art galleries. One possible conclusion from this is that so-called 'high' cultural activities like going to art galleries are not particularly important for children's educational outcomes. Yet prior research neglects to consider whether there is any relationship between reading and other indicators of cultural capital like going to the theatre or art galleries. DiMaggio (1982) showed through factor analysis the significant inter-correlations between different types of cultural activities, pointing out that the interrelation between different cultural practices is central to Bourdieu's thinking on cultural capital. With this in mind, this chapter studies the relationship between both children and parents' engagement in cultural activities, such as going to art galleries and theatres, and children's time reading, as well as their time doing homework and study, activities most directly connected to education.

Education is a driving focus in the daily lives of children, and pressures to succeed in education have intensified over the past several decades (Ennew, 1994; McDonald, 2001; Prout, 2005). More children are subject to more testing and assessment, and there has been a sustained increase in school attainment. Socio-economic differences persist, however, and gender differences in educational attainment at school have emerged. The extent to which these changes both influence children's time use and are in turn influenced by children's time use is examined in this chapter. This may be through changes in children's time doing homework or study, or through changes in activities linked to the acquisition of cultural capital such as reading or cultural participation in activities such as going to art galleries or theatres. This chapter explores the impact of changes in education on children's daily lives structured in three major parts focused on three key activity domains. The first part examines activities most directly linked to education, namely time at school, and time doing homework and study. The second part moves on to look at trends in children's daily time reading, and the third part children's monthly participation in cultural activities such as going to museums and art galleries.

Each of the three parts examines change over time in children's engagement in these different activities, decomposing trends according to children's age, gender and parental education. To understanding more about possible change or stability in the transmission of cultural capital between parents and children though time, parts two and three contain analyses of the influence of parents' engagement in cultural activities on children's engagement in those same activities at different points in time, paying close attention to differences associated with parent education. Lastly, the third part of this chapter explores the possible interconnections between daily reading and time doing homework with participation in other cultural activities such as going to art galleries by both children and parents.

Trends in time at school, doing homework and studying

Against a backdrop of rising attainment in school, and pressures to do well in school, the empirical analysis in this chapter opens with a study of trends over four decades from 1975 to 2015 in the time children spend in activities linked to their education. The imprint of education in children's daily life may be seen through the time they spend in a number of activities. Most obviously, and consuming the most amount of time, it is seen in the time children spend at school. This changed little over the past several decades at around 6 hrs 35 minutes. Figure 2.1 shows on average how much time children spent at school throughout the day in 1975, 2000, and 2015. It shows that the school day started and ended slightly earlier in 2000 and 2015 compared with 1975. A second notable change in the school day is that children no longer left school (to go home or elsewhere) at lunchtime in 2000 and 2015, which was more common in 1975. This probably reflects an increase in concerns for pupil safety outside school grounds during the school day, along with fewer mothers being at home during the school day due to increasing maternal employment. Despite these differences in the timing and structure of the school day, children's overall time at school remained fixed over this period. This is not surprising given that this time is highly regulated by education authorities. Unfortunately, there is extremely limited information about what children are doing when at school, and thus this time remains something of a black box in a child's day.

Figure 2.1: The school day in 1975, 2000 and 2015

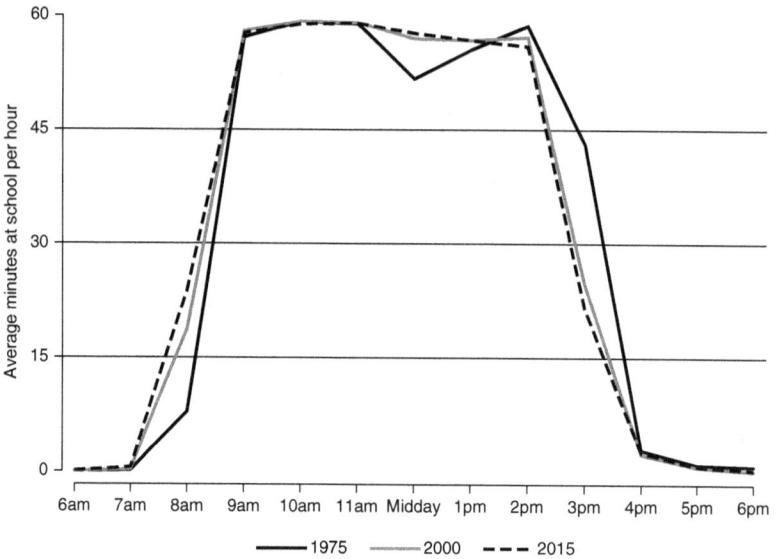

Beyond time at school, education influences children's daily life most directly through the time they spend doing homework and studying. Table 2.1 shows the average time children aged 8–11 years and 12–16 years spend doing homework on school and non-school days in 1975, 2000, and 2015. Children aged 8–11 years increased the time they spent doing homework on school days from 6 minutes in 1975 to 21 minutes in 2000, but there was little change between 2000 and 2015 (at 19 minutes). There was a comparable increase in homework time on non-school days also for children 8–11 years, rising from 3 minutes in 1975 to 12 minutes in 2000, though again changing little between 2000 and 2015 (at 14 minutes).

As expected, children aged 12–16 years spent significantly more time doing homework and study than younger children in all years on both school and non-school days (see Table 2.1). The general pattern of change is remarkably similar with a significant increase in the average time children aged 12–16 years spent doing homework between 1975 and 2000 on both school and non-school days. On school days, there was little change in homework time between 2000 and 2015, though there was a modest further increase over this period on non-school days (24 vs 33 minutes; p=.07). As a result, there was a much reduced, and no longer significant, difference between school and non-school days in the time children aged 12–16 years spent doing homework (39 vs 33 minutes).

Table 2.1: Average minutes in homework and study on school and non-school days in 1975, 2000 and 2015: children 8–11 and 12–16 years

	1975	2000	2015
School day	**Average minutes [95% CI]**		
8–11 years	6 [4–8]	21 [18–24]	19 [16–23]
12–16 years	21 [17–26]	41 [36–45]	39 [33–45]
Non-school day			
8–11 years	3 [2–5]	12 [9–15]	14 [11–17]
12–16 years	6 [3–9]	24 [19–28]	33 [25–41]

As expected, parental education was significantly associated with children's time doing homework and study, though this varied over time. The upper panel of Figure 2.2 shows trends in homework and study time in the UK separately for children whose parents have compulsory schooling only, and those with post-compulsory schooling. On school days, children with a parent with post-compulsory education averaged significantly more time doing homework in 1975 and 2000 (around 12 minutes), but not in 2015. In contrast, on non-school days, a relatively small difference in homework time linked to parental education in 1975 widened in 2000 and 2015. This was because the increase between 1975 and 2000 on non-school days in the average time children spend doing homework was larger for children with higher-educated parents (19 vs 10 minutes). Between 2000 and 2015, homework time on non-school days increased further by around 6 minutes for all children, irrespective of parent education; thus the significant difference in homework time on non-school days associated with parental education persisted.

Looking now at gender, the lower panel of Figure 2.2 shows trends for boys and girls separately. In 1975, boys and girls spent a similar amount of time doing homework, on both school and non-school days. Homework time increased between 1975 and 2000 for both boys and girls, but this increase was marginally higher among girls, and a significant gender gap thus emerged in homework time in 2000 that was sustained in 2015. On non-school days, gender differences increased further still between 2000 and 2015 (from 9 minutes to 13 minutes).

These results show, for the first time, long-term trends in children's average time doing homework and study. They provide some support

Figure 2.2: Average minutes children 8–16 years spend doing homework on school and non-school days in 1975, 2000 and 2015: parental education and child gender

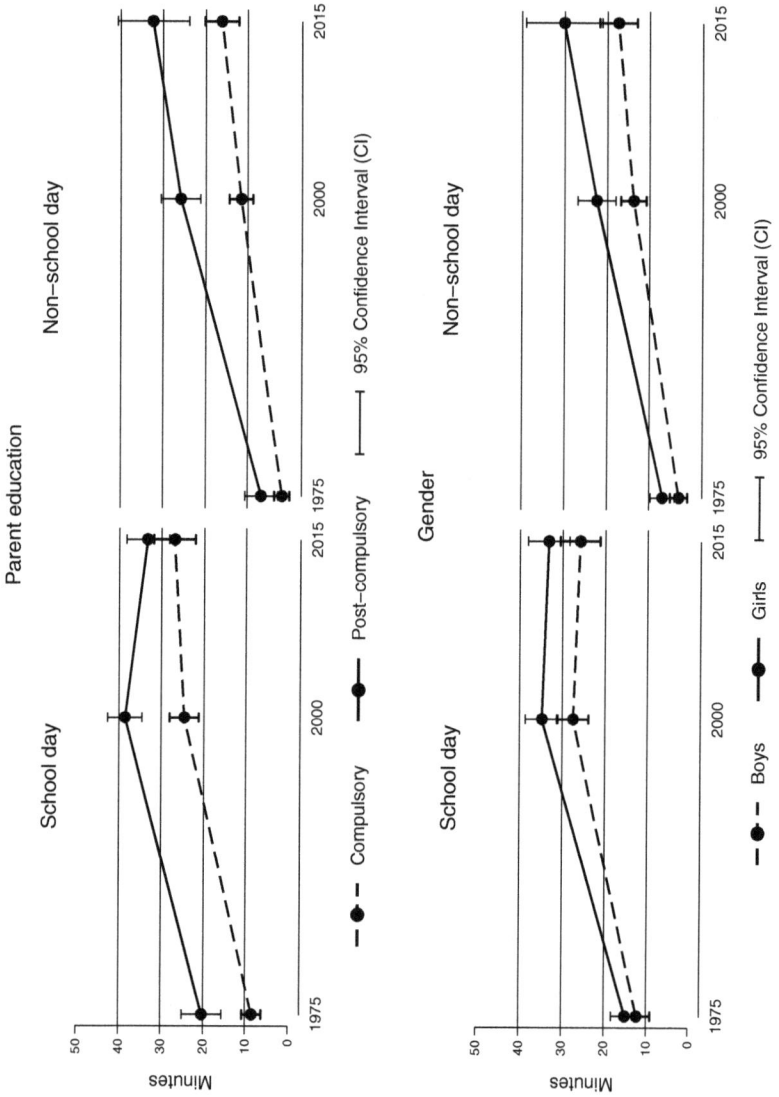

for the contention that education is consuming more of children's time outside school, but there is evidence also that there could be a limit to this. Average homework time increased between 1975 and 2000 for children irrespective of age, gender and parental education on both school and non-school days. Between 2000 and 2015, however, children's time doing homework has plateaued on school days, with further increases in this period concentrated on non-school days, particularly among girls and children aged 12–16 years. These results suggest a possible limit in the amount of time children have available, or are prepared to spend, doing homework on school days, though may also reflect change in the amount of homework received. Differences associated with parental education and gender broadly align with differences in educational outcomes associated with these factors. However, the association with parental education diverges on school and non-school days in 2015 (being insignificant in the former) despite the fact that differences in educational outcomes associated with socio-economic status have persisted and even widened.

Trends in children's daily time reading

Reading is another activity linked closely to children's education. Learning and developing reading competence and appreciation are core objectives of education, but time reading may also be viewed purely as a leisure activity pursued for pleasure and cultural enrichment. For this reason, measures of reading and the home reading environment have been prominent in research examining the influence of cultural capital for children's educational outcomes. As with homework, however, little is known about long-term trends in children's time reading, and about change in factors associated with children's time reading including the influence of parents' reading, which is a key component of the home reading environment. In this part of the chapter therefore, trends in children's average time reading between 1975 and 2015 are presented, decomposed by child age, gender and parental education. Following this, the influence of parents' reading on children's reading over four decades is analysed.

The measure of reading analysed here refers to time when reading was the main activity that children were engaging in, though it is not known if they were reading for pleasure or whether the reading was school related (though these need not necessarily be exclusive).[14] It may include, in recent years, time children spend reading using a device such as an e-reader or reading content on a website (Clark, 2011). It is not possible to know if children were reading paper-based material or reading on an electronic device like a computer, but if children recorded that reading was their main activity (rather than saying they were using a computer), then it is included in the measure of reading studied here.

Table 2.2 reports the average time children aged 8–11 years and 12–16 years spent reading on school and non-school days in 1975, 2000, and 2015. On school days, there was a significant, though small, increase between 1975 and 2000 in average time children aged 8–11 years spent reading, with no significant change between 2000 and 2015. In contrast, average time reading by children aged 12–16 years on school days did not change between 1975 and 2015. Consequently, on school days, children aged 8–11 years were spending significantly more time reading than children 12–16 years in 2000 and 2015, which was not the case in 1975. On non-school days in 1975 children aged 12–16 years spent significantly more time reading than children aged 8–11 years (19 vs 12 minutes). However, averaged reading time decreased significantly among children aged 12–16 years between 1975 and 2000 (with no change between 2000 and 2015), whereas there was no change in average time reading among children aged 8–11 years between 1975 and 2015. As a result, age was no longer significantly associated with average reading time on non-school days in 2000 or in 2015. The results across both school and non-school days show a small shift over time with younger children aged 8–11 years spending more time reading on average than children aged 12–16 years.

Differences through time associated with parental education and child gender in children's average time reading are shown in Figure 2.3. Parental education was not significantly associated with children's

Table 2.2: Average minutes reading on school and non-school days in 1975, 2000 and 2015: children 8–11 and 12–16 years

	1975	2000	2015
School day	Average minutes [95% CI]		
8–11 years	5 [3–7]	8 [6–10]	10 [7–14]
12–16 years	7 [5–9]	5 [4–7]	5 [3–7]
Non-school day			
8–11 years	12 [9–14]	10 [8–12]	12 [8–15]
12–16 years	19 [16–23]	12 [9–15]	10 [6–14]

Figure 2.3: Average minutes children 8–16 years spend reading in 1975, 2000 and 2015: parental education and child gender

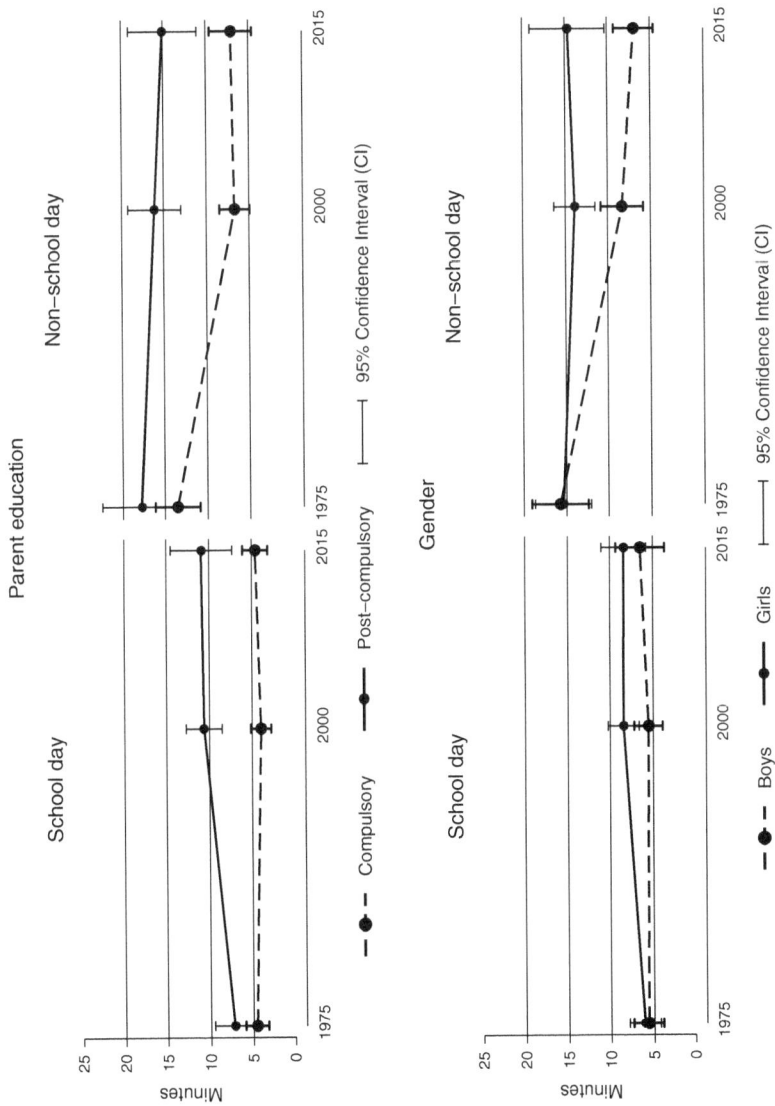

reading time on either school or non-school days in 1975. However, average reading time increased significantly between 1975 and 2015 on school days for children with relatively highly educated parents, and it decreased significantly on non-school days for children with parents with compulsory education only (with a much smaller insignificant decrease for those with post-compulsory education). These diverging trends have resulted in children with relatively highly educated parents spending significantly more time reading on school and non-school days in both 2000 and 2015. The lower panel of Figure 2.3 shows trends in reading for boys and girls. There was very little change in both boys' and girls' average reading time on school days, and little difference between boys and girls although a small gender gap was found in 2000. On non-school days, boys' average reading time decreased significantly between 1975 and 2000, and it decreased by a small amount further between 2000 and 2015. Girls' average reading time on the other hand did not change between 1975 and 2015, and consequently a significant gender difference in reading (with girls reading more than boys on average) emerged in 2000 and 2015.

Although reading is an activity distinct from time spent doing homework and study, they are in different ways linked to education, and patterns associated with both parental education and gender and these activities are very similar, suggesting a degree of complementarity in these activities, at least with respect to these characteristics. To consider this further, Figure 2.4 shows trends in these activities combined broken down by parental education and child gender. When combined, there is a significant and persistent gap in total time in these activities associated with parental education on school days, and a clearly widening gap on non-school days, over four decades. The results for child gender also underscore an emerging gender gap in activities linked to education in 2000 and 2015 on both school and non-school days, though this is more pronounced on non-school days.

Looking at children's time in activities linked to their education combined highlights a significant and widening influence of parental education and child gender on children's time in these activities. Underpinning this are notable differences in trends in these activities suggesting that, on non-school days in particular, rather than complementing each other, these activities may be in direct competition for some groups of children. Homework time increased for children aged 12–16 years while their average time reading decreased. Also, among boys and children whose parents have less education, increases in time doing homework are offset by decreases in time reading, with the result that total time in these activities remained comparatively unchanged

Figure 2.4: Average minutes children 8–16 years spend doing homework, study or reading in 1975, 2000 and 2015: parental education and child gender

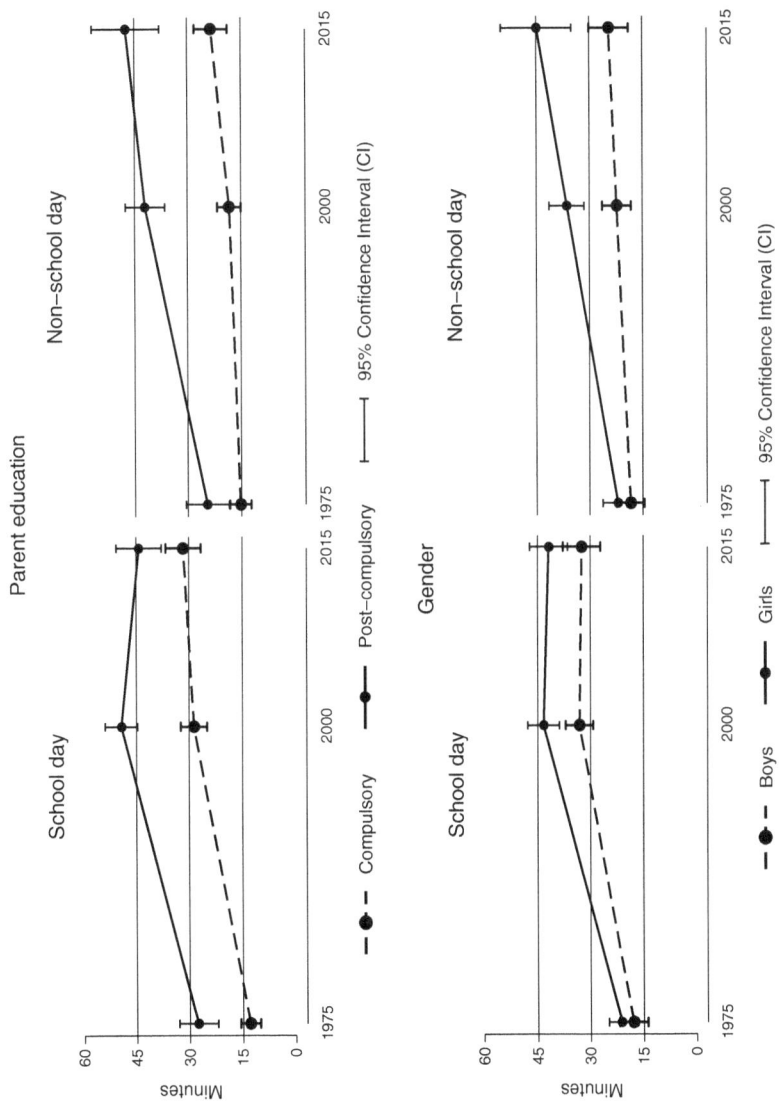

over time. Girls and those whose parents have relatively more education, on the other hand, have maintained consistent levels of average time reading alongside increases in time doing homework and study. These results highlight that while it is common to think of activities such as watching TV or playing video games as competing with homework, it is crucial also to recognise that spending time doing homework may crowd out, or limit, time in complementary activities such as reading.

The relationship between parent and child reading

The previous section shows that parental education is a major factor associated with the time children spend reading. A core tenet of Bourdieu's cultural theory of social reproduction is the argument that differences in outcomes associated with socio-economic position are linked not only to differences in economic resources, but also to differential amounts of cultural capital possessed by those from different social backgrounds. The foregoing analysis underscored the importance of parental education as a factor associated with children's time in education-related activities such as reading, which is a form of institutionalised cultural capital often used in research to identify the effect of cultural capital on children's outcomes. It is preferable, however, also to use parents' participation in cultural activities as an indicator of their cultural capital, along with activities relating to promoting a positive reading environment for children. Parents' engagement in reading is a core element of children's home reading environment (DeGraaf et al, 2000; Mullan, 2010), and this section examines the relationship between parent and child reading over four decades between 1975 and 2015.

To study the relationship between the daily reading of parents and children, families are split into two groups as follows: 1) families where no parent read on the diary day; 2) families where a parent read on the diary day. Table 2.3 contains information about the proportion of children aged 8–16 years who have a parent who spent any time reading during the diary day in 1975, 2000 and 2015, differentiating between families where parents have compulsory or post-compulsory education. In 1975, 71 per cent of children in families where parents have compulsory education only had a parent who read on the diary day. This decreased to 53 per cent in 2000, and further still to 37 per cent in 2015. Therefore, over four decades, the proportion of children who had a parent who read during the day almost halved in these families.

We can observe a similar pattern of change among children in families where at least one parent has post-compulsory education. It is striking

Table 2.3: Percentage of children 8–16 years with a parent who reads on a diary day in 1975, 2000 and 2015 in families where parents have compulsory only or post-compulsory education

	1975	2000	2015
	%		
Compulsory only	71 [66–76]	53 [50–57]	37 [33–42]
Post-compulsory	80 [74–86]	69 [66–72]	45 [41–50]

to see a huge decrease in the incidence of parent reading irrespective of parental education, in contrast to modest changes in children's time reading. In all years, the daily incidence of parent reading is higher in those families where parents have relatively more education though the difference is decreasing over time. Parent reading may therefore mediate the association between parental education and children's reading.

To explore this proposition, the following analysis compares differences in children's average time reading depending on whether their parents spent any time reading during the same day, differentiating between families where parents have compulsory education and those where at least one parent has post-compulsory education. Results displayed in Figure 2.5 show that in all years in families where parents have compulsory education only, children averaged more time reading when their parents also spent some time reading during the same day. This was the case also in families where at least one parent had post-compulsory education, except in 2015 where there was no significant difference in children's reading associated with parent reading. This suggests that the decrease in parent reading observed in 2015 had a significant effect on the influence of parents' reading for children, though only in families where parents have some post-compulsory education.

It is worth noting in addition here that parent reading was not significantly associated with children's time doing homework or study in any year, and this applied irrespective of parental education. This indicates some level of distinction in the influence of parents' reading between activities explicitly associated with school (and indeed set by schools) from cultural activities like reading where children may exercise more autonomy.

There has been clear change over time in the influence of parental education and parent reading on children's reading. In 1975, parental education was not significantly associated with children's reading, but children spent more time reading on average in families where

Figure 2.5: Association between parent and child reading in 1975, 2000 and 2015

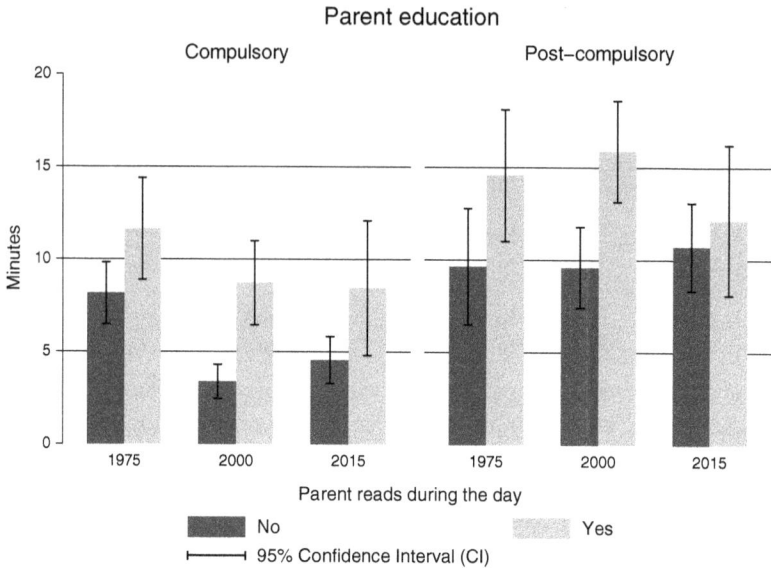

parents' also read on the same day (irrespective of the level of parental education). In 2000, parental education and parent reading were significantly positively associated with children's reading, whereas in 2015 the association between children's average time reading and parental education is concentrated primarily in families where no parent read on the diary day. Generally, these results highlight the importance of parents' engaging in reading as having a positive influence on children's reading, over and above whatever level of education parents have. It is especially notable in connection with this that the fall in children's average time reading in families where parents have relatively low education is most pronounced in cases where no parent reported reading on the diary day (see Figure 2.5).

Nevertheless, despite controlling for parent reading on the same day, which was significantly associated with their own education, parental education (cultural capital institutionalised) remained significantly associated with children's reading in 2000 and 2015. This runs counter to some prior research showing that the effect of parental education on indicators of children's cultural capital (including engagement in reading) is mediated entirely by parents' engagement in cultural activities (Sullivan, 2001). Sullivan's study, however, does not clearly distinguish between reading and engagement in other types of cultural activities like going to museums or galleries, which may prove important. To explore this further, the final part of this chapter now examines children's and their parents' engagement in other cultural activities.

Trends in children's participation in cultural activities: 2000 and 2015

Unlike reading, or homework and study, children's participation in certain cultural activities such as going to an art gallery or theatre, if they participate at all, is likely to occur relatively infrequently. Children taking part in time use surveys can report time they spend in cultural activities in their time diary, but on a randomly selected day for the population only a very small proportion will have done so. Therefore, supplementing the diary information, children (and their parents) provide further information about their participation in different cultural activities in the month prior to interview. The activities span a broad cultural spectrum including visiting art galleries, museums, or theatres, going to the cinema, and going to sporting events. They also answer a question about visiting libraries during the month. Prior research on cultural capital includes membership and use of libraries under the rubric of children's engagement in reading activities (Sullivan, 2001; Sullivan, 2007), and libraries have the potential, as *cultural intermediaries*, to develop cultural capital, in combination with social capital, in the public sphere (Golding, 2008). Information on child (and parent) monthly participation in cultural activities is available only in the later 2000 and 2015 surveys.

This part of the analysis commences with an overview of the proportion of children participating in the following four cultural activities: 1) visiting arts/culture venues (galleries, theatres, museums); 2) going to the cinema; 3) attending sports events; and 4) visiting libraries. Table 2.4 reports the proportion of children aged 8–11 years and 12–16 years participating in any of these cultural activities at least once in the month prior to interview in 2000 and 2015. Approximately one third of children in both age groups visited an arts/culture venue at least once during the month in 2000. There was a modest though significant increase for children aged 8–11 years in 2015 (rising to 43 per cent), with no significant change for children aged 12–16 years. Just under 30 per cent of children aged 8–11 years and 37 per cent of children aged 12–16 years went to the cinema at least once in the month prior to interview, with no change between 2000 and 2015 for children in either age group. It is notable that a higher proportion of

Table 2.4: Children's monthly participation in different cultural activities in 2000 and 2015: children 8–11 and 12–16 years

In past month, child visited:	8–11 years		12–16 years	
	2000	2015	2000	2015
	Average proportion [95% CI]		Average proportion [95% CI]	
Arts/culture venue	38 [34–42]	43 [38–48]	37 [33–40]	37 [33–42]
Cinema	27 [23–31]	28 [24–33]	37 [34–41]	37 [33–41]
Sports event	21 [18–25]	18 [14–21]	24 [21–27]	24 [20–27]
Library	51 [47–55]	41 [37–46]	56 [52–60]	33 [29–38]
Base (n)	736	514	789	598

children aged 8–11 years visited an arts/culture venue than went to the cinema, confounding general ideas of what is 'popular' in the cultural domain. This might reflect the influence of outreach programmes in museums and galleries in arranging visits by children from primary schools. Around one fifth of children aged 8–11 years and one quarter of children aged 12–16 years attended a sports event, and again there was no change in these proportions between 2000 and 2015.

In contrast to the stability in children's engagement in the foregoing cultural activities, there was a sharp decrease in children in both age groups visiting libraries between 2000 and 2015. In 2000, 51 per cent of children aged 8–11 years and 56 per cent of children aged 12–16 years visited a library at least once over a period of a month; this dropped to 41 per cent and 33 per cent respectively in 2015. The decrease was greatest for children aged 12–16 years who were slightly more likely to visit libraries than children aged 8–11 years in 2000. By 2015, a significantly higher proportion of younger children visited libraries than children aged 12–16 years. For children in both age groups, the prevalence of visiting libraries, a more common activity in 2000, was in 2015 closer to the proportion of children visiting art galleries, museums and cultural sites. The substantial drop in children visiting libraries aligns with reports of substantial cuts to public expenditure on libraries, and library closures.[15]

Girls were more likely to visit libraries than boys were in 2000 (58 per cent vs 49 per cent), but there was no gender difference in 2015 (39 per cent vs 35 per cent). This result echoes government statistics from the *Taking Part* survey, showing that decreases in library visits in England have been concentrated among girls, who were significantly more likely to use libraries (DCMS, 2015). Girls were also more likely to participate in arts and cultural activities in 2000 (41 per cent vs 34 per cent) and to go to the cinema (36 per cent vs 29 per cent). The gender gap in visiting arts/cultural venues narrowed slightly in 2015 (43 per cent vs 37 per cent) and was no longer significant. The proportion of boys going to the cinema increased in 2015 (34 per cent) to become similar to girls whose cinema attendance decreased slightly (31 per cent). Boys were significantly more likely to attend sporting events than were girls in both years. Taken together, therefore, except for attending sports events, children's engagement in these cultural activities was not associated with gender in 2015, although this was the case in 2000.

Parental education was positively associated with children's engagement in a range of cultural activities in both 2000 and 2015. Figure 2.6 shows the predicted probability (%) of children visiting arts/culture venues, cinema, sporting events or libraries during a month broken down across different levels of parent education.

In both years, children with more educated parents were more likely to visit an arts/culture venue. This association was noticeably stronger in 2015 as there was a significant increase in participation between

Figure 2.6: Parental education and children's predicted monthly participation in cultural activities

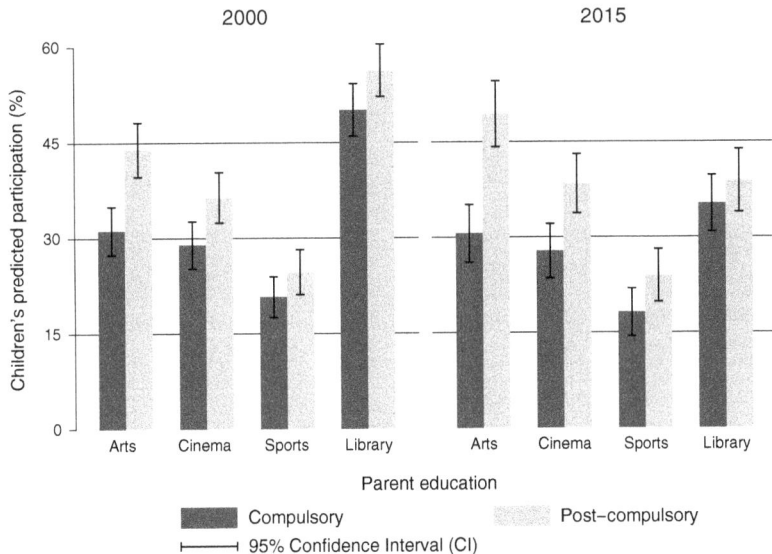

2000 and 2015 for children in relatively more educated families and no change for other children. Children with more educated parents were more likely to go to the cinema during the month in both 2000 and 2015, but parental education was not associated with attending sporting events in either year. Lastly, children with more educated parents were more likely to visit libraries in 2000, although the difference is comparatively small. By 2015, however, parental education was no longer significantly associated with children's visits to libraries as library visits decreased irrespective of parental education.

Parent monthly engagement in cultural activities

Bringing parent participation in cultural activities into the frame now, Table 2.5 reports on the proportion of children with parents who participated in different cultural activities during the month in 2000 and 2015. Looking first at children in families where parents have compulsory education, around 30 per cent had a parent who visited an arts or cultural venue, and this did not change significantly in 2015. In 2000, around 15 per cent had a parent who visited a cinema and 28 per cent who attended a sporting event. In 2015, the proportion of children in these families with a parent who visited the cinema increased to 20 per cent and the proportion with a parent who attended a sporting event decreased by ten percentage points to 17 per cent. Lastly, around one third of children in these families had a parent who visited the library, which dropped to around one fifth (19 per cent) in 2015.

Table 2.5: Percentage of children 8–16 years whose parents participate in different cultural activities in 2000 and 2015 in families where parents have compulsory only or post-compulsory education

In past month, parent visited:	Compulsory only		Post-compulsory	
	2000	2015	2000	2015
	Average proportion [95% CI]		Average proportion [95% CI]	
Arts/culture venue	27 [24–30]	31 [27–35]	48 [45–52]	52 [48–57]
Cinema	15 [12–17]	20 [17–24]	24 [21–27]	26 [22–30]
Sports event	28 [25–31]	17 [13–20]	33 [30–37]	30 [26–34]
Library	31 [27–34]	19 [16–22]	52 [48–45]	28 [24–32]

Across a wide range of cultural activities, children in relatively more educated families have parents who are more likely to participate. Half of all children in families with at least one parent with post-compulsory education have a parent who visited an arts/culture venue, around one quarter have a parent who visited the cinema, and one third who attended a sporting event at least once during the month. The proportions remained mostly unchanged between 2000 and 2015, although parent visits to libraries stand out as an exception here. In 2000, half of children in families where at least one parent has post-compulsory education had a parent who visited a library; this dropped to 28 per cent in 2015. Although still significant, the difference in parental visits to libraries associated with parental education narrowed substantially from 21 to 9 percentage points. These results reflect findings elsewhere showing that higher social classes are distinguished though participating in an extensive range of different cultural activities ranging from 'high-culture' activities such as visiting art galleries and theatres through to more popular forms of culture such as going to the cinema (Bennett et al, 2009).

Parental education is strongly associated with their engagement in different cultural activities, but Bourdieu's ideas also suggest that there is a strong correlation between parent and child participation in cultural activities; prior research to this study has supported this (Sullivan, 2001). To test this, variables indicating whether or not parents engaged in different cultural activities were added to models of children's probability of engaging in these same activities. Associations were very similar for mothers and fathers and are combined to consider the association with parents' engagement in general. Figure 2.7 shows children's predicted participation estimated by these models, for 2000 and 2015, which indicate how likely it is that children participate in a cultural activity if any co-resident parent did so in the previous month also. Without exception, the likelihood of a child participating in any cultural activity was significantly greater if their parent also participated in that activity in the previous month in both 2000 and 2015. Also without exception, the association between parent and child participation in cultural activities was greater in 2015 than it was in 2000. In some cases, this was because children's predicted participation increased among those whose parents also participated (arts/cultural venues and sports events), or it decreased among those whose parents did not participate (cinema and library). In contrast with parents' reading during the day, therefore, parents' engagement in cultural activities has a substantial and highly consistent effect on children's engagement on those activities. This strongly implies that cultural participation is a family-oriented area of activity in children's lives.

Figure 2.7: Association between parent and child participation in cultural activities during the month in 2000 and 2015

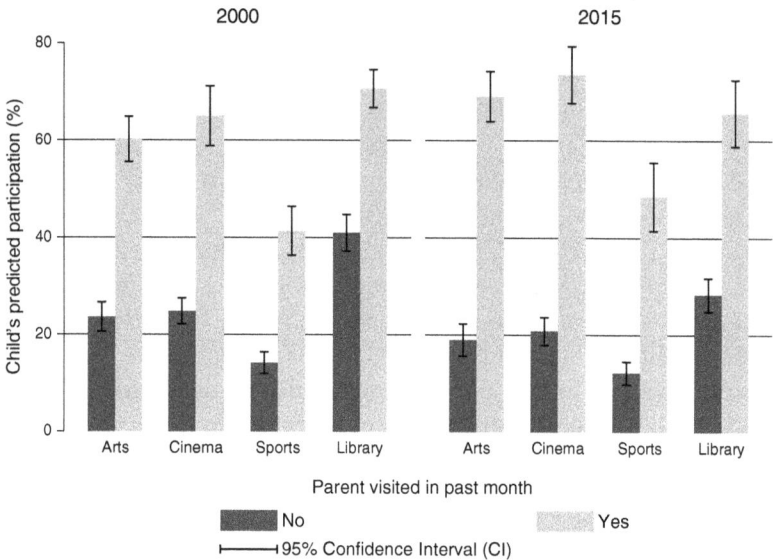

The results for visiting libraries merit close attention given the large decrease in visiting libraries since 2000. In 2000, there was a 72 per cent chance that a child visited a library during the month if their parent had also visited a library in the same period. This fell slightly to 66.5 per cent in 2015, but this was not a significant change. In contrast, children in 2000 had a 41.2 per cent chance of visiting a library if their parent did not visit a library, decreasing significantly to 29 per cent in 2015. Therefore, although lower, a substantial proportion of children would likely have visited a library in 2000 even if their parent did not visit a library indicating a degree of independence in this activity, which is less the case in 2015. It could be that with library closures more children have to travel longer to access a library, increasing the necessity for parents to accompany them, potentially restricting visits to libraries to those children whose parents can accompany them.

It was found earlier, as expected, that parental education was significantly associated with children's engagement in different cultural activities. After accounting for the influence of parents' engagement in these cultural activities, however, the direct positive effect of parental education diminished and in some cases was no longer significant. Parental education was no longer significantly associated with children's library visits in either 2000 or 2015 after controlling for parents' library visits. Parental education was also no longer significantly associated with children's visits to arts/cultural venues and cinemas in 2000, but remained significant in 2015, after controlling for parents' engagement in these cultural activities. Perhaps the key point here, however, is not that parental education is more or less important than parents' engagement in cultural practices. Rather, what is seen here is a robust connection between parent and child cultural practices, under-pinned by strong associations in both cases with parental education. The extent to which this has any bearing on children's educational outcomes remains a fiercely debated question (Kingston, 2001; Jæger and Breen, 2016). Though the analysis here does not consider edu-cational outcomes, aspects of children's daily time use linked directly to their education (homework, study, and reading) are studied. The final section of this chapter, therefore, explores links between child and parent cultural participation and children's daily time in activities connected to their education.

Cultural participation and daily time use

As already discussed, prior research highlights the importance of inter-correlations between participation in different cultural activities which aligns with Bourdieu's theoretical perspective that engagement in different cultural practices cohere in a structured way. A limited number of studies have found positive associations between children's engagement in cultural activities, such as going to galleries or museums, and children's engagement in reading (DiMaggio, 1982; Sullivan, 2001). Adding to this, the analysis in this section examines whether monthly participation in cultural activities (by both children and parents) is associated with children's daily time reading and, going further, examines associations with their time doing homework and study – activities directly linked to children's education.

Results in Table 2.6 show the differences in children's daily time reading, and doing homework and study associated with their monthly participation in cultural activities. Children who visited an arts/cul-ture venue or library in 2000 spent significantly more time reading (4.2 and 2.8 minutes respectively). Children's participation in these cultural activities in 2000 was moreover significantly associated with their time doing homework and study (4.7 and 9.6 minutes respect-ively). In 2015, however, there were no longer significant associations between participation in these cultural activities and children's daily time in activities connected to education. The association for library visits remains positive and comparatively large suggesting that the lack

Table 2.6: Association between children's monthly engagement in cultural activities and daily time in reading and homework in 2000 and 2015

Children's monthly cultural activities	Reading		Homework and study	
	2000	2015	2000	2015
Arts	4.2"	1.3	4.7˙	−3.5
Cinema	0.8	3.5	0.8	−0.3
Sports	−2.8˙	−3.6˙	2.3	−2.4
Library	2.8˙	3.4	9.6"'	5.8

Notes: Table shows the difference in children's average time reading and doing homework and study (in minutes) between children who participate in each cultural activity at least once in the month prior to interview and those who do not; *** p < .001; ** p < .01; * p < .05

Table 2.7: Association between parent monthly engagement in cultural activities and children's daily time in reading and homework in 2000 and 2015

Parents' monthly cultural activities	Reading		Homework and study	
	2000	2015	2000	2015
Arts	2.8	3.1	3.9	−1.9
Cinema	5.2"	3.8	−0.4	3.1
Sports	−1.4	−1.8	3.4	−4.8
Library	6.1"'	3.0	3.4	4.2

Notes: Table shows the difference in children's average time reading and doing homework and study (in minutes) between children with a parent who participated in each cultural activity at least once in the month prior to interview and those who do not; *** p < .001; ** p < .01; * p < .05

of significance arises from the decrease in the proportion of children who visit libraries in 2015.

Turning to other results in Table 2.6, visiting cinemas has no significant effect on children's daily time reading or doing homework and study, but note that attending sporting events was negatively associated with daily time reading in both 2000 and 2015. This domain of cultural participation is concentrated among boys who also spend less time reading, particularly on non-school days (see Figure 2.3).

Table 2.7 reports the difference in children's average daily time reading and doing homework and study in 2000 and 2015 depending on whether their parents participated in each cultural activity during the month. Broadly, the results show a very limited degree of association between parents' monthly engagement in cultural activities and children's daily time reading, which are restricted to 2000 only. Children in families where a parent went to the cinema or library averaged significantly more time reading (5 and 6 minutes respectively) than children whose parents did not engage in these activities during the month. The positive association with parent library visits serves to underscore the potential role libraries can play in supporting parents to promote children's reading, but this is no longer significant in 2015 as both parent and child visits to libraries have fallen. The result for parents' visits to the cinema is perhaps surprising, though this could perhaps reflect a type of crossover effect due to books being adapted for the screen. Again, however, this is no longer significant in 2015. Lastly, Table 2.7 shows that children's daily time in homework and study is not significantly associated with parent participation in any cultural activity in either 2000 or 2015.

Overall, associations between both children's and parents' cultural participation and children's daily time use in activities linked to education are limited and not consistent over time. Children's visits to arts/culture venues were positively associated with their daily time reading and doing homework and study, but in 2000 only. Parents' engagement in these high-culture activities had no effect on children's daily time in these activities in either 2000 or 2015. Parent participation in any cultural activity indeed had no discernible effect on children's time doing homework or study in any year. Parental education remains therefore a key significant factor associated with children's time in this domain. Although this analysis does not directly address possible links between parental cultural capital and children's educational outcomes, it does raise questions as to how parental cultural capital might influence children's daily lives in relation to their education. Cultural participation is clearly a major component of shared family life that is strongly associated with parents' level of education, but it does not appear to be directly associated with children's daily time in activities related to their education.

Conclusion

Education forms a major part of children's daily lives occupying a significant amount of their time. In terms of the time children spend at school, this is mostly unchanged over time. As there have been no substantial changes in the rules governing children's time at school this should not be surprising. Of course, what children do when at school has changed often in many ways over the past several decades (Chitty, 2009), which is arguably of more importance in understanding changes in children's daily lives relating to education. Nevertheless, the constancy of time at school as a structural feature in the daily lives of children is clear, echoing the striking conformity found in the basic structure of adults' daily time use (Vagni and Cornwell, 2018).

Beyond school, education impacts on children's daily lives most prominently through time they spend doing homework and study, and there have been significant increases over time concentrated between 1975 and 2000 on school days (no overall change between 2000 and 2015), and over four decades on non-school days (1975–2015). These results point simultaneously to the impact on children's time use from increased school workloads (especially for children in secondary schools), but also highlight that there are certain limits to this, as evidenced by the relative lack of change on school days between 2000 and 2015.

The time children spend engaging in different cultural activities may also influence their education by developing their cultural capital. The time children spend reading is a key activity in this regard, alongside participation in a range of cultural activities such as going to art galleries or museums. Unlike time doing homework and study, there has been no comparable increase in children's average daily time reading. In fact, on non-school days, as time doing homework and study has increased, the time children in secondary school spend reading has decreased. The encroachment of education on the daily lives of children is not visible therefore through children spending more time reading, in stark contrast to their time doing homework and study. There has been, moreover, very little change in children's monthly participation across a range of different cultural activities between 2000 and 2015. The major exception here is children's visits to libraries, which decreased significantly during this period.

Gender has emerged as key determinant of children's time in daily activities linked to their education. Although both boys and girls have increased their time doing homework and study, the increases, especially on non-school days, have been greatest for girls, leading to an emerging, indeed widening, gender gap in time in these activities. A significant gender difference has emerged in daily time reading also on non-school days, flowing in this instance from significant decreases in boys' daily time reading. These changes have occurred against a backdrop of girls outperforming boys in school attainment, although this is not evidence of a direct causal link between these changes. These results must be understood in the wider context of gender differences in other areas of children's time use (analysed throughout this book), and subject choice in further and higher education continues to be highly gendered with girls significantly less likely to pursue educational pathways leading to (comparatively high-paying) careers in engineering, science or technology (Cassidy et al, 2018).

Persistently over time, children with relatively more educated parents spent more time doing homework and study, spent more time reading and were more likely to engage in a range of different cultural activities. Parental education, therefore, is positively associated with children's engagement in activities linked to education *and* culture. There is some indication, moreover, that the influence of parental education on children's time doing homework and study has increased, in that a significant difference associated with parental education emerged on non-school days in 2000 and 2015 as time in these activities increased. In this sense, children from different social backgrounds are diverging in terms of the time they spend in this activity linked to education. On top of this, children with parents who have higher education spent more time reading in 2000 and 2015, where there was no significant association between parental education and children's average daily reading time in 1975. Overall, especially on non-school days, children in different socio-economic backgrounds were clearly diverging in the average time they devoted to homework, study, and reading combined over four decades between 1975 and 2015. There is no indication, however, that socio-economic differences in children's monthly participation in cultural activities widened between 2000 and 2015.

Parents' own engagement in cultural activities is intertwined with, and arguably mediates, the connection between their formal education and children's engagement in cultural activities. In line with theoretical expectations and prior research, we have seen that parental education is positively associated with parents' engagement in cultural activities, and, in turn, that parents' engagement in different cultural activities was significantly associated with children's engagement in those same activities. The analysis of these relationships over time, however, provided a new perspective, showing some divergence between daily time reading and participation in other types of cultural activities. Parental education has become a more significant factor in determining children's time reading outside school, whereas their own reading has become less significant in this regard, as their own engagement in reading has declined, especially among parents with relatively higher levels of education. Parent reading in families where parents have relatively less education remains an important determinant of children's time reading in these families, but formal parental education has become, over the past couple of decades, comparatively more important in influencing children's engagement in reading.

Parents' participation in various cultural activities is consistently positively associated with children's engagement in these activities in both 2000 and 2015, and accounting for this diminishes the direct influence of formal parental education in 2000; this accords with the findings from other research on this topic conducted around this time (Sullivan, 2001). However, in 2015 parental education remains significantly associated with children's attendance at galleries and museums, and cinemas, after controlling for parents' participation in these activities. We see again therefore that parents' formal education has become relatively more salient over time in determining children's engagement in certain cultural activities.

The influence of cultural capital for children's educational outcomes remains contested and the subject of ongoing empirical investigation (Jæger and Breen, 2016). The results presented in this chapter suggest that education and culture occupy relatively distinct spheres in children's daily lives, with parental education acting as a kind of linchpin connecting the two. Participation in various cultural activities by parents and children, which is highly correlated, has little direct influence on children's daily time doing homework and study, or reading, though parental education is significantly associated with activities linked to both education and culture. This does not neutralise cultural capital as a potentially important factor in children's educational outcomes, however, nor is it necessarily inconsistent with Bourdieu's thinking, which nowhere posits any kind of rationally informed exchange between time in these separate domains. It demonstrates rather, that particular forms of cultural engagement in the daily lives of children are a constituent part of family life, which helps to shape children's outlook on, and engagement with, their social world as they navigate their way through formal education.

Notes

[1] https://www.gov.uk/government/collections/statistics-gcses-key-stage-4#gcse-and-equivalent-results,-including-pupil-characteristics
[2] https://www.education-ni.gov.uk/publications/children-and-young-peoples-strategic-indicators-2016-update
[3] https://www.gov.uk/government/collections/statistics-key-stage-2
[4] Scotland has only recently begun to publish data on primary school attainment.
[5] http://gov.wales/statistics-and-research/academic-achievement-pupil-chracteristics/?tab=previous&lang=en
[6] https://www.gov.uk/government/collections/statistics-gcses-key-stage-4#gcse-and-equivalent-results,-including-pupil-characteristics
[7] http://www.gov.scot/Topics/Statistics/Browse/School-Education/TrendData
[8] http://gov.wales/statistics-and-research/academic-achievement-free-school-meals/?tab=previous&lang=en
[9] https://www.education-ni.gov.uk/articles/school-performance

[10] http://gov.wales/statistics-and-research/academic-achievement-free-school-meals/?tab=previous&lang=en

[11] https://www.gov.uk/government/statistics/national-curriculum-assessments-at-key-stage-2-2015-revised

[12] https://www.education-ni.gov.uk/publications/children-and-young-peoples-strategic-indicators-2016-update

[13] https://www.gov.uk/government/collections/statistics-gcses-key-stage-4#gcse-and-equivalent-results,-including-pupil-characteristics; https://assets.publishing.service.gov.uk/government/uploads/system/uploads/attachment_data/file/219306/sfr03_2012_001.pdf

[14] Chapter 6 examines levels of enjoyment of time reading, highlighting stark differences in comparison with time doing homework and study, suggesting that the measure of reading we use is capturing reading for enjoyment.

[15] https://www.cipfa.org/about-cipfa/press-office/latest-press-releases/decade-of-austerity-sees-30-drop-in-library-spending

3

Time for Health

Over the past several decades, increasing overweight and obesity in childhood has become a major public health concern. In the UK, as in many other countries, rates of overweight and obesity among children increased substantially in the closing decades of the 20th century (Chinn and Rona, 2001; Lobstein et al, 2003). There were further increases in the early 2000s, up to 2004, but rates of overweight and obesity appear to have stabilised thereafter, even decreasing slightly in recent years (Bradshaw et al, 2016). In England, throughout the 2000s, around three in every ten children aged 2–15 years were classified as being overweight or obese (HSE, 2016[1]). Scotland and Wales report a similar proportion of children aged 2–15 years as being overweight or obese (SHS, 2016;[2] WHS, 2012[3]). A number of other health problems are linked with unhealthy weight among children, including cardiovascular disease and type 2 diabetes, and it can lead to further health problems in later life (Ebbeling et al2002; Han et al, 2010).

As well as their physical health, concern about children's mental health and well-being is now a public health issue (DHSC, 2015). Around one in ten children aged 5–16 years in the UK have some form of recognised mental health problem (Rees and Main, 2016). Relative to the clear upward trend in the prevalence of overweight and obesity among children, and associated health problems, there is more uncertainty around trends in mental health problems among children. As Rees and Main (2016) report, some studies find that there has been little change between 1999 and 2014, but others find that there has been a long-term increase in prevalence of mental health problems among adolescents, both in the UK and in other countries. Data from the most recent Mental Health of Children and Young People, England (MHCYP)[4] shows that the prevalence of children aged 5–15 years with any mental health disorder increased by 1.5 percentage points (from 9.7 per cent in 1999 to 11.2 per cent in 2017). The increase was higher for girls than boys (1.8 vs 1.2 percentage points) and was higher for children aged 11–15 years than for children aged 5–10 years (2.2 vs 1.1 percentage points). The increase was highest for girls aged 11–15 years, increasing from 9.6 per cent in 1999 to 13 per cent in 2017.

Both scholars and public health agencies acknowledge that how children spend time can influence a wide range of health outcomes (Hills et al, 2007; PHE, 2013). Numerous studies have found that engagement in physical activity is associated with improved health outcomes for school-aged children (Janssen and LeBlanc, 2010; Jimenez-Pavon et al, 2010; Hills et al, 2011), whereas time in sedentary activities is associated with increased weight and other health problems (Tremblay et al, 2011; Carson et al, 2016). As well as physical health, time use has an influence on children's mental health and well-being (Rees and Main, 2016). Multiple studies have found positive associations between time spent in screen-based activities and hyperactivity/inattention, internalising problems and indicators of psychological well-being, though with no association for depression, eating disorders, or low self-esteem (Suchert et al, 2015).

A large body of evidence, therefore, highlights significant associations between children's time use and a range of different health outcomes. This raises the question as to whether changes in how children spend their time can help explain negative trends in various health outcomes. Yet we know very little about the extent to which children's time use in connection with their health actually has changed. A basic question, therefore, remains largely unanswered, which is whether children's daily lives have become more sedentary, and whether they are spending less time in physical activities over time, coinciding with negative trends in physical and mental health outcomes.

Two key factors may have contributed to increases in children's time in sedentary screen-based activities and spending less time in physical activity outdoors. One is technological change and the second relates to parental concerns for children's safety particularly affecting the time they spend outdoors. There can be little doubt that technological change over the past several decades has given children access to an increasing range of options for spending time in screen-based activities. In the mid-1970s TV was the dominant media technology occupying children's leisure time indoors (Livingstone, 2009a). By the turn of the millennium, TV was already competing with other devices, such as video-game consoles and computers, for children's time in the home (Livingstone, 2002). From the millennium onwards, home-ownership of computers increased dramatically, from 44 per cent in 2000 to 83 per cent in 2014 (ONS, 2002; ONS, 2014b), and over 90 per cent of children in the UK now access the internet at home (Ofcom, 2015). Increased access to, and use of, multiple new technologies, lies behind concerns that children are spending excessive amounts of time in sedentary screen-based activities, at the expense of physical activities, with possibly negative consequences for their health (Palmer, 2007).

Technological change is not the only issue at play in debates about change in children's time in physical activities however. Many physical activities typically occur outdoors, thus raising concerns for children's safety arising from perceived dangers associated with traffic, strangers, or crime in the local neighbourhood. Hillman et al's 1990 study, *One False Move*, revealed a striking decrease in independent active travel (walking and cycling) among children between 1971 and 1990, alongside increased use of cars for travel, highlighting parental concerns for children's safety, particularly road safety, as a key determinant of these trends. Shaw et al (2013) update these trends and find broadly that there was relatively little change in children's independent mobility between 1990 and 2010, with significant decreases in independent mobility holding between 1971 and 2010. They show also that parents spontaneously mention concern for their children's safety in relation to restrictions they place on their children's independent mobility.

Parental concerns for children's safety are also thought to impact negatively on children's time in physical play outdoors (Gill, 2007; Faulkner et al, 2015), often coinciding with time when they are unsupervised (Kelly et al, 1998). Several studies reveal a generational decline in children's play outdoors as recounted by parents' comparisons with their own childhood (McNeish and Roberts, 1995; Valentine and McKendrick, 1997; Karsten, 2005). Children spending more time in organised sporting activities might counter this, however (Finch, 2002). Organised sport resolves potentially competing concerns about children's health and their safety outdoors in that it offers children an opportunity to engage in a physical activity but within a controlled environment typically supervised by adults. There is some limited evidence to support the view that children in the UK have increased their participation in sport since the 1980s (Dallman et al, 2005).

The active playful child is an enduring image of a childhood (Wyness, 2006), but some argue that children's daily lives, over the past several decades, have become less active, and more confined to the home (for example, Hillman et al 1990; Valentine, 2004; Gill, 2007). This has potentially negative consequences for their health and well-being, as a large body of empirical research connects children's time use with various health outcomes. Spending time in physical activities is widely viewed as positively associated with good health outcomes, whereas spending excessive amounts of time in sedentary screen-based activities is negatively associated with different physical and mental health outcomes. Consequently, there is a strong suspicion that negative trends in certain health outcomes (for example, childhood obesity and mental health problems) correspond with children leading lives that are less active and spending increasing time in screen-based activities, linked to technological change and parental concerns for children's safety.

This chapter scrutinises the empirical basis for this by examining trends in the time children spend in screen-based activities and in a range of different physical activities, over four decades between 1975 and 2015. The chapter looks at overall trends for younger (8–11 years) and older (12–16 years) children, and analyses differences relating to socio-economic background. Children in lower socio-economic groups are especially at risk of being overweight or obese (Shrewsbury and Wardle, 2008; El-Sayed et al, 2016), and are more likely to experience mental health problems (Rees and Main, 2016). Studies, furthermore, show that children in lower socio-economic groups spend more time in screen-based activities (Hofferth, 2010), though there is little evidence that children's engagement in physical activities is associated with socio-economic status (Biddle et al, 2011).

This chapter will also examine trends separately for boys and girls. Boys and girls differ markedly in terms of how they spend their time (Maudlin and Meeks, 1990), with boys typically spending more time both in physical activities and in screen-based activities. The prevalence of obesity among children is very similar between boys and girls (Bradshaw et al, 2016), suggesting that gender differences in time use may have little bearing on certain physical health outcomes. There are gender differences in the prevalence of certain mental health disorders, however, with higher rates among boys (Rees and Main, 2016). Recall though from earlier in this chapter that increases in mental health problems between 1999 and 2017 were greater among girls, especially older girls aged 11–15 years. In fact, the gender differences in mental health problems have diminished somewhat among older children (11–15 years).[5] In 1999, 13.1 per cent of boys and 9.6 per cent of girls aged 11–15 years had some mental health condition. The corresponding figures for 2017 were 14.2 per cent and 13.0 per cent respectively. Gender differences in mental health conditions, with boys outnumbering girls, persisted among younger children (5–10 years).

As in the previous chapter, the analysis is not solely interested in outlining trends in children's activities, but also seeks to understand more about the relationship between activities within each domain over time, and the influence of parents' engagement in similar activities. Therefore, following the analysis of trends in screen time and physical activities, the chapter moves on to explore the relationship between children's engagement in these contrasting, supposedly conflicting, areas of time use. The results from a novel of analysis of the relationship between children's monthly engagement in sporting activities and daily screen time are set out. The final section addresses questions concerning the relationship between parents' engagement in sporting activities and children's physical activity and screen time. Note that, with respect to parents' screen time, parents' time watching TV with children is taken up in Chapter 4 and their time using technology such as smartphones in the presence of children is examined in Chapter 5.

Trends in screen time

The analysis of children's time use relating to their health begins with an examination of trends in their total screen time between 1975 and 2015. The measure of screen time studied here is comprised of time when the child's main or primary activity is watching TV, playing video games, or using computers. In 1975, screen time was composed entirely of time watching TV, whereas in 2000 and 2015 it also includes time playing video games and using computers (Chapter 5 takes up the study of change in different types of screen-based activities in 2000 and 2015). Although not the total of all sedentary activity, which can include time doing homework and reading (see previous chapter), it is the single largest component of all sedentary activity.

Table 3.1 shows average screen time (in minutes) for children aged 8–11 years and 12–16 years on school and non-school days in 1975, 2000, and 2015. On school days, surprisingly, screen time did not change significantly between 1975 and 2000 for children in either age group, and between 2000 and 2015 screen time decreased significantly for children 8–11 years (-17 minutes), remaining largely unchanged for children aged 12–16 years. Therefore, against the pervasive view that screen time has risen inexorably over the past several decades, on school days at least there has been little change in screen time, with an actual decrease of half an hour between 1975 and 2015 among children aged 8–11 years.

In contrast, between 1975 and 2015, screen time on non-school days increased for children in both age groups, but the increase was greater for older children (12–16 years). There was, in 1975, no real difference in screen time between children 8–11 years and 12–16 years on either school or non-school days. By 2015, children aged 12–16 years spent more time in screen-based activities on both school and non-school

Table 3.1: Average minutes screen time on school and non-school days in 1975, 2000 and 2015: children 8–11 and 12–16 years

	1975	2000	2015
School day	**Average minutes [95% CI]**		
8–11 years	134 [123–145]	120 [112–128]	103 [93–112]
12–16 years	135 [121–149]	133 [124–141]	139 [128–150]
Non-school day			
8–11 years	186 [170–202]	203 [191–215]	229 [214–243]
12–16 years	182 [165–198]	223 [211–235]	249 [232–265]

days. Screen-based activities therefore have emerged as a major site for age-based distinctions in children's leisure time, over a period when technology and the online world (as opposed to the outside world) have become increasingly central to the formation of identity in childhood and youth (Livingstone, 2009b) (and see Chapter 5).

Figure 3.1 probes further into trends in screen time, breaking them down by parental education to examine differences broadly relating to socio-economic status. The results reveal a persistent difference in screen time on both school and non-school days associated with parental education. On school days in 1975, children with parents with only compulsory schooling spent 17 minutes more in screen-based activities. This difference dropped to 9 minutes in 2000, and was insignificant, because of a decrease in screen time between 1975 and 2000 for children with parents with relatively less education (−14 minutes). Between 2000 and 2015, however, screen time for children with relatively highly educated parents decreased significantly by 13 minutes with no change for children whose parents had compulsory education only, resulting in the re-emergence of a significant, and larger, parent-education difference of 26 minutes in 2015.

On non-school days, screen time increased for all children irrespective of parental education between 1975 and 2015, although the increase was most significant in the 1975–2000 period for children with relatively highly educated parents, and most significant in the 2000–2015 period for children whose parents had relatively less education. Looking across school and non-school days, these results suggest that the link between parental education and children's screen time in the UK was, to some extent, diminishing up to 2000, but that between 2000 and

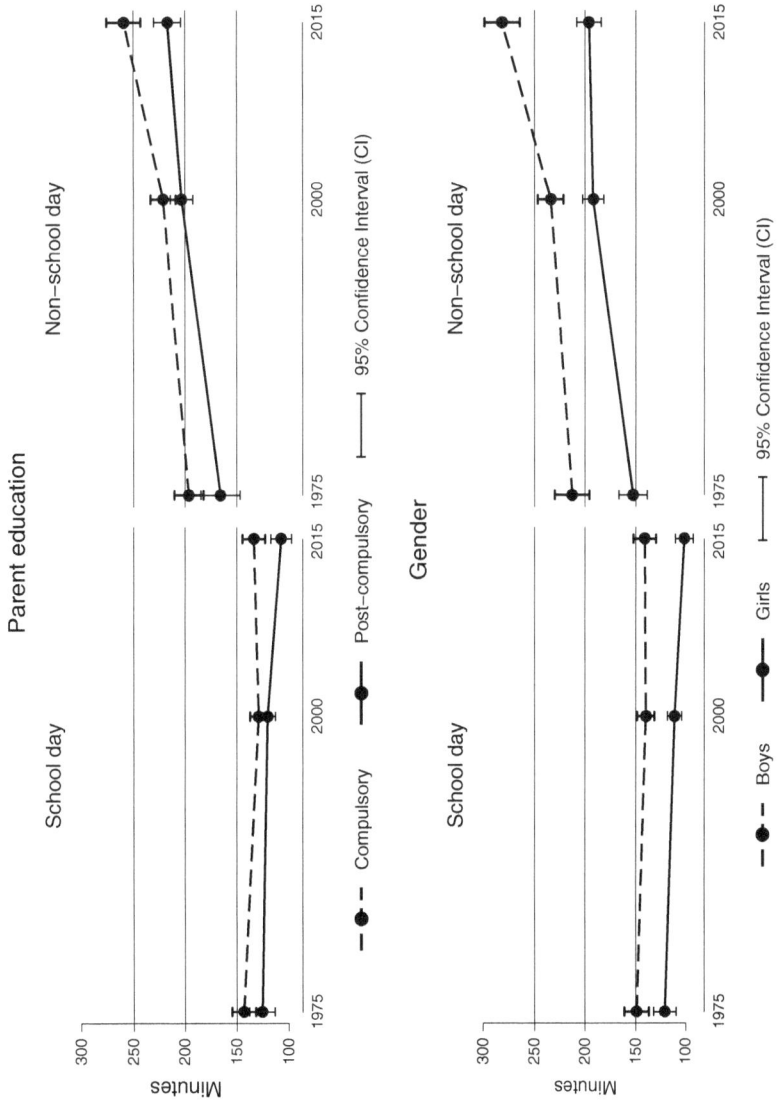

Figure 3.1: Average minutes children 8–16 years spend in screen time on school and non-school days in 1975, 2000 and 2015: parental education and child gender

2015 children's screen time became increasingly polarised in terms of differences associated with parental education.

Looking now at child gender, Figure 3.1 also shows that on school days there was no significant change in boys' screen time between 1975 and 2015. Girls in 2015, on the other hand, spent 19 minutes less in screen-based activities than girls in 1975. In contrast, on non-school days, girls' screen time increased by 40 minutes between 1975 and 2000, while the increase for boys in the same period was lower (21 minutes). Between 2000 and 2015, however, boys' screen time increased significantly, by 47 minutes, whereas girl's screen time did not change. Overall, between 1975 and 2015, boys' and girls' screen time increased by 68 minutes and 43 minutes respectively on non-school days. Chapter 5 probes further into gender differences in changes between 2000 and 2015 by examining trends in different screen-based activities.

These results show for the first time that there are limits to the extent to which children are spending more time in screen-based activities, when this is their main activity, and that the increases are concentrated in particular on non-school days. It is striking considering the proliferation of different types of technology available to children that their total time in screen-based activities remained mostly unchanged on days when they are at school and in fact decreased for younger children, girls, and those with relatively highly educated parents. This might reflect the constraints flowing from time spent at school, but it may also reflect the influence of parents in restricting children's time in screen-based activities on school days and directing them to time in other activities. The picture on non-school days, however, more closely resembles the widespread view that children are spending increasing time in screen-based activities. This raises questions about the alternatives that are available to children on the days when they have most free time.

Trends in physical activities

Time in physical activities is the second major dimension of daily life linked to health. This section builds upon the foregoing section on trends in screen time by analysing trends in children's time in a range of different physical activities. These are time in sport and exercise, time in out-of-home play, and time in active travel (walking and cycling).

Sport and exercise

Children's time in sport and exercise includes any time they spend in activities such as running or jogging, biking, playing ball games, general fitness activities, or swimming. It can include time when children are engaging in organised sporting activities supervised by an adult as well as time in informal sport and exercise such as skateboarding or playing a sport with friends, though it is not possible to distinguish in the data between organised or informal time in sport and exercise. Note also that any time children are doing sport at school may be recorded as time in 'classes' and is thus included in the measure of time at school. Therefore, the measure of time in sport and exercise studied here is necessarily restricted to time outside school.

Table 3.2 shows the average time children aged 8–11 years and 12–16 years spend in sport and exercise (in minutes) on school and non-school days in 1975, 2000, and 2015. On school days, between 1975 and 2000, average time in sport and exercise (outside school) increased for both groups. Sport time increased further between 2000 and 2015 on school days, though this increase was larger (and statistically significant) for children aged 8–11 years (10 minutes) than for children aged 12–16 years (7 minutes). Children in both age groups spent more time in sport and exercise on non-school days in each year. As on school days, there was a significant increase in time in sport and exercise between 1975 and 2000. However, unlike school days, there was no real change in time in sport and exercise between 2000 and 2015 on non-school days for children in either age group.

Figure 3.2 decomposes trends in sport based on parental education and child gender. Unlike screen time, there was no difference in

Table 3.2: Average minutes spent doing sport and exercise on school and non-school days in 1975, 2000 and 2015: children 8–11 and 12–16 years

	1975	2000	2015
School day	Average minutes [95% CI]		
8–11 years	6 [3–9]	16 [13–20]	27 [20–33]
12–16 years	13 [9–17]	22 [17–27]	29 [23–36]
Non-school day			
8–11 years	25 [20–30]	47 [40–54]	50 [41–60]
12–16 years	46 [37–55]	57 [50–65]	52 [45–60]

Figure 3.2: Average minutes children 8–16 years spend doing sport on school and non-school days in 1975, 2000 and 2015: parental education and child gender

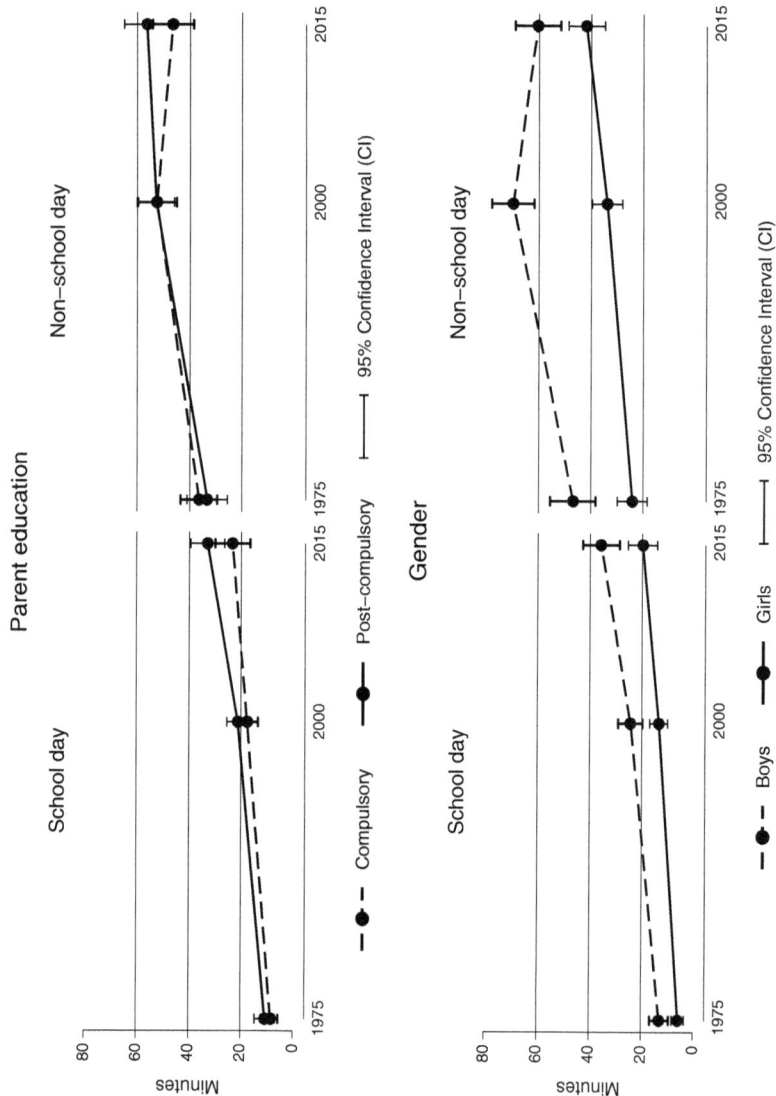

children's time in sport linked to parental education in any year on either school or non-school days, and thus trends were similar for children irrespective of parental education. In contrast, there were large and persistent gender differences. Boys spent more time in sport than girls did on both school and non-school days at all points in time, although the gender gap was markedly narrower on school days. Girls, however, have significantly increased their time in sport and exercise on both school and non-school days both between 1975 and 2000 and between 2000 and 2015. Therefore, limited change in sport between 2000 and 2015 on non-school days is concentrated among boys, whose time in sport decreased slightly in this latter period (−5 minutes), though this was not statistically significant.

Out-of-home play

Relative to sport and exercise, out-of-home play comprises a more ambiguous set of activities in terms of the physical nature of the activity. While it will include physical play, it can also include relatively passive games and forms of play, and although occurring outside the home it does not only include time outdoors. Data limitations in all surveys preclude the possibility of clearly identifying time when children are outdoors and being able to differentiate between more or less physical types of play. Though not ideal in terms of capturing physical play (which can of course occur within and around the home), this broad measure of time in games and play beyond the home will include physical play, and crucially is comparable across all surveys. In addition, leaving aside the physical aspect of this time, studying trends in out-of-home play will provide some insight into the curtailment of children's time outside the home over the past several decades.

Table 3.3 shows the average time children aged 8–11 years and 12–16 years spent in out-of-home play on school and non-school days in 1975, 2000, and 2015. On school days, there was no change in time in out-of-home play between 1975 and 2000. Children aged 8–11 years spent on average around 20 minutes in this activity in both years, whereas children aged 12–16 years spent approximately half as much time as younger children in out-of-home play in 1975 and 2000. There was a significant decrease between 2000 and 2015, however, in children's average time in out-of-home play in both age groups.

On non-school days, there has been a steady decline in out-of-home play over four decades between 1975 and 2015. Children aged 8–11 years spent on average 92 minutes in out-of-home play on non-school days in 1975, which dropped to 52 minutes in 2000,

Table 3.3: Average minutes in out-of-home play on school and non-school days in 1975, 2000 and 2015: children 8–11 and 12–16 years

	1975	2000	2015
School day	Average minutes [95% CI]		
8–11 years	23 [18–28]	21 [17–26]	12 [7–17]
12–16 years	10 [5–14]	12 [8–15]	3 [1–5]
Non-school day			
8–11 years	92 [75–108]	52 [44–60]	28 [21–34]
12–16 years	45 [31–59]	23 [18–28]	8 [5–11]

and dropped again to 28 minutes in 2015. There were decreases of comparable magnitude for children aged 12–16 years also, though again they consistently averaged less time in this activity than younger children. This broad activity encompasses more than physical play outdoors, but these trends are certainly in alignment with a widespread view that children's play outdoors has decreased substantially over time.

In absolute amounts, as time in out-of-home play decreased over time so too have age differences associated with time in this activity, primarily because younger children's time in this activity decreased to a greater extent than older children (albeit from a much higher level). However, the overriding pattern here is not so much about a homogenisation of time in play across age groups over time (as found for sport), but rather the steady disappearance of time in this activity for children in all age groups. Reports of the supposed disappearance of children's play have a long history (see Roberts, 1980: 26–39), and no doubt the nature of play changes, but these results nevertheless present a stark picture of decline in the amount of time children spend in an activity that is intimately tied to commonly shared understandings of what childhood is.

Children in families where at least one parent has some post-compulsory education spent less time in out-of-home play in 1975 than those with no parent who has post-compulsory education, especially on non-school days, but there was no longer any difference in out-of-home play in 2000 or 2015 on either school or non-school days (see Figure 3.3). Note that on non-school days children in relatively highly educated families spend significantly more time in play at home

Figure 3.3: Average minutes children 8–16 years spend in out-of-home play on school and non-school days in 1975, 2000 and 2015: parental education and child gender

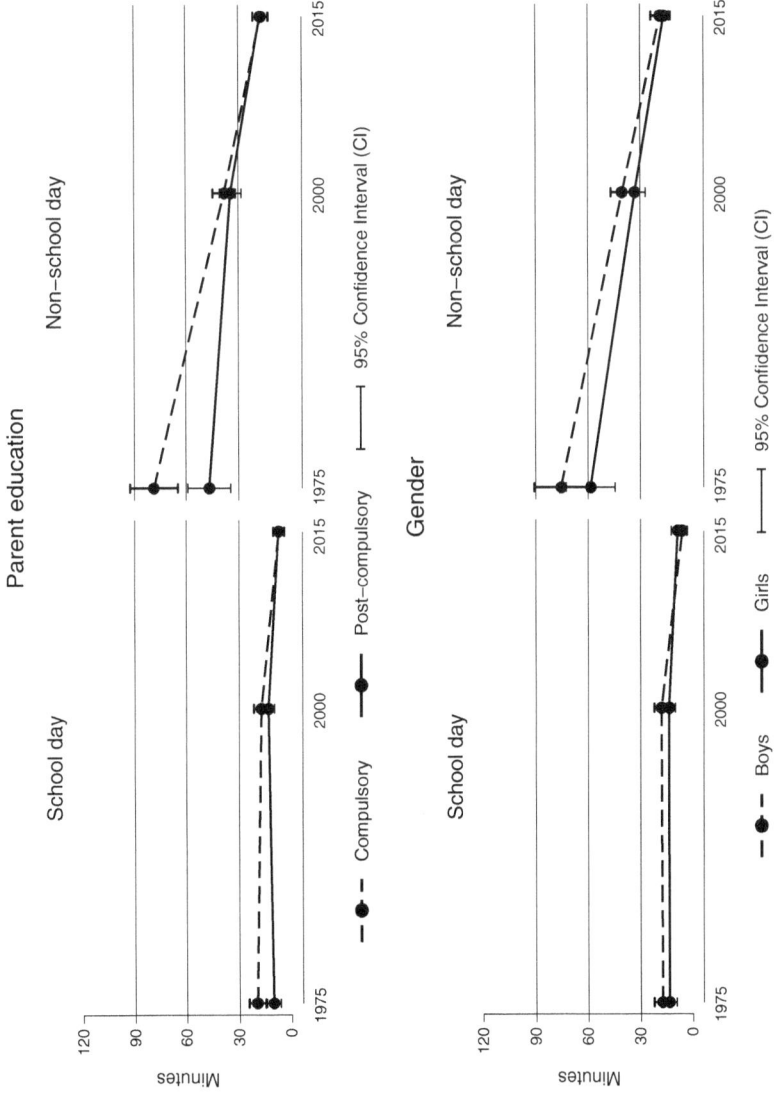

in 1975, and that parental education was not significantly associated with the total time children spend playing.[6] Notably, despite parents expressing stronger concerns for girls' safety compared with boys (Valentine, 2004), there were no significant gender differences in the time children spent in out-of-home play. The difference was greatest in 1975 on non-school days with girls spending 17 minutes less time in this activity than boys, but this difference was not statistically significant. As time in out-of-home play decreased between 1975 and 2015, however, differences linked to gender (and parent education) have disappeared.

Finch (2002) has suggested that increasing time in organised sports may substitute for decreasing time in more informal out-of-home play. The trends for time in sport and out-of-home play do provide some support for this. To consider this further, Figure 3.4 combines the results for sport and exercise with out-of-home play to provide an overview of trends in the total time in these activities. It shows that the total time in these activities combined increased on school days between 1975 and 2000 for children in both age groups, underpinned by an increase in time in sport with no change in out-of-home play. Between 2000 and 2015, however, there was little change in total time in these activities, as further increases in time in sport offset decreases in out-of-home play.

On non-school days, the results show a substantial decrease in total time in these activities, driven by decreases in time in out-of-home play that were not offset by increases in time in sport. These results should be interpreted with caution with respect to drawing conclusion about trends in children's time in total physical activity for reasons already noted. Nevertheless, they do show that children's engagement in sport has become the dominant component of their physical activity, and there have been only modest increases in time in this activity between 2000 and 2015.

Active travel

Children's daily time in active travel is the last component of time in physical activities examined here. The analysis of trends in active travel time uses data collected in the location field of the time diary where respondents could record their location or, when travelling, mode of transport. The 1975 survey did not collect this information, and therefore the focus here is on trends in active travel time between 2000 and 2015. Active travel is time when children report walking or cycling as their mode of transport. Table 3.4 shows the average time children

Figure 3.4: Average minutes in sport and out-of-home play combined on school and non-school days in 1975, 2000 and 2015: children 8–11 and 12–16 years

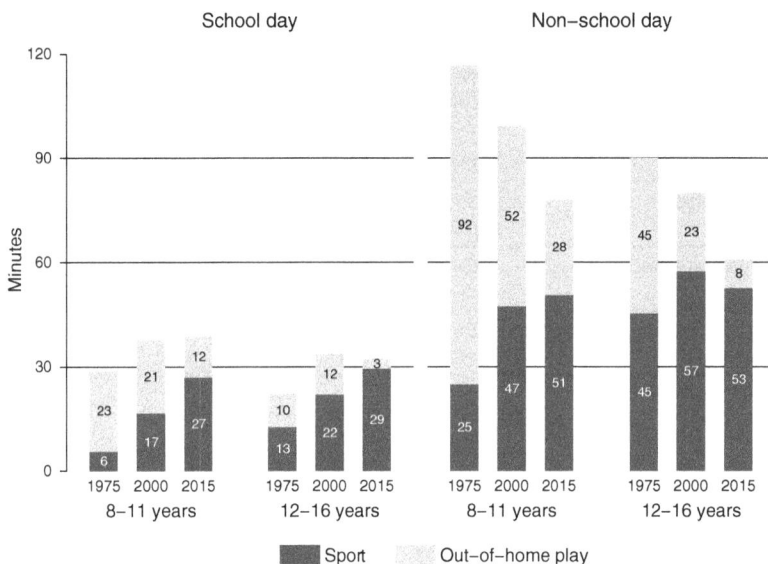

aged 8–11 years and 12–16 years spend in active travel (walking/cycling) in 2000 and 2015 on school and non-school days. To provide a complete picture of trends in travel time, Table 3.4 also shows results for children's time travelling by car or other vehicle, trends in time using public transport, and total travel time (which includes time when children did not specify their mode of travel in the diary).

The results are striking and reinforce the results for out-of-home play set out in the previous section. Children in both age groups spent significantly less time in active travel in 2015 compared with 2000, on both school and non-school days. For example, active travel on school days by older children (12–16 years) decreased from 45 minutes in 2000 to 32 minutes in 2015, with an even greater decrease on non-school days. The decrease on school days for children aged 8–11 years was lower but still statistically significant, and there was a substantial decrease on non-school days comparable with the decrease for children aged 12–16 years (44 minutes in 2000 vs 20 minutes in 2015).

Total travel time was very similar on school days between 2000 and 2015. For children aged 8–11 years, small increases in travel by car or using public transport offset decreasing time in active travel. Children aged 12–16 years also spent slightly more time using public transport in

73

Table 3.4: Average minutes in different modes of travel on school and non-school days in 2000 and 2015: children 8–11 and 12–16 years

| | 8–11 years | | 12–16 years | |
	2000	2015	2000	2015
School day	**Average minutes [95% CI]**		**Average minutes [95% CI]**	
Active travel (walk/cycle)	27 [24–30]	21 [17–25]	45 [41–50]	32 [28–37]
Car/vehicle	25 [22–28]	27 [23–30]	19 [16–22]	21 [17–24]
Public transport	5 [3–6]	8 [5–11]	22 [19–26]	27 [22–32]
Total (including unspecified mode)	64 [60–68]	66 [61–72]	94 [88–100]	92 [86–99]
Non-school day				
Active travel (walk/cycle)	44 [37–50]	20 [17–24]	53 [47–59]	23 [19–28]
Car/vehicle	47 [42–52]	45 [39–50]	40 [36–45]	36 [31–41]
Public transport	6 [3–9]	4 [2–7]	12 [9–15]	12 [6–19]
Total (including unspecified mode)	107 [98–115]	78 [71–85]	115 [107–123]	83 [74–92]

2015 (27 minutes) compared with 2000 (22 minutes). On non-school days, decreasing time in active travel underpins a significant decrease in total travel time for children in both age groups. As we will see in more detail in the following chapter, a significant increase in the time children spend at home between 2000 and 2015 absorbs this decrease in total travel time (see also Mullan, 2019).

Decreases in time in active travel were found for children irrespective of parental education, but on non-school days the decrease in active travel was significantly greater for children in families where parents have compulsory education only (−36 minutes) compared with children in families with relatively more highly educated parents (−17 minutes). In fact, children in the former group averaged significantly more time in active travel than those in the latter group in 2000 (on both school and non-school days), but this was no longer the case on either day in 2015. Lastly, unlike time in sport and exercise as the main activity, gender was not significantly associated with children's time in active travel on any day in both 2000 and 2015.

The relationship between sport and screen time

This chapter has shown that screen time increased between 1975 and 2015, though this was concentrated on days when children were not at school, and was most pronounced among certain groups (boys, children aged 12–16 years, and those whose parents have compulsory education only). The results for physical activities showed an increase in time in sport and exercise between 1975 and 2000, with little change between 2000 and 2015. In contrast, time in out-of-home play decreased between 1975 and 2000, and further between 2000 and 2015. Moreover, active travel decreased significantly between 2000 and 2015. Though there is no comparable data for 1975, it is highly likely that average active travel time would have been higher in 1975 than in 2000 (see Hillman et al, 1990; Pooley et al, 2005). Flowing from these changes, children's daily time in physical activities is increasingly concentrated in sport and exercise, which tends to be organised and under adult supervision, and which changed little between 2000 and 2015. It would seem therefore that between 2000 and 2015 children are spending more time at home in screen-based activities (Chapter 4 studies trends in time at home), at the expense of spending time in informal physical activities outside the home, such as play and active travel.

Whether these trends in screen time and physical activity are connected or not remains an open question. As already noted, some argue that technological change has led to children spending more time in screen-based activities at the expense of time in physical activities (for example, Palmer, 2007). There is evidence that children who spend more time in physical activities spend less time in sedentary activities, but the association is small (Marshall et al, 2004) and not consistent across countries (Melkevik et al, 2010). Only a limited number of empirical studies have addressed this question, however. This section therefore presents a novel analysis of the relationship between children's engagement in sport and screen time in the UK. The analysis uses data on children's monthly engagement in sport collected in the UK Time Use Surveys in 2000 and 2015 to differentiate between children who are relatively more engaged in sporting activities during the month and those who are relatively less engaged at each of these points in time (details are provided in the following discussion). The analysis then compares daily time use patterns in 2000 and 2015, including screen time, for children who are relatively more or less engaged in sport during the month.

There were fewer sporting activities specified in the questionnaire for the 2015 survey than in the 2000 survey, and to ensure comparability

Table 3.5: Distribution of the number of times children 8–16 years engage in different sporting activities: boys and girls in 2000 and 2015

	Boys		Girls	
	2000 (%)	2015 (%)	2000 (%)	2015 (%)
None	6.3	10.3	13.5	16.0
1–14 times	45.8	48.9	55.9	54.9
15–30 times	27.1	26.4	20.5	18.7
31+ times	20.9	14.5	10.1	10.4
Mean	18.8	16.3	12.5	12.5
Median	14	12	8	8

Notes: Weights applied

across surveys only those sporting activities listed in both surveys are considered. These are swimming, aerobics and weights, cycling, team games, racquet games, golf, walking, and running. The total number of times children engage in these different sporting activities during the month is then calculated. Table 3.5 contains information about the distribution of the total number of times children engage in different sporting activities during the month for boys and girls in 2000 and 2015.

Nearly all children engage in some sporting activity at least once during the month. Around 94 per cent of boys in 2000 engaged in at least one sporting activity during the month, though this dropped slightly to close to 90 per cent in 2015. These proportions are closely comparable with similar data reported elsewhere (DCMS, 2015). The most common level of engagement in sporting activities by boys was between 1–14 times during the month, and this increased slightly from around 46 per cent in 2000 to around 49 per cent in 2015, with just over one quarter of boys engaging in a sporting activity between 15–30 times during the month in both 2000 and 2015. The proportion of boys highly engaged in sport (31 or more times per month) decreased from 21 per cent in 2000 to 14.5 per cent in 2015. Overall, the average (mean) number of times boys engaged in sporting activities decreased from 18.8 to 16.3, and the median from 14 to 12 times.

As with average time per day in sport and exercise, the average (mean) number of times girls engage in different sporting activities is lower than boys in both 2000 and 2015 (12.5 times per month). Compared with boys, a higher proportion of girls either do not engage in any sporting activities or do so between 1 to 14 times per month, while fewer engage in sport between 15 to 30 times per month or more. Unlike boys, whose monthly engagement in sport decreased between 2000 and 2015, girls' monthly engagement in sport did not change significantly over this period. There is a trace of this in the results for children's time in sport and exercise on the diary day. Although there was no significant decrease in boys' time in sport and exercise on the diary day, there were diverging patterns for boys and girls between 2000 and 2015 on non-school days, with an increase for girls and a decrease for boys (see Figure 3.2).

It is reasonable to expect a direct positive correlation between children's total time in sport and exercise, and the total number of times they engage in sporting activities throughout the month. These are after all, simply two different ways of measuring children's engagement in the same broad activity. Though there is data for two days in a single week (a weekday and a weekend) for each child only, using this information we can explore the relationship between total time in sport and exercise (summed over the two days available) and the total number of times children engage in sport during the month. Crucially, as well as looking at time in sport and exercise, it is possible to examine the relationship between children's monthly engagement in sport and their daily time in other activities, including screen-based activities. Although a direct relationship between indicators of the *number of times* engaging in sporting activities and the *total time* in sport and exercise may be expected, there is no equivalent direct relationship with time in other activities. Of particular interest here is whether there is any link between general engagement in sport (indicated by the number of times doing sport during the month) and daily screen time.

For the analysis, children are divided into two approximately equal groups. One group contains children who report up to the median number of times engaging in sporting activities per month, and the second contains children who report doing sporting activities for more than the median number of times per month. This is done separately for 2000 and 2015, and for boy and girls (Table 3.5 reports the median values for each sub-sample). Children in these groups are compared with respect to their average time in sport, screen time, non-screen leisure, and active travel. Table 3.6 shows, for boys and girls in 2000 and 2015, the difference in total time in these activities (summed across the two diary days) between those relatively highly engaged in sporting activities throughout the month (greater than the median) compared with those relatively less engaged (median or less).

As expected, boys who are relatively highly engaged in sport during the month spend significantly more time in sport and exercise (summed over two days) in both 2000 (55.8 minutes) and 2015 (70.6 minutes).

Table 3.6: Association between monthly engagement in sport and daily average minutes in sport, screen time, non-screen leisure and active travel: boys and girls in 2000 and 2015

	Boys		Girls	
	2000	*2015*	*2000*	*2015*
Sport	55.8***	70.6***	4.4	27.1**
Screen time	−67.2**	−55.4*	12.4	−29.6
Non-screen leisure	5.5	−11.9	−9.0	10.3
Active travel	30.6**	1.0	1.2	7.3

Notes: Table shows the difference in the average minutes summed over two days between those who report greater than the median number of times engaging in sport during the month and those who report the median or less. *** p < .001; ** p < .01; * p < .05

In addition to this, there is a significant negative association with total screen time. Boys who engage in sport for in excess of the median number of times per month (14 times per month in 2000, 12 times per month in 2015) average around one hour less screen time in both 2000 and 2015 than boys relatively less engaged in sport throughout the month. In contrast to screen time, boys' monthly engagement in sport was not significantly associated with total time in non-screen leisure activities. Time in active travel was positively associated with monthly engagement in sport, but in 2000 only. Therefore, as well as children's average time in active travel decreasing between 2000 and 2015, it has become less connected to boys' general engagement in sporting activities.

Girls' monthly engagement in sport, however, was not as strongly associated with their daily time use. There was no significant difference in average time in sport and exercise between girls relatively highly engaged in sport during the month and those less so in 2000. It could be, given girls' lower engagement in sport relative to boys', that it would be necessary to observe girls' daily time use over a longer period (perhaps one complete week) in order to find a significant link between the total number of time girls engage in sporting activities and their total time in sport and exercise. It is important to note here, however, that the measure of daily time in sport excludes any time in sport during school. Having said that, there was a significant positive association between monthly and daily measures of engagement in sport in 2015, even though there was no significant increase in the average number of times girls engage in sporting activities during the month (see Table 3.5). This might reflect a deepening of girls' engagement in sport where a given level of engagement has a stronger impact on daily time in sport outside school, underpinning the modest increase in girls' average time in sport between 2000 and 2015 already shown (see Figure 3.2). Girls' monthly engagement in sport also has no significant impact on their daily screen time (though there is a substantial negative difference in 2015), non-screen leisure, or active travel.

Parents' engagement in sport and children's sport and screen time

Parents can play a major role in influencing their children's engagement in physical activity (Edwardson and Gorely, 2010; Cheng et al, 2014; Lindqvist et al, 2015). This can be in the form of support and encouragement for children to engage in sport and physical activity, including transporting children to organised sporting activities, being involved in organising sport for their children, and modelling engagement in sport and physical activity themselves. The final section of this chapter investigates whether parents' engagement in sport has a positive modelling effect on children's engagement in sport and on their daily time use more generally. First, the association between parent and child monthly engagement in sport is analysed. Following this, the influence of parent monthly engagement in sport and children's daily time use is studied. It has already been shown that to some extent, especially for boys, engagement in sport displaces screen time. Whether parents' engagement in sport has any similar effects is an open question; further study of this will provide new insights on the possible influences of the wider family context for children's daily activities.

As for children, the total number of times mothers and fathers engage in sporting activities during the month is computed using data from the 2000 and 2015 surveys. Table 3.7 shows the distribution of the number of times parents engage in different sporting activities throughout the month. Compared with children, more parents did not report engaging in any of the sporting activities considered here. In 2000, just over 40

Table 3.7: The number of times parents engage in different sporting activities: 2000 and 2015

	Fathers		Mothers	
	2000	2015	2000	2015
None	41.8	33.3	43.5	32.5
1–14 times	40.4	39.4	40.0	41.3
15–30 times	12.9	18.3	12.1	20.0
31+ times	4.9	9.0	4.5	6.2
Mean	7.3	10.6	7.0	9.6
Median	2	4	2	4

per cent of both fathers and mothers did not report engaging in any sporting activity during the month. This decreased significantly, with around a third of both fathers and mothers not reporting engaging in sporting activities in 2015.

Offsetting this were increases in the proportion of mothers and fathers engaging in sporting activities at least 15 times per month. Overall, the average and median number of times mothers and fathers engaged in a sporting activity during the month increased between 2000 and 2015. Finally, it is notable that, unlike children, there was no significant gender difference in engagement in sporting activities between mothers and fathers.

Replicating the approach taken with children (see previous section), parents are split into two groups: 1) those who report the median or lower number of times engaging in sport during the month; and 2) those who report above the median number of times engaging in sport during the month. These broadly capture, respectively, relatively low and high engagement in sport by parents during the month. As shown in Figure 3.5, there was a significant association between parent and child monthly engagement in sport. Children whose parents (both mothers and fathers) report relatively high level of engagement in sport during the month (above median) average significantly more times doing sport during the month than those whose parents are relatively less engaged in sport during the month (median or below). Equally applying to both girls and boys in 2000 and 2015, both mothers' and fathers' monthly engagement in sports was positively associated with children's monthly engagement in sport.

This clear relationship breaks down, however, when looking at the influence of mothers' and fathers' monthly engagement in sport and children's daily time use (see Table 3.8). Neither mothers' nor fathers' monthly engagement in sport is significantly associated with boys' or girls' average daily time in sport. There is some evidence that children with mothers who are relatively more engaged in sporting activities throughout the month spend less time in screen-based activities and more time in non-screen leisure. The differences are not always significant, however, but the size of the differences is not negligible. The influence of fathers' monthly engagement in sport on children's daily time use, in comparison with mothers' engagement, is more limited.

Conclusion

Concerns around children's health have surfaced in recent decades against a backdrop of increasing childhood obesity and related illnesses

Figure 3.5: Association between parent and child monthly engagement in sporting activities

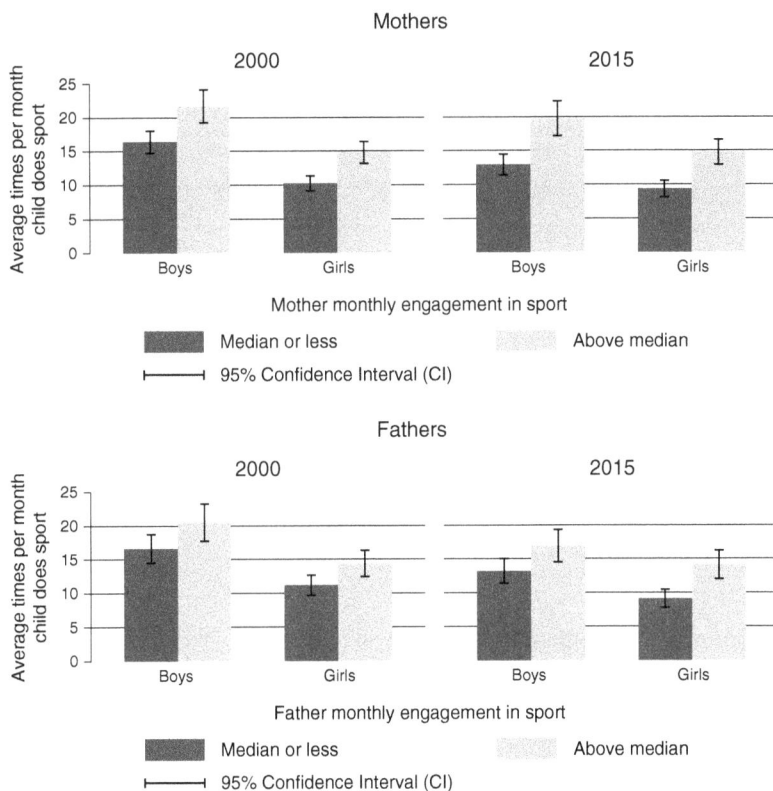

alongside the rising prevalence of mental health problems among children. An extensive body of empirical research shows links between children's engagement in physical and sedentary activities as having a positive and negative association respectively with various health outcomes. Attention has thus turned to questions about the extent to which changes in how children spend their time connects to changes in health outcomes. This chapter sought to contribute here by providing an extensive analysis of how children's time in screen-based activities (the major form of sedentary activity in a child's day), and their time in a range of different physical activities changed over four decades between 1975 and 2015. The overarching aim of this chapter has been to assess the extent to which children's daily lives have become more sedate and/or less active over time.

There was a substantial difference in trends in health-related activities between school and non-school days. On school days, time in

Table 3.8: Association between mothers' and fathers' monthly engagement in sport and children's average minutes in sport, screen time and non-screen leisure: boys and girls in 2000 and 2015

	Boys		Girls	
	2000	*2015*	*2000*	*2015*
Mothers' monthly sport				
Sport and exercise	8.2	19.3	7.9	−5.0
Screen time	−34.6	−73.6"	−35.2˙	−27.0
Non-screen leisure	39.6	30.4	24.3	51.3˙
Active travel	9.0	16.0˙	17.8˙	2.9
Fathers' monthly sport				
Sport and exercise	9.5	−14.2	7.2	−6.7
Screen time	−3.1	−16.4	6.4	16.4
Non-screen leisure	17.6	3.2	−24.8	1.9
Active travel	15.9	4.1	1.0	5.7

Notes: Table shows the difference in the average minutes summed over two days between those whose mothers/fathers report greater than the median number of times engaging in sport during the month and those whose mothers/fathers report the median or less. *** p < .001; ** p < .01; * p < .05

screen-based activities (when these are the primary activity) has not increased over four decades, and it has even modestly decreased among younger children (8–11 years). Conversely, children's average time in sport increased significantly over this period, though the increase was concentrated in 1975–2000 period for children aged 12–16 years. Partially offsetting this, children's time in out-of-home play decreased with total time in physical activities (sport and out-of-home play) remaining unchanged. Active travel time did decrease, however, between 2000 and 2015. Overall then, there is little evidence to support the view that children's daily lives have become markedly less active on school days, with evidence in fact to support the view that younger children, at least, are leading more active lives, spending more time in sport and less time in screen-based activities.

The picture on non-school days differs markedly however. Here there was a clear increase in total time in screen-based activities, particularly between 2000 and 2015, in tandem with substantial decreases in the time children spend in out-of-home play and active travel. Average time in sport, however, increased significantly between 1975 and 2000, but remained unchanged between 2000 and 2015. These diverging changes in different types of physical activity underscore that children's time here is composed increasingly of engagement in organised sporting activities with children spending less time in informal physical activity (Finch, 2002). This most likely reflects the influence of parental concerns for children's safety, limiting the time they can spend outdoors playing and in active travel such as walking or cycling to and from school.

There were persistent and substantial gender differences in children's time in screen-based activities and sport, with boys consistently spending more time in these activities over time on both school and non-school days. Girls are gradually spending more time in sport over the past four decades, on both school and non-school days, and the gender gap narrowed between 2000 and 2015 on non-school days but it remains large. There were no gender differences, however, in active travel, and gender differences in out-of-home play, again favouring boys and concentrated on non-school days, diminished over time, as time in this activity all but vanished, with no significant gender difference in 2015. There remains a considerable distance to travel to equalise daily time in sport for boys and girls. It is important to note, however, that children's engagement in sporting activities during school was not captured in time diaries and it is highly likely that gender differences in time in sport when children are at school will be lower.

Socio-economic inequalities in child health outcomes, with children in lower socio-economic groups faring worse, may be related to differences in how they spend their time. The only significant difference found in connection with parental education related to children's time in screen-based activities, with no significant association with time in sport, active travel, or time in out-of-home play (except in 1975). Across all years, on both school and non-school days, children with more educated parents spent less time in screen-based activities than those whose parents had no post-compulsory schooling. It would be misguided, however, to conclude from this that socioeconomic differences in health outcomes relate directly to how children spend their time and specifically to the differences in time in screen-based activities associated with parental education found here. Differences in screen time associated with parental education predate the rise in obesity and mental health problems that currently dominate public concern about children's health. Differences in screen time associated with parental education, moreover, do not have a counterpart in children's time in physical activities. Rather than being related to children's engagement in physical activities, socio-economic differences in screen time are most likely entwined with inverse differences in children's time doing homework, study or reading; that is, other types of sedentary activity that are in direct competition for children's time and attention when at home.

The question as to whether increases in screen time between 2000 and 2015 on non-school days have come at the expense of time in physical activities is a difficult one to provide a clear answer for. Time spent only in informal physical activities (active travel and out-of-home play) decreased, where time in sport did not, but it seems unlikely that this is a direct result of increases in screen time. If it were, it would be difficult to explain why increases in screen time between 2000 and 2015 on non-school days were concentrated among boys and children whose parents have compulsory education only, whereas decreases in active travel and out-of-home play were found irrespective of child gender and parental education. There was, moreover, little change between 2000 and 2015 in average time in screen-based activities for girls and for children whose parents have some post-compulsory education, yet there were significant decreases in active travel and out-of-home play among these groups.

Nevertheless, for boys at least, there was a significant negative relationship between engagement in sporting activities and time in screen-based activities. Boys who were relatively more engaged in sport during the month spent more time in sport (outside school) on the diary day and less time in screen-based activities. This suggests that daily time in sport directly competes with time in screen-based activities among boys who are most engaged in sport in general. This raises the possibility that increases in boys' screen time on non-school days between 2000 and 2015 might have stunted further increases in boys' time in sport during this period which was observed among girls whose screen time remained unchanged.

Efforts to increase routine engagement in sport might therefore help in limiting screen time, but it is far from clear whether increasing time in sporting activities will ever be sufficient to overcome significant decreases in other informal physical activities. It is apparent that increases in sport do not compensate for decreases in informal physical activities, highlighting a clear limitation in the capacity of sport to offer enough opportunities for children to engage in physical activity on any ordinary day. This may be due to a lack of accessible facilities, or the availability of activities that are feasible given constraints on parents' time and other resources. Parents' engagement in sport is likely to be instrumental here: there was a highly significant positive association between parent and child monthly engagement in sport. Promoting sport is important, but unless underlying and deeply embedded concerns around children's safety outdoors are addressed in our society, it is unlikely that significant change will occur in the time children spend outdoors in informal physical activities like regular walking, cycling or outdoor play and running about. The responsibility for this should not rest solely with parents.

Notes

[1] https://digital.nhs.uk/catalogue/PUB30169
[2] http://www.gov.scot/Publications/2017/10/2970/downloads
[3] http://www.gov.scot/Publications/2017/10/2970/downloads
[4] https://digital.nhs.uk/data-and-information/publications/statistical/mental-health-of-children-and-young-people-in-england/2017/2017
[5] https://digital.nhs.uk/data-and-information/publications/statistical/mental-health-of-children-and-young-people-in-england/2017/2017
[6] The sole exception here is on school days in 2000, where children in relatively more educated families spend less time in play (probably as they spend more time in homework).

4

Time for Family

The previous two chapters each addressed questions concerning children's activities, or, to put it in other words, what children do. This chapter marks a departure from these chapters by bringing contextual features of children's daily lives into view. Context here refers to information about the location where activities occur and information about who else is present during the activity. The focus in this chapter is on the context of daily life linked to family, in particular concentrating on the time children spend at home and with parents. The chapter uses data collected from both children and parents to create comparable measures of co-location and time in shared family activities covering a period of four decades between 1975 and 2015, thereby enabling analysis of long-term trends in children's time use connected to family. The analysis in this chapter is restricted, however, to measures of time when children are co-located with their parents at home because of data restrictions in the earliest survey detailed in the next section. Chapter 5 will take up the study of change in children's total time with parents across all locations, and other dimensions of the social context of daily life, using available comparable data in recent years.

This chapter is organised in three major parts looking at separate, though connected, elements of the family context of children's daily lives. The first part sets out an analysis of long-term trends between 1975 and 2015 in the time children are at home, distinguishing between time when parents are also at home and time when they are not at home. In addition to considering total time with parents, the analysis differentiates, in two-parent families, between time when children are with their mothers only, with their fathers only, or with both parents, enabling the analysis of patterns in the gender division of parents' time with school-age children at home. The second part brings together the analysis of trends in major activities covered in previous chapters with the analysis of trends in time at home with and without parents in this chapter. This exploratory analysis provides further insights into trends in major activities, highlighting connections between children's activities and the family context, and re-examines key factors associated with children's time use across varying social contexts. Lastly the third part, using data on time in daily activities provided by both parents and children, presents the results of an analysis of long-term trends in children's time in shared activities when at home with parents together over four decades between 1975 and 2015.

Change in children's time with and without parents at home

Previous chapters revealed that children are spending more time in screen-based activities and doing homework (activities taking place mostly at home) and less time in out-of-home play and active travel. The possible influence of parental concerns for children's safety and technological change were highlighted as key factors leading to children to spending more time at home, typically under parental supervision. Research on trends in parents' time with children shows that over the past several decades they are spending more time doing childcare (Gershuny, 2000; Gauthier et al, 2004; Sayer et al, 2004) and spending more time with children in general (Genadek et al, 2016; Neilson and Stanfors, 2017). It is interesting to note that rather than drawing attention to parental concerns for children's safety, this body of research from the perspective of parents suggests that these increases may stem from changing parenting norms valorising spending time with children together as a family.

This prior research on trends in parents' time with children focuses on care provided by parents to younger children and little is known about change in the time older school-age children spend with their parents in the UK (or elsewhere). Children's care needs change at different stages of their development (Waldfogel, 2006) and trends in time in direct childcare activities (feeding, cleaning, or reading to children) decrease as children grow older (Craig and Bittman, 2008). Added to this, as they get older, children spend more time away from their parents and this is an essential part of their development as adolescents seeking more autonomy (Steinberg, 2002). This raises a question therefore about whether older school-aged children are spending more time at home when their parents are not at home. Though not comprising all the time children are away from their parents, spending time at home when parents are not also there is an important aspect of children's development of autonomy, but we know next to nothing about how this may have changed over the past several decades.

Addressing this, this chapter investigates trends over four decades between 1975 and 2015 in the time children spend with their parents at home, and time when children are at home and their parents are not at home. Time-diary data provided by both children and parents are used to measure time when they are together at home, and time when children are at home and their parents are not at home. This represents a departure from most previous research on trends in the time parents and children are together, which uses measures based solely on parents' reports of time being with children. Sandberg and Hofferth (2001) are a rare example of using data from children to measure time with parents. Using data from both children and parents allows a distinction between times when they are together, in a broad sense, from time when they are not together, which is a critical distinction for older children.

The analysis of trends between 1975 and 2015 in the time children spend with and away from parents is restricted to time at home because the 1975 survey provides limited information about children's locations outside the home and children were not able to indicate directly when they were with their parents. Despite this restriction, when awake and not at school, children are at home for a large portion of the day and have been shown to view time at home as integral, even synonymous, with family time (Christensen et al, 2000). Although this focus on time at home is somewhat restrictive, the data available does permit a study of trends in this substantial aspect of the social context of children's daily lives over four decades between 1975 and 2015. Nevertheless, this chapter does not study change in the total time children are with their parents or not with their parents (at home and at other locations); this is taken up in the following chapter for 2000 and 2015 where appropriate data are available.

As already noted, as children get older, it is expected that they spend less time with their parents, so it is necessary to decompose trends for children in different age groups (Larson and Richards, 1991; Lam et al, 2012). With respect to parental education, the increasing importance of education for child outcomes may have led to parents 'investing' more time in their children's education and development (Ramey and Ramey, 2009), and there is evidence that the positive trend in certain elements of parental time devoted to children is greater for more educated parents (Altintas, 2016; Sullivan, 2010). Again, however, extant research here tends to focus on parents of younger children, and less is known about the possible influence of parental education on the time older school-aged children in the UK spend with their parents, and indeed not with their parents.

In addition to studying trends in children's time with parents at home, the analysis will differentiate, in two-parent families, between time when children are with their mothers only, with their fathers only, or with both parents, allowing us to study patterns in the gender division of parents' time with school-age children at home. The analysis here will explore associations between maternal employment and children's time with mothers and fathers over time. The labour force participation of mothers has been increasing in the UK over many decades, though it was always comparatively high among mothers with school-aged children.[1] There is concern in some quarters that mothers' increased time in paid work might come at the expense of time with children. These concerns have proven unwarranted, however. Paid work (especially part-time) often coincides with children's time in school, employed mothers prioritise time with children outside of paid work (often by sacrificing time in leisure and sleep), and fathers have increased their time with children (Presser, 1989; Bianchi, 2000; Craig, 2007). Again, however, extant research here concentrates on families with younger children and little is known about associations between maternal employment and the time older school-age children spend with co-resident mothers and fathers in two-parent families.

Time at home with and without parents

Table 4.1 reports the average time children aged 8–11 years and 12–16 years spent at home (awake) in 1975, 2000 and 2015 on school and non-school days, differentiating between time with and without parents. The average time both groups spent at home with parents on school days changed little over four decades. For younger children (8–11 years), this decreased by small amounts between 1975 and 2000 (−10 minutes) and between 2000 and 2015 (−7 minutes), leading to an overall decrease between 1975 and 2015 of around 17 minutes, which was marginally statistically significant (p=0.05). For older children (12–16 years) there was a small decrease between 1975 and 2000 (−14 minutes), partly offset by an increase of 6 minutes between 2000 and 2015 (yielding an overall insignificant decrease of 8 minutes between 1975 and 2015). These diverging trends between 2000 and 2015, though small, did lead to the emergence of a significant age gap on school days with children aged 12–16 years spending significantly more time at home with parents in 2015 (23 minutes) than children aged 8–11 years. It is important to bear in mind however that this is restricted to time when children are at home (see Chapter 5 for further analysis of children's total time with parents in 2000 and 2015).

Children aged 8–11 years were also spending less time at home when parents were not at home in both 2000 and 2015 than in 1975, and therefore were spending significantly less time at home in total. The time children aged 12–16 years spent at home when parents were not at home has not changed between 1975 and 2015, though as expected this was higher than for children aged 8–11 years across all years.

All children spent more time at home, both with and without parents, on non-school days in all years. Trends in time at home with parents are comparatively similar for children in both age groups. There was a significant decrease in time at home with parents between 1975 and 2000. The next chapter shows that this is not all the time that children spend with their parents as this includes time spent together outside the home. Unfortunately, it is impossible to construct a comparable measure of this in 1975 and therefore to conclude whether this decrease in time with parents at home was offset by an increase in time with parents outside the home, perhaps with no overall change in time with parents. Nevertheless, it remains the case that children were spending less time at home with their parents in 2000 than was the case in 1975.

Between 2000 and 2015, there was a significant increase in time at home with parents. Results in Table 4.1 show that this reversal was most pronounced for children aged 12–16 years, so much so that time at home with parents on non-school days was actually slightly higher

Table 4.1: Average minutes at home with and without parents on school and non-school days in 1975, 2000 and 2015: children 8–11 and 12–16 years

	8–11 years			12–16 years		
	1975	2000	2015	1975	2000	2015
At home	Average minutes [95% CI]			Average minutes [95% CI]		
School day						
With parents	270 [261–279]	260 [249–271]	253 [237–268]	283 [273–294]	269 [257–281]	275 [260–291]
Not with parents	44 [39–50]	35 [30–41]	32 [26–39]	52 [45–59]	57 [50–64]	54 [45–63]
Non-school day						
With parents	401 [383–418]	370 [354–387]	391 [369–413]	361 [343–378]	337 [322–352]	369 [348–390]
Not with parents	85 [76–94]	66 [58–75]	73 [60–85]	104 [95–113]	93 [83–102]	107 [93–121]

in 2015 than in 1975, whereas children aged 8–11 years still spent less time at home with parents in 2015 than they did in 1975. Flowing from this, age-related differences in time at home with parents on non-school days have diminished substantially. In 1975, on non-school days, children aged 12–16 years spent 40 minutes less time on average at home with parents than children aged 8–11 years. By 2015, this difference reduced by half to 22 minutes and was no longer significant. Children's time at home when parents are not at home is greater on non-school days, but differences associated with age group and patterns of change over time closely mimic patterns found on school days.

Figures 4.1 and 4.2 show a decomposition of trends for parental education and child gender in children's time at home with parents and not with parents respectively. Broadly, on school days there was very little difference in children's time at home with parents and not with parents associated with parental education and child gender. A significant gap associated with parental education did emerge in 2015 where children with parents who have compulsory education spent significantly more time at home with parents (29 minutes) than children with at least one parent who has post-compulsory education. A reverse of this was found on non-school days, however. In 1975 and 2000 children with parents who have only compulsory education spent significantly less time with parents at home (−37 in 1975 and −33 minutes in 2000) than children with parents with post-compulsory education. However, this gap disappeared in 2015 following a significant increase of 40 minutes between 2000 and 2015 in the time children in families with relatively less education spent at home with parents. A similar significant increase in this time over this period was found also for boys, though there was no significant difference in time at home with parents associated with gender in any year. Lastly, it is striking that there was no significant difference in the time children spent at home when parents were not also at home associated with parent educational or gender (see Figure 4.2).

Time with mothers and fathers in two-parent families

Figure 4.3 provides a further breakdown of children's time at home with parents in families with both a co-resident mother and father, differentiating between time children are at home with both parents, their mothers only, or their fathers only, or neither parent in 1975, 2000, and 2015 on school days and non-school days. For most of the time when at home with parents, children in both age groups, at each year, on both school and non-school days, are mostly with both their mother and father, or their mother only. Not surprisingly therefore,

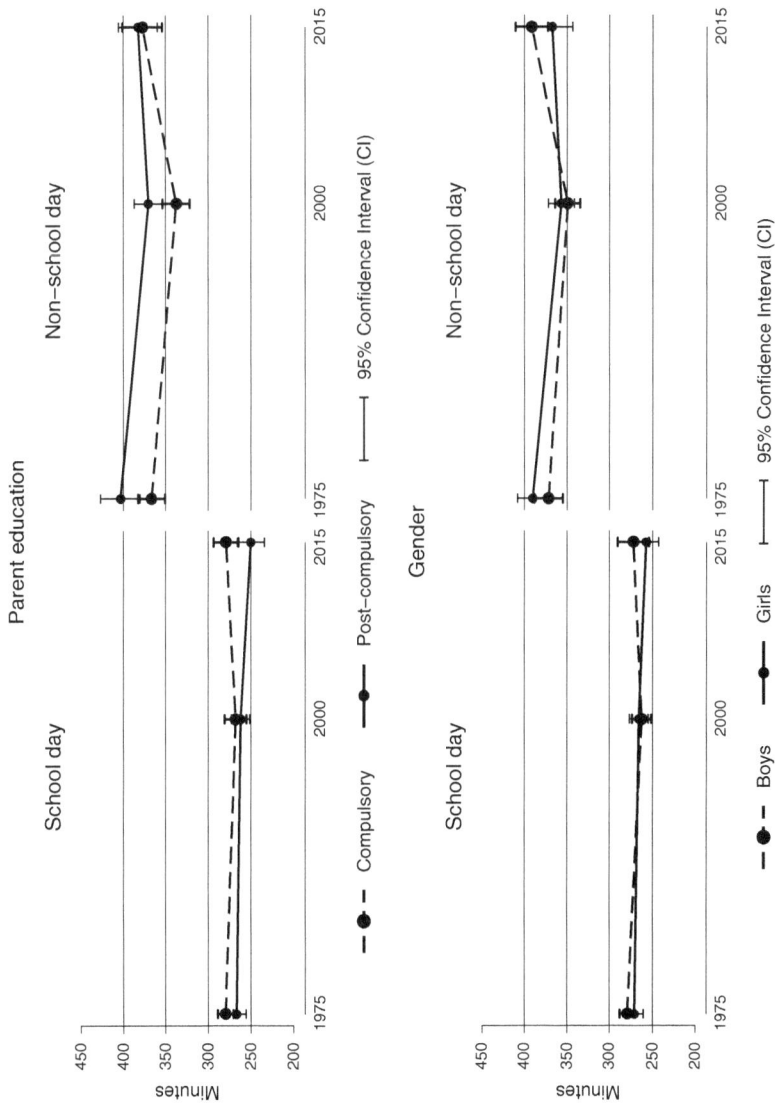

Figure 4.1: Average minutes children 8–16 years spend at home with parents on school and non–school days in 1975, 2000 and 2015: parental education and child gender

Figure 4.2: Average minutes children 8–16 years spend at home when parents are not home on school and non-school days in 1975, 2000 and 2015: parental education and child gender

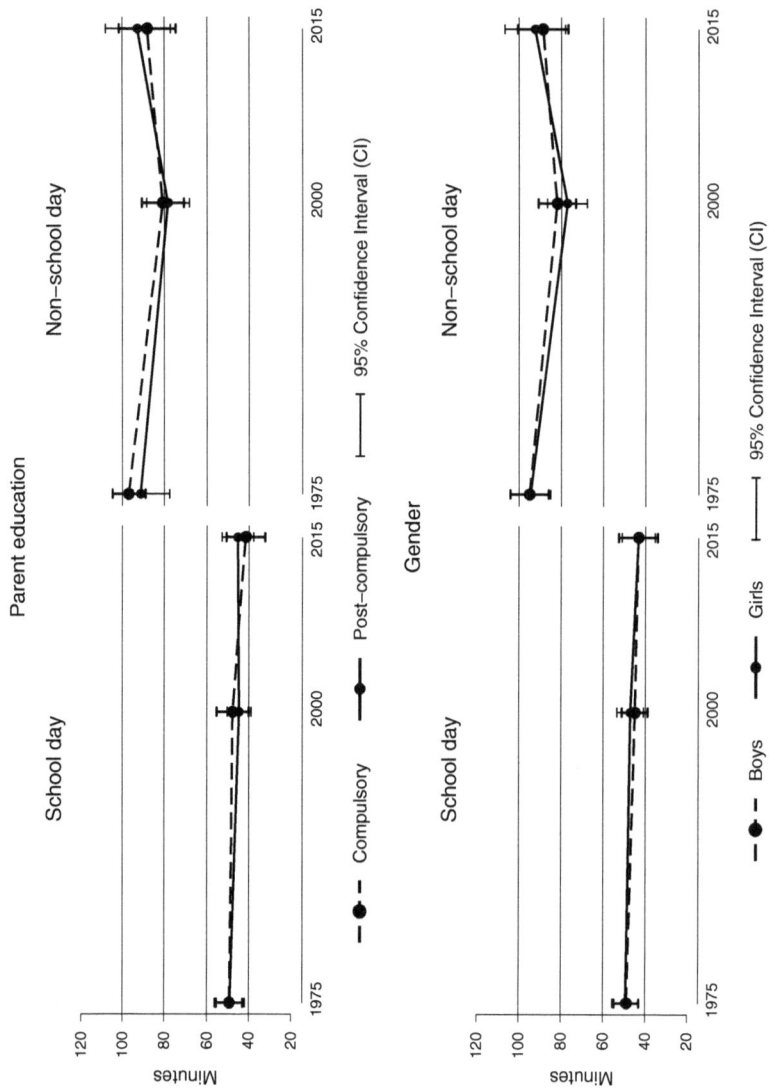

Figure 4.3: Average minutes at home with mothers, fathers, both parents and neither parent on school days and non-school days in 1975, 2000 and 2015: children 8–11 and 12–16 years

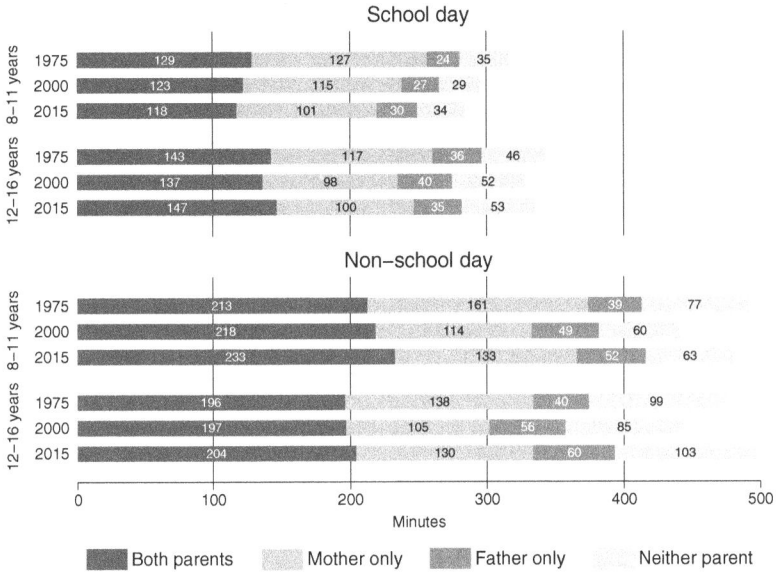

changes in overall time at home with parents are concentrated in time with both parents or with mothers only. A small portion of children's time at home with parents is time when only the father is at home. There was no change in this on school days, but there was an increase on non-school days in the time children in both age groups were at home with fathers only between 1975 and 2000.

These results are broadly congruent with research on the gender division of parental care (in families with younger children) showing that mothers spend substantially more time alone with children than fathers do, while fathers' time with children occurs predominantly when the mother is also present (Craig, 2006). Although modest, changes in the time children spend with mothers and fathers alone accords with expectations arising from mothers' increased engagement in the labour force. However, the increases between 2000 and 2015 in time with mothers on non-school days are surprising. It is worth noting here that mothers' overall time at home did not change between 2000 and 2015, implying that the increase children's time at home with mothers during this period arises because children are spending more time at home independent of factors linked directly to mothers' time at home (such as mothers' engagement in paid work).

To examine associations with mothers' employment, Figure 4.4 shows results differentiating between children with mothers who are not in paid work and those whose mothers are in paid work. On both school and non-school days, in all years, children with employed mothers spent less time with both parents and with mothers only at home, and more time at home with fathers only or at home with neither parent. Time at home only with mothers decreased between 1975 and 2000 irrespective of mother's employment status, but interestingly this decrease was most pronounced among children whose mother is not in paid work. For example, on school days there was a decrease between 1975 and 2000 in children's time at home with mothers only, both for employed and non-employed mothers. In fact, the decrease is larger for children with non-employed mothers (−24 minutes) than for employed mothers (−14 minutes). In contrast, time at home only with fathers increased between 1975 and 2000. Yet again, surprisingly, the increase is greatest in families where the mother is not in paid work. Therefore, the overall increase in the time children spend with fathers between 1975 and later years cannot be attributed solely to increases in mothers' labour force participation, and may perhaps be linked to changing social norms around fathering in general.

Figure 4.4: Average minutes children 8–16 years spend at home with mothers, fathers, both parents and neither parent on school days and non-school days in 1975, 2000 and 2015 by mothers' employment status

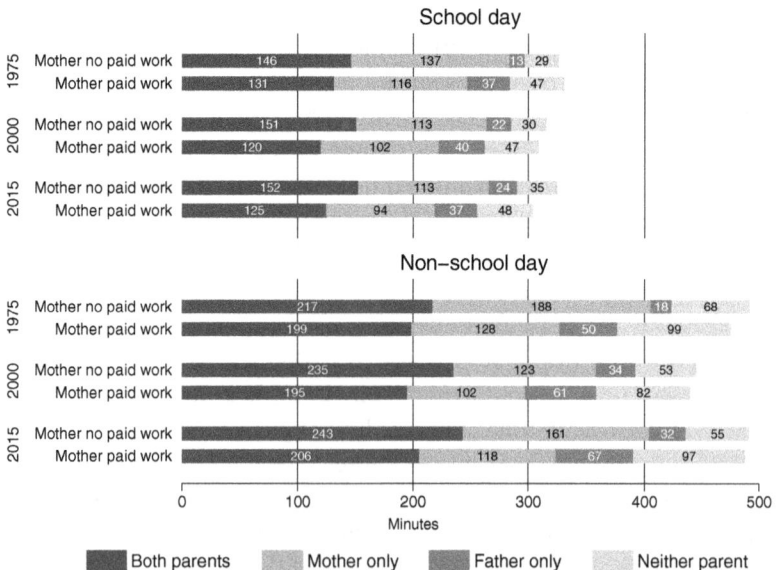

In a number of key respects, the results on non-school days are very similar to those on school days. In all years, on non-school days, children with employed mothers spend less time at home both parents and with mothers only, more time at home with fathers only and more time at home with neither parent. Children's time alone with mothers at home decreased between 1975 and 2000 irrespective of mother's employment status (again being greater in families with non-employed mothers). Again, children's time with fathers alone increased between 1975 and 2015 in families with non-employed mothers (almost doubling from 18 minutes to 32 minutes), though there was also a significant increase in children's time with fathers alone at home in families with employed mothers on non-school days (from 50 minutes to 67 minutes).

Overall, change in children's total time at home with parents, and total time at home, is very similar for children with employed and non-employed mothers on non-school days. Children's total time at home decreased between 1975 and 2000, irrespective of mother's employment, and increased between 2000 and 2015, again irrespective of mother's employment. Yet although children with employed and non-employed mothers are spending more time at home in 2015 compared with 2000, the social context of this time differs based on the employment status of mothers. Specifically, this increase is concentrated in time with mothers only in families with non-employed mothers (rising from 123 minutes to 161 minutes), whereas in families with employed mothers this increase is distributed more evenly across the different social contexts identified here.

Trends in children's activities in context

The context of daily life, such as location and who else is present, does not sit apart from children's activities. Context and activity are in many ways intimately bound together. In an obvious sense, certain locations are conducive to spending time in certain activities. Screen time and time doing homework typically occurs at home, whereas sport and physical activities most often take place outside home. The same activity, moreover, can be qualitatively different by virtue of taking place in different locations, such as eating at school or at home compared with eating in a restaurant. Similarly, the presence or absence of others may shape the character or experience of time in different activities. Time spent in leisure activities when in the presence of parents, for example, may differ qualitatively from time in those same activities when away from parents, as conversely the qualitative experience of parents' leisure time can differ depending on whether or not children are also present (Craig and Mullan, 2013).

This part of the analysis revisits trends in select activities examined in the previous two chapters by mapping information about the family context onto these, differentiating between time at home both with and without parents, and time in other locations. Doing so adds a further layer to our understanding of change in children's time use by drawing out the contextual dimensions running alongside time in different activities. Rather than simply evaluating change in total time, here the analysis moves on to examine whether change in time in activities is concentrated within certain social contexts. Differentiating between social contexts also allows for further exploratory analysis of the influence of key factors, such as parental education and maternal employment on children's time use. For example, parental education is positively associated with children's time doing homework, study and reading, but little is known about whether this applies only to time when children are with parents or if it covers time when children are not with parents. It is especially important, it will be shown, to understand how social context and activity intersect when considering the influence of mothers' employment on children's time use (Mullan, 2009; Gracia and García-Román, 2018).

Not all activities covered in previous chapters are analysed here, and the focus is on home-based activities: screen time, time doing homework and study, and reading. As noted previously, it is not possible to identify time when children are with parents outside the home in the 1975 survey. For completeness, however, time when children are engaging in these activities outside the home is distinguished in the analysis. Lastly rounding out the analysis in this section, trends in children's time in domestic activities and non-screen leisure activities (not considered in previous chapters) across social contexts are presented.

Screen time in context

Not surprisingly, most of children's screen time occurs at home when parents are also at home, and consequently overall trends in screen time are concentrated during time at home with parents (see Figure 4.5). For children aged 12–16, however, the increase in screen time outside the home formed the major component in the increase in total screen time between 1975 and 2000. This might reflect increased time in screen-based activities at other people's homes (friends or family). Around the year 2000, many families with children had computers at home though only around half had access to the internet (see Chapter 5 for more details). These changes may therefore reflect children spending more time in screen-based activities, particularly those associated with

Figure 4.5: Trends in screen time in context

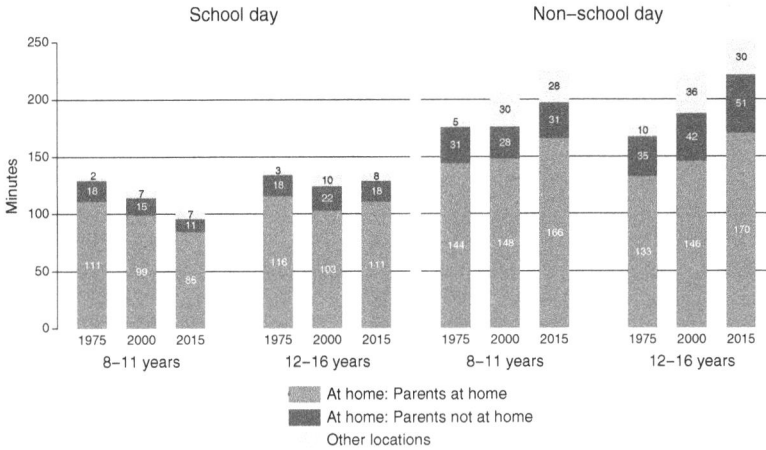

computers and the internet, at other locations with access to these (at the time) new technologies.

The increase in screen time on non-school days between 2000 and 2015 was entirely concentrated in time spent at home with parents among children aged 8–11 years, whereas there were increases in time at home both with and without parents for children aged 12–16 years. This coincides with, and overlaps, the increase in time at home already shown. Half of the total increase in time at home between 2000 and 2015 for children aged 8–11 years was composed of additional time in screen-based activities. For children aged 12–16 years, close to two thirds of the increase in time spent at home between 2000 and 2015 was composed of more screen time.

The analysis of screen time in Chapter 3 showed significant differences in screen time associated with gender and parental education. Girls spent less time in screen-based activities and further analysis of the context of screen time shows that this is concentrated in screen time at home (both when parents are also at home and when they are not). Parental education was negatively associated with children's screen time, as children with parents who had no post-compulsory education spent more time in screen-based activities than children with parents with some post-compulsory education. In contrast with child gender, however, social context of screen time does also matter.

To consider this further, Table 4.2 shows the difference in screen time in different contexts, as well as total screen time, associated with parental education. On school days, parental education was negatively associated with total screen time in 1975 and 2015 (see Figure 3.1 in

Table 4.2: Trends in screen time in context: parental education

Day type	Year	At home		Other locations	Total
		Parents at home	Parents not at home		
School day	1975	−20.6˙	2.4	−0.1	−18.4˙
	2000	−6.8	−3.0	2.1	−7.7
	2015	−30.2˙˙˙	2.3	−0.8	−28.7˙˙˙
Non-school day	1975	−30.8˙˙	−2.7	−0.1	−33.6˙˙
	2000	−1.9	−3.1	−13.8˙˙	−18.7˙
	2015	−25.7˙˙	−7.6	−5.7	−39.0˙˙

Note: Table shows the difference in average screen time in different contexts between children whose parents have some post-compulsory education compared with those whose parents do not. *** $p < .001$; ** $p < .01$; * $p < .05$

the previous chapter), and Table 4.2 shows that this was concentrated entirely in screen time at home when parents are also there, with no differences in screen time in other contexts associated with parental education. There was no significant difference in average screen time associated with parental education on school days in 2000, and this was the case across different social contexts.

Parental education was negatively associated with total screen time in all years on non-school days (see Table 4.2 and Figure 3.1). In 1975, and 2015, differences associated with parental education were concentrated on screen time at home when parents are also there. In 2000, however, the association with parental education (which was lower than other years) was concentrated in screen time at other locations. This coincides with an increase in children's screen time outside the home around this time (see Figure 4.3) perhaps reflecting a lack of access to new computer and video-game technology at home for some children. Indeed, screen time outside the home was higher among children with parents who have relatively less education (36 vs 24 minutes). Note also, that between 1975 and 2000, screen time at home with parents increased in families where parents have some post-compulsory schooling (124 to 137 minutes) with a modest decrease in relatively less educated families (149 to 141 minutes). Therefore, changing technology around 2000 appears to have increased screen time at home in families where parents have some post-compulsory education, and increased screen time outside the home in other families. By 2015, the difference in screen time linked to parental education was comparable to that in 1975, shifting back to being concentrated during time at home with parents.

Table 4.3: Trends in screen time in context: maternal employment

Day type	Year	At home		Other locations	Total
		Parents at home	Parents not at home		
School day	1975	−5.3	7.8"	−1.8	0.7
	2000	−9.4	7.9"	5.8"	4.2
	2015	−10.5	11.0"'	−0.7	−0.2
Non-school day	1975	0.8	12.4"	−4.5	7.2
	2000	−14.9	8.9'	3.1	−2.9
	2015	−5.7	20.9"'	1.7	16.9

Note: Table shows the difference in average screen time in different contexts between children whose parents have some post-compulsory education compared with those whose parents do not. *** $p < .001$; ** $p < .01$; * $p < .05$

Looking now at maternal employment, Table 4.3 reports the difference in screen time across different social contexts between children with a mother in paid work and those with a mother not in paid work. Overall, there was no significant association between maternal employment and children's screen time on school or non-school days in any year. Children with employed mothers do, however, spend significantly more time in screen-based activities at home when parents are not at home. This was offset by a negative (though not significant) association between screen time at home with parents, leading to no significant difference in total screen time associated with mothers' employment. Lastly, we can see that screen time at other locations in 2000 was also positively associated with maternal employment particularly on school days.

Homework, study and reading in context

Like screen time, most of children's time linked to their education outside of classes (homework, study and reading) is when they are at home and their parents are there too. However, as shown in Figure 4.6, boys' and girls' time in these activities at home when parents are not also there, and at other locations, increased in 2000 and 2015. Indeed, the additional time in these activities in 2015, especially on non-school days, was concentrated during time when children were at home but not with their parents, or during time at other locations. Figure 4.6 also shows that girls' additional time in these activities in 2000 and 2015 cuts across time at home with and without parents, and time at other locations.

Figure 4.6: Trends in homework, study and reading in context

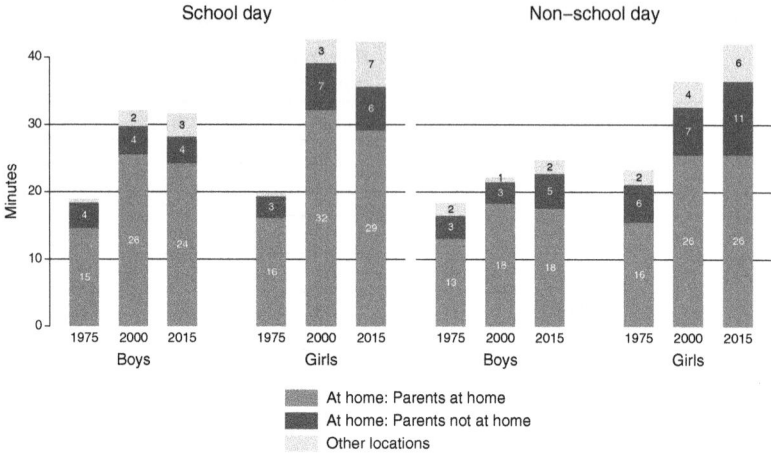

Table 4.4: Trends in homework and reading in context: parental education

Day type	Year	At home		Other locations	Total
		Parents at home	Parents not at home		
School day	1975	12.4***	2.7*	0.1	15.2***
	2000	16.3***	1.9	2.3*	20.5***
	2015	9.7**	0.2	2.7	12.6**
Non-school day	1975	8.9**	1.6	1.8	12.3**
	2000	16.5***	3.6**	2.8***	23.0***
	2015	11.6***	6.2*	4.4	22.2***

Note: Table shows the difference in average time in homework, study and reading in different contexts between children whose parents have some post-compulsory education compared with those whose parents do not. *** $p < .001$; ** $p < .01$; * $p < .05$

Parental education is positively associated with time in activities linked to children's education (see Figure 2.1 and Figure 2.3 in Chapter 2), and results in Table 4.4 show that on school days this was concentrated in time at home with parents in all years. On non-school days, differences associated with parental education emerged during time at home when not with parents, and to a lesser extent in time in other locations, with increases in time in these activities concentrated among children with relatively highly educated parents. Results for maternal employment are shown in Table 4.5. In 1975, children whose mothers were in paid work averaged less time in activities linked to education, with this trend concentrated during time at home with parents.

Table 4.5: Trends in homework and reading in context: maternal employment

Day type	Year	At home		Other locations	Total
		Parents at home	Parents not at home		
School day	1975	−8.3**	0.8	−0.1	−7.6**
	2000	−8.5**	4.6***	1.4	−2.5
	2015	−6.7*	4.2**	−3.2	−5.7
Non-school day	1975	−5.9*	−0.6	−1.3	−7.8**
	2000	−4.1	2.4*	−0.5	−2.2
	2015	−5.4	4.9*	−5.6	−6.2

Note: Table shows the difference in average time in homework, study and reading in different contexts between children whose mother is in paid work compared with those whose mother is not. *** p < .001; ** p < .01; * p < .05

Mothers' employment was not significantly associated with children's time in these activities in 2000 and 2015. However, children's time in these activities was relatively more concentrated during time at home when parents were not also there rather than when they were there.

Domestic activities and non-screen leisure in context

Screen time and time doing homework, study and reading are concentrated during time spent at home. This part of the analysis on children's time use in context looks at two broad activities that occur as much outside the home as inside. The first is time in domestic activities, which includes cleaning, doing laundry or caring for children, and shopping. The time children spend in domestic activities is an important dimension of their family life as they contribute to household domestic work, particularly around the home, helping parents and developing skills and responsibilities (Mayall, 1994). Mimicking adults, children's time in domestic activities is strongly gendered with girls more involved than boys in these activities (Maudlin and Meeks, 1990; Brannen, 1995), though gender differences in domestic activities have diminished over the past several decades (Mullan, 2019). Figure 4.7 shows the average time boys and girls spend in domestic activities when at home with and without parents, and at other locations, in 1975, 2000 and 2015 on school and non-school days.

As expected, girls spend significantly more time in domestic activities in all years on both school and non-school days. With respect to trends over time, there has been little change in time in domestic activities

Figure 4.7: Trends in domestic activities in context

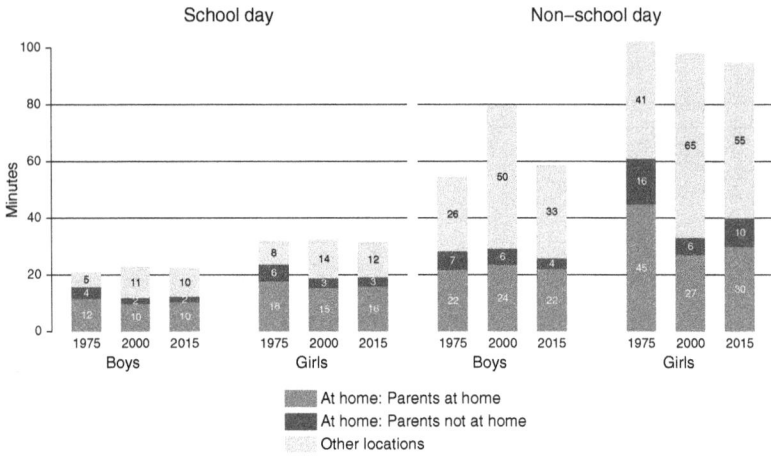

on school days for either boys or girls. On non-school days, however, the time boys spent in domestic activities outside the home (pre-dominantly shopping) increased significantly by just over 20 minutes (with no change in time spent in domestic activities at home). Girls also increased their time in domestic activities outside the home (by 20 minutes), but time in domestic activities at home decreased by a greater amount (28 minutes). Time in domestic activities outside the home decreased between 2000 and 2015, especially among boys. These results show a clear increase in children's exposure to consumer culture particularly in the 1975–2000 period (Buckingham, 2011). Decreasing time shopping between 2000 and 2015 may be in response to changing economic conditions in these years, with economic growth around the turn of the millennium contrasting with a weaker economy following the financial crisis from 2007 onwards, though also possibly tied to the increase in online shopping.

Lastly, this section looks at children's total time in non-screen leisure in context. This time encompasses a very broad group of activities, including not only children's time in sport, but also time in hobbies, games and play, and social activities. The average time, children aged 8–11 and 12–16 years spend in non-screen leisure across different contexts, in 1975, 2000 and 2015 on school and non-school days, is shown in Figure 4.8. In contrast with screen time and activities linked to education, most time in non-screen leisure occurs outside the home. On school days, average non-screen leisure for children aged 8–11 years increased between 1975 and 2015, concentrated in time

Figure 4.8: Trends in total non-screen leisure in context

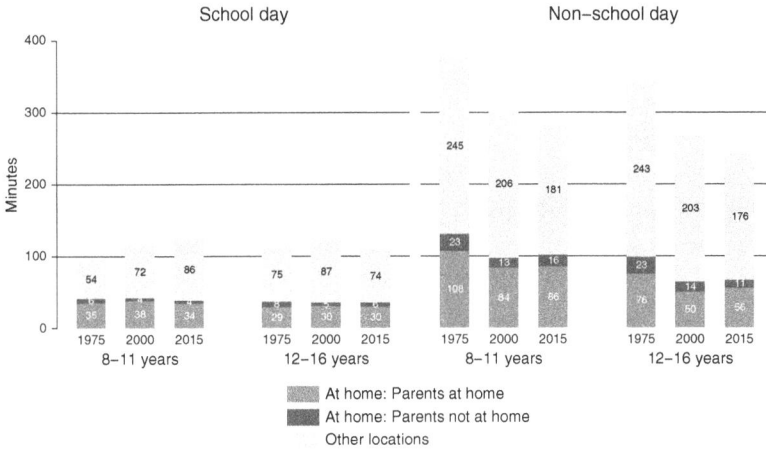

outside the home, which is the inverse of trends in screen time for these children (see Table 3.1 in previous chapter). For children aged 12–16 years, there was no significant change in non-screen leisure in any context, which again is broadly the reverse of trends for screen time on non-school days (see Table 3.1).

There was a substantial drop on non-school days in non-screen leisure between 1975 and 2000 for children in both age groups, both when at home and in other locations. The increase in domestic activities outside the home over the same period accounts for part of this decrease, alongside increases in screen time at other locations (see Figure 4.5). Between 2000 and 2015, there were further decreases in non-screen leisure for both age groups, though these were concentrated entirely on time outside the home. Therefore, increasing screen time at home over this latter period appears to come at the expense of children spending time in domestic activities (shopping) and non-screen leisure activities outside the home.

Shared activities

The final area of children's daily time use connected to the family addressed in this chapter concerns the time children and parents spend together at home doing the same activities, focused on shared time eating and watching TV together. These activities typically are regarded as a focal component of family life, and are highly valorised (Daly, 1996), and time in these two activities form the major component of all time in shared activities at home (Mullan and Chatzitheochari, 2019). The time that parents and children spend eating together is considered beneficial to children's health and well-being (Harrison et al, 2015; Dallacker et al, 2018), and participation in family meals is one of a number of indicators used to measure child well-being in the UK (ONS, 2014a). It is important to bear in mind, however, that there can be wide variation in the experience of family meals: it is not necessarily always a positive experience (Murcott, 1997). Time watching TV, in contrast, is construed often in a negative light as not being 'quality' time, but the time families spend watching TV together is a longstanding, widespread and valued shared family activity, associated with a number of indicators of positive family functioning (Morley, 1988; Kubey, 1990; Coyne et al, 2014). Other shared activities, such as travelling together or time in other shared leisure activities, are not as comparable across the three surveys due to differences in the collection of contextual data outside the home.

The measures studied here relate to time when children and parents are together at home and report eating or watching TV at the same time. Again, time at home is considered in order to maximise the comparability of measures over the longer period from 1975 to 2015. The measure of shared activities studied here might include time when children and parents are not engaged in the activity together. They might, for example, be engaging in these activities at home at the same time, but in different rooms. As such, these measures provide an upper bound on the total time parents and children spend eating or watching TV together. Crucially, the measures, though broadly specified, are comparable across time. First trends in eating together are looked at, and then time watching TV together.

Eating together

It is often stated, and often as a matter of fact, that families are spending less time eating together although there is very little data and empirical research on trends in the time families spend in this way (Murcott, 1997). Beginning to address this gap, Mestdag and Vandeweyer (2005) found that the average time families ate together in Belgium did decrease significantly between 1966 and 1999. In the UK, Cheng et al (2007) found that average time spent eating at home by working-age adults (20–59 years) also decreased significantly over a similar period (between 1975 and 2000), but they did not look specifically at eating with family nor did they consider changes in children's time eating at home. This section addresses this by looking directly at trends in the time children and parents spent eating at the same time when at home. Table 4.6 shows the average time in shared eating for children aged 8–11 and 12–16 years on school and non-school days in 1975, 2000 and 2015. The results show that, between 1975 and 2000, average minutes shared eating decreased significantly on both school and non-school days for children in both age groups. In contrast to the earlier period however, shared eating did not change significantly between 2000 and 2015 for children in both age groups on school days, but there was an increase in time eating with parents between 2000 and 2015 on non-school days for children aged 8–11 years (with no change for children aged 12–16 years). Despite this, on both school and non-school days, all children averaged less time in shared eating in 2015 compared with 1975.

There are few age differences in shared eating on school days, but on non-school days, in all years, children aged 12–16 years spend less time in shared eating with their parents than their younger counterparts (see Table 4.6). Trends in time in shared eating are very similar for boys and girls, but there was an increase in shared eating for boys only on non-school days, with no change for girls. Consequently, there was no difference in shared eating between 1975 and 2015 for boys, though girls in 2015 spent less time eating at home with their parents than girls in 1975. Turning to parent characteristics, Figure 4.9 shows trends in shared eating broken down by maternal employment (upper panel) and parent education (lower panel).

Looking first at maternal employment, Figure 4.9 shows that the significant decrease in shared eating on school days between 1975 and 2000 was concentrated in families where the mother was not in paid work. In these families, there was a decrease of 8 minutes in average

Table 4.6: Average minutes in shared eating on school and non-school days in 1975, 2000 and 2015: children 8–11 and 12–16 years

	1975	2000	2015
School day	**Average minutes [95% CI]**		
8–11 years	20 [17–23]	15 [13–16]	16 [14–19]
12–16 years	18 [16–21]	14 [12–15]	13 [11–15]
Non-school day			
8–11 years	32 [29–36]	20 [18–22]	27 [23–30]
12–16 years	25 [22–28]	17 [16–19]	18 [16–20]

time in shared eating compared with 3 minutes for children in families with a mother in paid work. Consequently, there was no longer a significant difference associated between shared eating and maternal employment in 2000 and in 2015 on school days. There is no evidence here, therefore, to suggest that change in shared eating may be linked to increasing maternal employment. On non-school days children in families with a mother not in paid work spent more time in shared eating in 1975 and 2000 (6 minutes and 4 minutes respectively) compared with children whose mother was in paid work. Between 2000 and 2015, however, there was a modest increase in shared eating, which was slightly higher and more significant for children whose mother was in paid employment. As a result, maternal employment was not significantly associated with shared eating on non-school days in 2015.

The lower panel of Figure 4.9 shows results for parental education. On school days, average time in shared eating was very similar between families with different levels of parental education. On non-school days, however, parent education was positively associated with time in shared eating in 1975, 2000 and 2015, though the gap somewhat narrowed in 2000. Increasing time in shared eating on non-school days between 2000 and 2015 was concentrated among children with relatively more educated parents, thereby widening the gap in time in shared eating associated with parental education in 2015 to become again similar to that found in 1975 (7 minutes). These results echo those showing a significant association between education and the time parents' report eating when with children (Jarosz, 2017).

As well as looking at trends in the average time in shared eating, it is worth considering trends in the extent to which children spend any time in shared eating at home with their parents. Much of the previous research on the positive effects of family meals on child outcomes uses indicators of the frequency of family meals, over a period of a week for example. The data used here does not allow construction of that measure, but does allow examination of the simple prevalence of reporting eating at home with parents during the day. Figure 4.10 shows the daily participation rate of shared eating for children aged 8–11 and 12–16 years on school and non-school days in 1975, 2000 and 2015. It shows that daily participation in shared eating increased significantly on school days between 1975 and 2000 for children in both age groups, rising from 49 per cent to 62 per cent for children aged 8–11 years, and from 47 per cent to 55 per cent for children aged 12–16 years. It also increased over this period on non-school days for children aged 12–16 years, though remained largely unchanged for children aged 8–11 years. These results demonstrate that, as the average time in shared eating decreased between 1975 and 2000, the prevalence

Figure 4.9: Average minutes children 8–16 years spend in shared eating on school and non-school days in 1975, 2000 and 2015: maternal employment and parental education

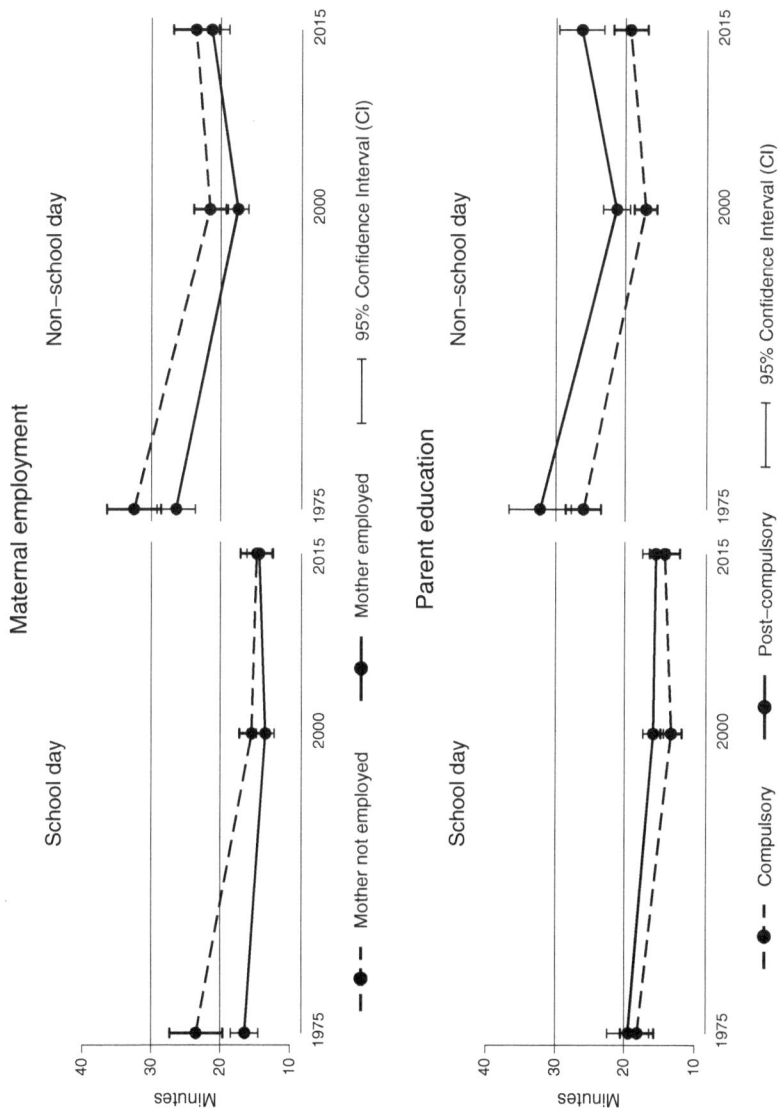

Figure 4.10: Daily participation rate (%) in shared eating on school and non–school days in 1975, 2000 and 2015: children 8–11 and 12–16 years

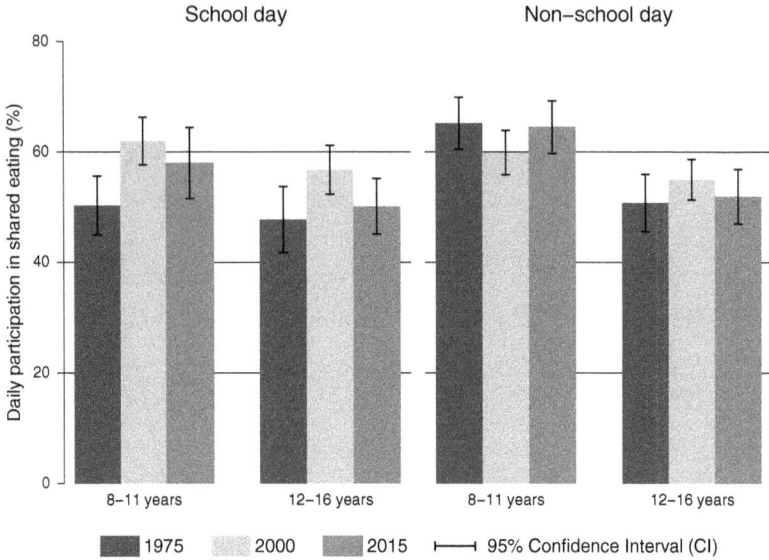

of children reporting any time in shared eating has not decreased. They suggest that family meals, although not declining in prevalence, have become shorter in duration, which fits with parents' sense of struggle in trying to set aside time in busy schedules for family mealtimes (Daly, 2001). They do not fit, however, with the view that all shared eating in the family has become a markedly rarer occurrence over time.

Watching TV together

Technological change is affecting how we watch TV in ways that may affect both children and parents, and the time they spend watching TV together. In particular, there has been an increase in the use of computers and mobile devices to watch TV at a time and place of one's choosing, using streaming and catch-up services (Ofcom, 2017). This could influence shared family TV viewing as it makes watching TV alone easier, or it enables parents and children to watch different programmes on different devices while together. Ofcom (2017) reports that watching TV alone at least once per week is very common in the UK (87 per cent for adults, 93 per cent for teenagers), while half of households with children aged 12–15 years watched TV on different devices while together with other family members at least once per week.

Table 4.7: Average minutes shared TV on school and non-school days in 1975, 2000 and 2015: children 8–11 and 12–16 years

	1975	2000	2015
School day	Average minutes [95% CI]		
8–11 years	57 [49–66]	37 [32–42]	25 [20–30]
12–16 years	63 [53–72]	40 [35–46]	30 [25–36]
Non-school day			
8–11 years	73 [62–84]	48 [43–54]	49 [43–55]
12–16 years	70 [60–79]	52 [46–57]	45 [39–51]

Table 4.7 shows clearly that the average time children and parents spend watching TV together at home has decreased significantly since 1975. On school days, there have been significant decreases in shared TV time between 1975 and 2000 and between 2000 and 2015 for children aged 8–11 and 12–16 years, and no difference associated with child age in any year. Shared TV time also decreased between 1975 and 2000 on non-school days, but there was no real change between 2000 and 2015, with children in each age group spending a similar amount of time in shared TV time in all years. Therefore, the possible influence of technological change over the past decade on family TV viewing is limited.

Analysis of gender differences in shared time watching TV reveals that boys spent more time in shared TV than girls did in 1975 (and more time watching TV in total; see also Chapter 5), but the decrease in shared TV between 1975 and 2000, on both school and non-school days, was especially pronounced among boys with no significant change for girls. The lack of change in shared TV between 2000 and 2015 was found for both boys and girls, and gender was not significantly associated with shared TV in 2000 and 2015 on either school or non-school days. With respect to parent characteristics, Figure 4.11 shows trends in shared TV broken down by maternal employment (upper panel) and parental education (lower panel).

There was very little difference in shared TV associated with maternal employment on either school or non-school days in any year (see Figure 4.11, upper panel). Children in families with a mother in paid work averaged slightly less time in shared TV in each year on school days (about 7–8 minutes), though this was statistically significant in

Figure 4.11: Average minutes children 8–16 years spend in shared TV on school and non-school days in 1975, 2000 and 2015: maternal employment and parental education

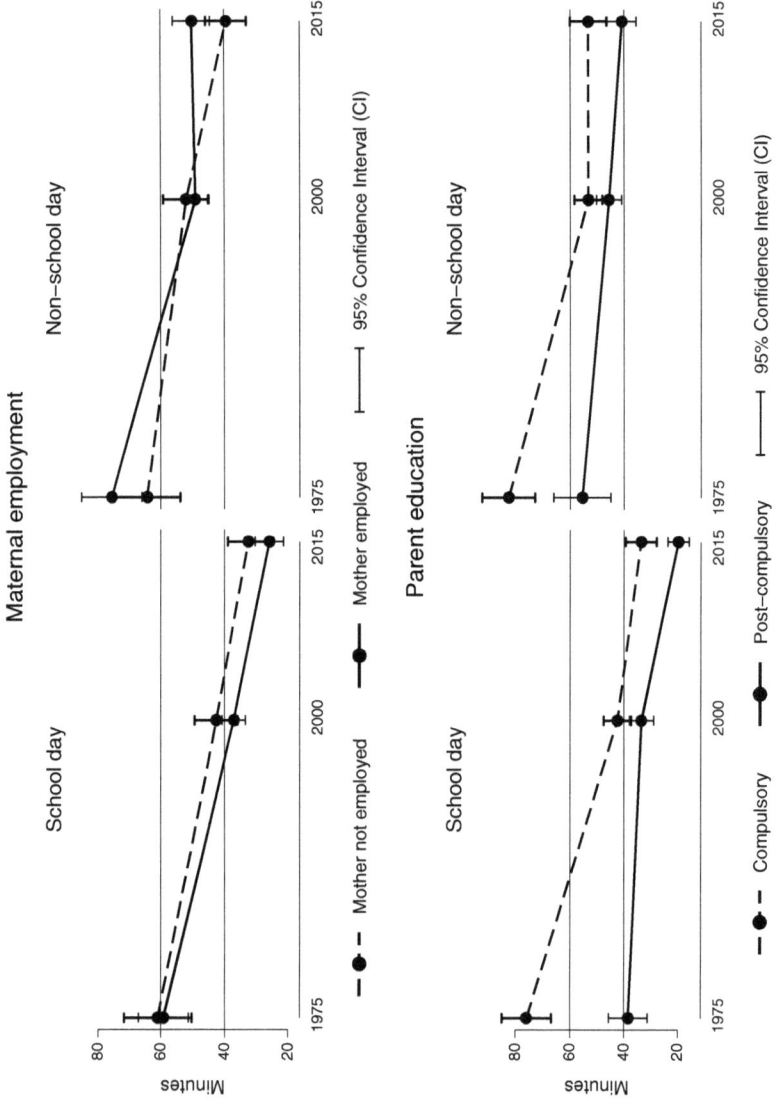

2015 only (p < .05). On non-school days in 1975, children in families with a mother in paid work spent more time in shared TV (10 minutes) but this was not statistically significant, and there was no significant association between maternal employment and shared TV in 2000 or 2015 on non-school days.

Children in families where both parents had completed only compulsory education spent more time in shared TV than children whose parents have some post-compulsory education (see Figure 4.11, lower panel). This difference is greatest in 1975 (30 and 20 minutes on school and non-school days respectively), but the decrease in shared TV between 1975 and 2000 was concentrated among families where parents have compulsory education only. Nevertheless, there remains a significant, though much smaller, difference in shared TV (7–10 minutes), associated with parental education on both school and non-school days in 2000 and 2015.

Conclusion

This chapter has foregrounded the family context of children's daily lives with a focus on children's time at home and time with parents. Much written about this area of children's lives is from the perspectives of parents, in research on changes in the time parents spend with young children and changes in the gender division of labour in families with children. This chapter takes the perspective of school-aged children, examining change in the time children aged 8–16 years spend with their parents at home, changes in their time with mothers and fathers, and changes in the time children are at home when their parents are not at home.

Mirroring the stability of time at school over the past several decades, children's waking time at home with their parents on school days changed remarkably little over four decades between 1975 and 2015. Changes in children's time use will of course generate much more attention and debate, but it is worth acknowledging that the basic structural contours of a child's school day have remained mostly unchanged over the past several decades (see also Figure 1.1).

Days when children are not at school, in contrast, have witnessed significant changes in the time children are at home with their parents. In 2000, children spent less time at home with parents than children in 1975. It is impossible to know from the available data whether children were spending less or a similar amount of time with their parents outside the home in 1975 than in 2000, and thus spent less time with their parents overall. The examination of changes in children's activities in context revealed that children in 2000 were spending more time in screen-based activities (likely occurring at indoor locations outside the home) and substantially more time in domestic activities (primarily shopping) outside the home than children in 1975, the latter of which likely includes time when children are with their parents.

Between 2000 and 2015 there was a subsequent reversal of this trend, with a significant increase in the time children spent at home with their parents, which (as Chapter 5 will show) accounts for an overall increase in this period in the time children spend at the same location as their parents. This increase in time at home with parents on non-school days coincides with children spending more time in activities such as homework, study, and screen-based activities, and less time in active travel and out-of-home play. It is perhaps obvious to point this out, but it serves to underscore that change between 2000 and 2015 across a diverse range of activities does share a common underlying component, in that children are spending more time at home with parents. Changes relating to children's education, technological change, and concerns for children's safety probably coalesce in influencing this return to the home.

Looking closer at time at home with parents in two-parent families, children aged 8–16 years spend a substantial amount of time at home with their mothers only, or with both their mothers and fathers together, with a small portion of this time spent with fathers only. This composition broadly mirrors the gender division of parental time with (primarily younger) children (Craig and Mullan, 2011). Also in accordance with prior research (for a review see Offer, 2018), the time children aged 8–16 years spend at home with only their fathers increased between 1975 and 2015. This increase, however, was modest, concentrated on non-school days, and concentrated in the 1975–2000 period, with little change between 2000 and 2015. Mothers' employment had a substantial impact on the time children spent at home with parents particularly on non-school days, associated with children spending less time with mothers only (and both parents to a lesser extent), and with spending more time at home with fathers only. Notably, however, children's time at home only with fathers increased irrespective of mothers' employment status, suggesting that there is no relationship between this change and mothers' increasing participation in the labour market.

This chapter brought to light a hidden aspect of the context of children's daily life relating to the time they spend away from their parents. Spending time away from parents helps children develop a sense of independence and responsibility as they grow and develop through adolescence (Larson and Richards, 1991; Steinberg, 2002).

Unsurprisingly therefore, children aged 12–16 years consistently spend more time at home without parents than children aged 8–11 years, and this is higher on non-school days for all children. Children with employed mothers spend more time alone with their fathers and at home without their parents; this combines to ensure that mothers' employment is not significantly associated with the overall time children spend at home. Mothers' employment has little effect on the total time children spend in screen-based activities and homework and study, but children with employed mothers spend significantly more time in these activities when they are not with their parents. Mothers' employment, therefore, primarily influences the social context of children's daily life rather than children's total time in key activities.

A further core element of family life studied in this chapter was the time children and parents spend together in shared family activities. There is a widespread idea that family life has become more time-pressured as dual-earner families have become the norm, with family time squeezed out due to time pressures associated with paid work. Very little is known, however, about the extent to which shared family time has changed over the past several decades. This chapter examined two major components of shared family time at home: shared time eating and shared time watching TV. The time when children and parents are eating together at home decreased between 1975 and 2000, but changed little between 2000 and 2015. The family meal has far from disappeared, as the proportion of children who spent time eating at home with their parents changed little over four decades. Shared time watching TV also decreased as children's average time watching TV steadily decreased (parents' time watching TV changed little between 1975 and 2015). Shared time watching TV changed little between 2000 and 2015, however, and it remains a key component of family life. This is a partial picture however, as it does not consider shared time outside the home. Research, including that on shared time outside the home, shows increases between 2000 and 2015 in time in shared non-screen leisure activities (Mullan and Chatzitheochari, 2019). Chapter 5, focusing on the use of technology in daily life, next extends this analysis of change in the social context of children's daily lives, looking at time across all locations with parents, time with friends, siblings and others children know, and time alone, and revisits time in shared family activities both at home and elsewhere.

Note

[1] https://www.ons.gov.uk/employmentandlabourmarket/peopleinwork/employmentandemployeetypes/articles/familiesandthelabourmarketengland/2017

5

Time for Technology

Over the past decade, children's access to and use of the internet and mobile devices has increased dramatically. Ofcom (2015) reports that around two thirds of children aged 8–15 years had access to the internet at home in 2005, rising to nine in every ten children by 2015. At the end of the first decade of the new millennium, smartphones were still relatively novel and the iPad had just been released on the market, but children very quickly took possession of, and began using, these devices. Smartphone ownership among children aged 8–11 years rose from 13 per cent in 2010 to 24 per cent in 2015. Comparable figures for children aged 12–15 years are 35 per cent and 69 per cent respectively. Furthermore, children in the UK have a high rate of smartphone ownership compared with children in other European countries (Mascheroni and Ólafsson, 2016). In addition, there have been markedly steep increases in children's access to and ownership of tablet computers in recent years. Ofcom report that around 5 per cent of children aged 5–15 years had access to a tablet in 2010, which increased to 80 per cent in 2015, and children's ownership of tablets rose from 2 per cent to 40 per cent over the same period (Ofcom, 2015). Running parallel with these changes in the available hardware, internet speeds and capacities have improved steadily, enhancing the functionality of mobile devices, with the consequence that children increasingly use these devices to access the internet (Livingstone et al, 2014).

The UK Time Use Surveys, collected around 2000 and 2015, capture these changes in children's access to computer technology and the internet in the home. Table 5.1 shows the proportion of children living in a home with a computer and access to the internet at each time point, broken down by child age and parental education. In 2000, around 70 per cent of children aged 8–11 years and 81.5 per cent of children aged 12–16 years lived in a house with a computer. In 2015, almost all children in both age groups lived in a house with

Table 5.1: Children's access to computers and the internet at home in 2000 and 2015: child age and parental education

	Computer at home		Internet access at home	
	2000	2015	2000	2015
	Proportion [95% CI]		Proportion [95% CI]	
Child age groups				
8–11 years	70.4 [66.9–73.6]	95.7 [93.3–97.2]	48.7 [45.0–52.4]	97.1 [95.0–98.4]
12–16 years	81.5 [78.6–84.1]	97.6 [95.9–98.6]	56.5 [53.0–60.0]	99.0 [97.8–99.6]
Parental education				
Compulsory	66.3 [62.8–69.7]	95.4 [93.2–96.9]	41.9 [38.4–45.6]	97.5 [95.7–98.5]
Post-compulsory	85.3 [82.4–87.7]	98.4 [96.7–99.3]	63.1 [59.5–66.5]	99.3 [97.7–99.8]

a computer (96 per cent and 98 per cent respectively). Around half of children aged 8–16 years lived in homes with access to the internet in 2000, but nearly all children aged 8–16 years had access to the internet at home in 2015.

There was some evidence of a digital divide in 2000, with access to computers and the internet significantly lower in families where no parent has post-compulsory education. In 2000, 63.1 per cent of children who had a parent with some post-compulsory education had access to the internet at home, compared with 41.9 per cent of children who had no parent with post-compulsory education. In 2015 however, as access to computers and the internet approached complete saturation, the digital divide in access has all but disappeared. Note also in connection with this that higher household income was positively associated with children's access to a computer and the internet in 2000 but not in 2015.

There is less direct information about children's access to, or own-ership of, new mobile devices in the later survey. There are questions about whether the household accesses the internet using different devices such as smartphones and tablets, and information about the number of mobile phones in the household, which provide some indication about children's access to these mobile devices. Table 5.2 shows the proportion of children living in homes that use smartphones and tablets to access the internet, again broken down by child age group and parental education. Table 5.2 also shows the proportion of children in homes with one or more mobile phones per person aged 8 years and over. This is a crude indicator of children's access to and

Table 5.2: Children's access to tablets, smartphones and mobile phones on school and non-school days in 2015: children 8–11 and 12–16 years

	Access internet using tablet	Access internet using smartphone	At least one mobile phone per person 8+ years
	Average proportion (%) *[95% CI]*		
Child age groups			
8–11 years	73.0 *[68.4–77.0]*	82.1 *[79.9–85.5]*	37.4 *[32.8–42.2]*
12–16 years	70.0 *[65.7–74.0]*	85.3 *[81.9–88.1]*	71.9 *[67.7–75.8]*
Parental education			
Post-compulsory	75.3 *[71.0–79.1]*	85.0 *[81.4–88.1]*	54.1 *[49.4–58.7]*
Compulsory	67.5 *[62.9–71.7]*	83.1 *[79.3–86.4]*	58.3 *[53.6–62.9]*

potential ownership of mobile phones, though there are surely cases of households with at least one phone per person aged 8+ years where parents use more than one mobile phone (such as a separate phone for work) and where the children do not own a mobile phone. Equally, children could have ready access to a phone in families where there is less than one phone per person aged 8+ years, if parents let children use their phone, for example.

Around 70 per cent of children live in households that access the internet using a tablet, with just over 80 per cent in households that access the internet using a smartphone. Accessing the internet using a tablet is higher in households with parents who have some post-compulsory education (75.3 per cent) than in households where no parent has (67.5 per cent), but there is no difference in accessing the internet using a smartphone associated with parental education. A higher proportion of older children aged 12–16 years live in households where there is at least one mobile phone per person (71.9 per cent) compared with children aged 8–11 years (37.4 per cent), which is an indicator of potential phone ownership among children. This strongly aligns with other data showing high levels of phone ownership among older children (Ofcom, 2015; Mascheroni and Ólafsson, 2016). Potential phone ownership is not significantly associated with parental education, though it is slightly higher in families where no parent has post-compulsory education (58.3 per cent) than in families with some post-compulsory education (54.1 per cent). Note also that there is no significant difference between boys and girls in potential phone ownership, though the proportion is slightly higher for girls than for boys (59 per cent vs 54 per cent).

The proliferation of computers and new mobile devices over the past couple of decades has given rise to a number of questions of concern surrounding the time children spend using screen-based technologies. One question relates to the total amount of time children spend in screen-based activities, including time using mobile devices such as smartphones and tablets, with concern widespread that this time is excessive. Following on from this, there are questions surrounding the influence of mobile devices on children's time in other activities and on their social interactions. In connection with this, there is concern that children's time spent using devices comes at the expense of time spent on other important activities, particularly physical activities, and that time on devices is having a negative impact on the time children spend with others in face-to-face interactions. This chapter addresses each of these questions. Change in children's screen time between 2000 and 2015, looking at different components of screen time including time using mobile devices such smartphones and tablets, is taken up in the next part of the chapter. The relationship between children's time using devices and time in other activities, including time in sport, is then studied. The third and final part of the analysis in this chapter looks at changes in the social context of children's daily lives between 2000 and 2015, investigating overlaps between these changes and children's time using computers, smartphones, and tablets.

Revisiting trends in screen time

The analysis in Chapter 3 found that there was little change in children's total screen time on school days, but that it increased significantly on non-school days. Trends in total screen time are only part of the story of change in screen-based activities, however. Looking only at total screen time can mask change in time in different screen-based activities. A number of sources have shown that, since 2000, children's time watching TV decreased and their time using computers and the internet, and playing video games increased (Silva et al, 2014; Ofcom, 2015; Bucksch et al, 2016). These studies, however, use measures of time in screen-based activities based on unreliable recall questions, and it is not possible to combine measures of time in different screen-based activities used in these studies to form a composite of total screen time. The data used here allows the construction of reliable measures of time in different screen-based activities and the ability to combine these to form a measure of total time in screen-based activities. Therefore, we can observe not only trends in total screen time, but also changes in time spent on the different components of total screen time.

To see this, Figure 5.1 shows trends in children's total screen time between 1975 and 2015, differentiating between time watching TV, using computers, and playing video games as a main activity. In 1975, children's screen time was comprised entirely of time watching TV, but in 2000 children aged 8–16 years spent less of their time watching TV, with an increase in time using computers and playing video games. Children's time watching TV decreased again between 2000 and 2015, alongside further increases in their average time using computers and playing video games. The results shown here for trends in children's time watching TV differ from the basic conclusion drawn by Marshall and colleagues that children's time watching TV changed little between 1949 and 2004 (Marshall et al, 2006). Most studies included in their review used responses to single questions about time watching TV in broad ranges (for example, up to 2 hours ['low users'], more than 4 hours ['high users']). It is certainly possible however, that there was significant change in the average amount of time children spent watching TV within these bands, and the results here suggest that this may be the case.

Trends in different screen-based activities are very similar among children in different age groups, but on school days in 2015 children aged

Figure 5.1: Average minutes children 8–16 years spend watching TV, using computers and playing video games on school and non-school days in 2000 and 2015

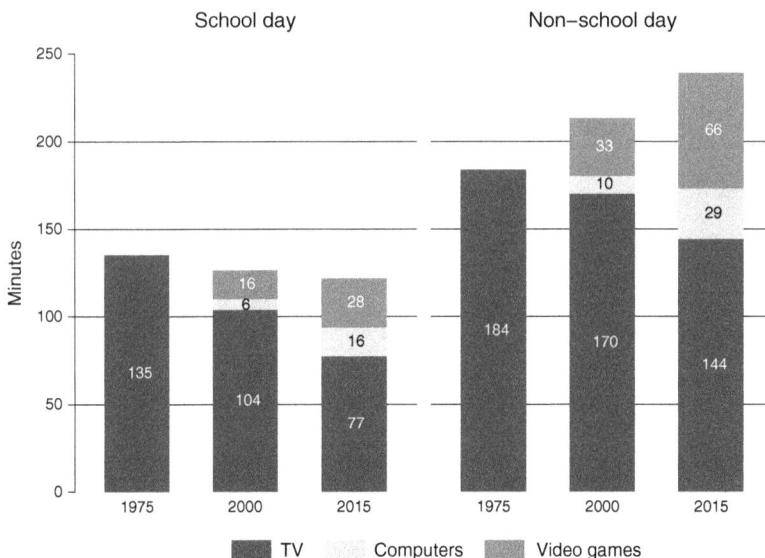

8–11 years spent less time watching TV than children aged 12–16 years (69 minutes vs 84 minutes), which largely underpinned the diverging trends on school days in total screen time for children in different age groups found in Chapter 3. In contrast to age, there were substantial differences in trends in different screen-based activities depending on gender. Recall from Chapter 3 that boys consistently spent more time in screen-based activities than girls did. Figure 5.2 shows trends in different screen-based activities for boys and girls. It reveals that gender differences in total time in screen-based activities in 2000 and 2015 were mainly concentrated in time playing video games, with very little difference between boys and girls in time watching TV or using computers. Increases in total time in screen-based activities on non-school days between 2000 and 2015, therefore, were concentrated among boys and concentrated in time playing video games. Consequently, over four decades, the gender difference in screen time has transferred from time watching TV to time playing video games.

Time using devices (smartphones, tablets, computers)

A key issue with the story of trends in screen time so far presented here (and in Chapter 3) is that it ignores the time children use new mobile devices such as smartphones and tablets. With the expansion of the

Figure 5.2: Average minutes boys' and girls' spend watching TV, using computers and playing video games on school and non-school days in 2000 and 2015

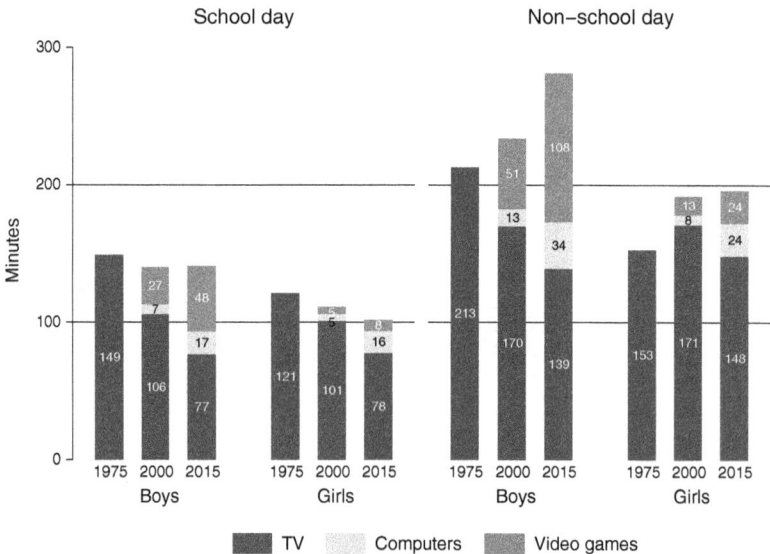

internet to almost every home in the UK, along with the advent of powerful internet-enabled mobile devices, 'screen time' has expanded to include not only screen-based activities, but time when children are using devices while engaging in many other activities. There is much interest and concern about how much time children spend using devices, often framed in terms of time spent using the internet or online. Ofcom (2015) reports that children aged 8–11 years spend around 11 hours per week and children aged 12–15 years spend 19 hours per week using the internet. A further Ofcom study[1] reports that children aged 6–15 years spend 15.5 hours per week using computers and mobile devices (excluding communication activities, but including social media), and again older children report more time using devices.[2] Children aged 6–11 years spend 12 hours per week using devices, while children aged 12–15 years spend close to 21 hours per week using these devices.

The latest UK Time Use Survey (2014–15) provides a further source of information on the time children spend using devices such as smartphones and tablets. This survey included a field in the time diary for respondents to indicate any time during the day when they were using a digital device (smartphone, tablet or computer). This additional information is used to compute the total time children spend using devices during the day. Table 5.3 reports the average time children aged 8–11 and 12–16 years spend using devices (computers, smartphones, tablets) on school and non-school days. Children aged 8–11 years spent on average just over one hour (74 minutes) using a device on school days, and on school days children aged 12–16 years spent three hours (178 minutes) using a device. Children in both age groups spent significantly more time using devices on non-school days. In relative terms, this increase was higher among children aged 8–11, where it almost doubles.

Whether or not children are spending 'too much' time using devices, or what indeed constitutes 'too much' time, is an ongoing subject of public and academic debate. The results shown here cannot address this directly, but these debates should be informed by reliable estimates of the time children spend using devices. The estimates reported here range from just over one hour (for children 8–11 years on school days) to around 3 hours 45 minutes (for children 12–16 years on non-school days). Viewed in isolation from other areas of children's time use, this is a substantial amount of time, comparable in magnitude to children's total time in screen-based activities (for example, TV and video games). It will be shown in the next section that much of the time children spend using devices coincides with time in screen-based activities such as watching TV and playing video games. By no means all the time

Table 5.3: Average minutes using devices (smartphones, tablets, computers) on school and non-school days in 2015: children 8–11 and 12–16 years

	School day		Non-school day	
	8–11 years	12–16 years	8–11 years	12–16 years
	Average mins *[95% CI]*		Average mins *[95% CI]*	
Total device use	74	178	129	224
	[63–85]	*[159–198]*	*[113–146]*	*[205–243]*
Number of mobile phones in household				
Less than one per person 8+ years	62	125	109	218
	[49–74]	*[100–151]*	*[90–128]*	*[179–256]*
One or more per person 8+ years	91	203	132	229
	[67–114]	*[176–230]*	*[105–159]*	*[202–256]*
Access internet at home using tablet				
Do not access internet using tablet	59	175	117	187
	[39–79]	*[140–211]*	*[83–152]*	*[149–224]*
Access internet using tablet	79	179	134	241
	[66–93]	*[157–201]*	*[117–151]*	*[220–262]*

children spend using devices therefore constitutes 'additional' screen time, and it will become clear that the remainder of children's device use is distributed across time in many different other activities.

Before considering that, it is worth noting that the estimate of total time using devices does not distinguish between using a smartphone, tablet or computer, though it is possible to explore the influence of access to some of these devices using the available information. Table 5.3 also shows differences in the average time using devices associated with access to mobile phones and tablets (as outlined previously). Looking first at mobile phones, children in families where there is one or more mobile phone per person average significantly more time using devices on school days. This difference is greater for older children (78 minutes) than for children aged 8–11 years (29 minutes). However, increased access to mobile phones is not significantly associated with children's total time using devices on non-school days. In contrast, access to tablets is positively associated with device use on non-school days only, but this is concentrated among children aged 12–16 years. Although access to a tablet is modestly positively associated with the total time children aged 8–11 years spend using devices, this is not statistically significant. Therefore, the time children 12–16 years spend using devices is positively associated with access to mobile phones on school days and tablets on non-school days.

An extended measure of screen time

The additional information about device use in the latest UK Time Use Survey allows us to construct a broader measure of screen time for 2015, incorporating time in screen-based activities, both when using devices and not using devices, together with time using devices during time in other non-screen activities. Therefore, this measure adds to the previous measure of screen time studied (see also Chapter 3) by incorporating children's use of devices during time in other non-screen activities. Table 5.4 shows the average time children aged 8–11 and 12–16 years spend in screen-based activities (for example watching TV, or playing video games) as their main activity, differentiating between time when they are also using a device (smartphone, tablet) and time when they are not using a device, along with average time using a device during other non-screen activities on school and non-school days in 2015.

For children in both age groups, and on both school and non-school days, a substantial amount of children's time using devices overlaps with time in screen-based activities, such as watching TV and playing video games (see Mullan 2018 for more details). Consistently on both school and non-school days, this comprised around one third of time in screen-based activities for children aged 8–11 years, and 45 per cent of all time in screen-based activities for children aged 12–16 years. The remainder of children's time using devices occurs when they are engaging in other non-screen activities, highest among children aged 12–16 years. Again, this does not differ greatly between school and non-school days, for children in both age groups, revealing that the increase in time using devices on non-school days is concentrated during time when children are engaging in screen-based activities, such as watching TV or playing video games.

As well as age differences in the time children spend using devices during other non-screen activities, there was a significant gender difference in this time (see Figure 5.3). On both school and non-school days, girls spend significantly more time using devices during time in non-screen activities than boys. Boys, on the other hand, spend more time using devices when they are engaging in screen-based activities, particularly on non-school days. This is concentrated during time playing video games (see Figure 5.2 and Mullan, 2018). Also shown in Figure 5.3 is total time in screen-based activities in 2000, to compare with the extended measure of total screen time combining screen-based activities with time using devices in 2015. We can see that on both school and non-school days, for both boys and girls, once time

Table 5.4: Average minutes screen time when not using a device, using a device and other time using a device on school and non-school days in 2015: children 8–11 and 12–16 years

	School day		Non-school day	
	8–11 years	12–16 years	8–11 years	12–16 years
	Average mins [95% CI]		Average mins [95% CI]	
Screen time no device	66 [57–75]	75 [67–83]	143 [130–156]	133 [118–148]
Screen time using device	38 [31–44]	60 [50–69]	86 [73–98]	112 [97–127]
Other time using device	36 [27–45]	119 [103–135]	44 [33–55]	112 [99–126]

using devices during other non-screen activities is incorporated, total screen time is substantially higher in 2015 than in 2000.

It is questionable, however, whether this is a valid comparison and if this is a valid 'increase', as devices such as smartphones and tablets did not exist in 2000. It is more useful perhaps to think of these results as highlighting how screen time has evolved alongside developments in new mobile technology, enabling the use of screen-based devices during time in non-screen activities. It is notable that, unlike time when screen-based activities are the main activity, the total time using devices is not significantly associated with gender, suggesting that time using devices is qualitatively distinct from time in screen-based activities such as watching TV or playing video games. The composition of time using devices differs between boys and girls, however, as girls spend significantly more time using devices during non-screen activities than boys and less of their time using devices during time in screen-based activities. The following section examines this in more detail looking at the different non-screen activities that children engage in when using devices.

Device use and children's time in other activities

One of the major concerns surrounding children's use of mobile devices such as smartphones and tablets is that it may be crowding out or displacing time in other activities. What is clear, however, from the foregoing analysis is that children use devices for a substantial amount of time when they are engaging in activities that are not screen-based, covering a wide range of different activities throughout the day (Mullan, 2018). Looking closer at this time now, Figure 5.4

Figure 5.3: Average screen time incorporating time using devices for boys and girls 8–16 years on school and non-school days in 2015

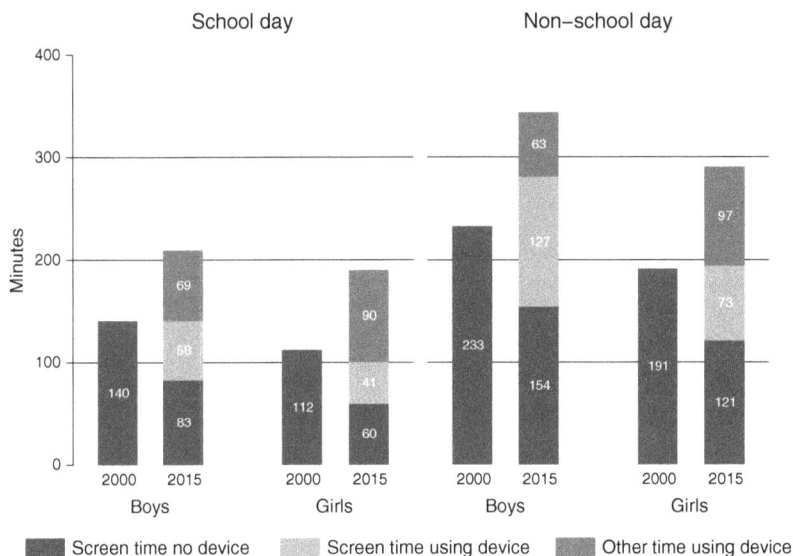

shows the average time boys and girls spend in a range of different activities outside school, both when using and not using a device on school and non-school days. It shows clearly that children use devices when they are spending time across a wide range of different non-screen activities throughout the day.

Children are using devices for a relatively large portion of the time they spend doing homework and study, especially on non-school days where about one third of all time in this activity is carried out when children are using a device. Unfortunately, it is impossible to tell from the available data if children are using the device to help with their homework (for example using the internet for research), or if time using a device distracts them from doing homework (for example, using a smartphone to interact with friends through social media). It is interesting, nevertheless, to note that the increases in time doing homework on non-school days between 2000 and 2015, particularly among girls (see Figure 2.2), coincide with children spending more time using a device when doing homework. Time using devices also overlaps with children's time reading. This is highest for girls on non-school days though in absolute terms it is not a large amount of time. Again, unfortunately it is impossible to know if children are reading using devices or if they are multitasking. Looking across other activities shown in Figure 5.4, time using a device comprises a small portion of total time in these activities.

Figure 5.4: Boys' and girls' average time using a device and not using a device when doing different activities outside school on school and non-school days in 2015

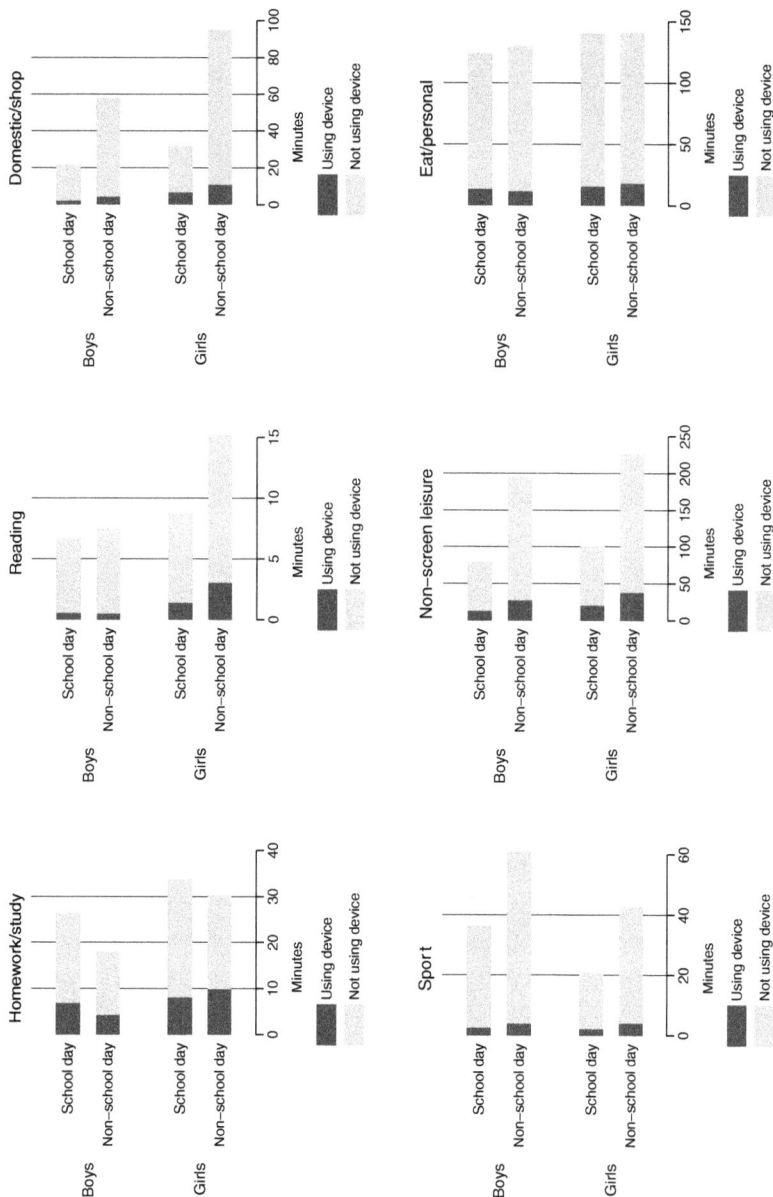

Recall that girls spend more time using devices during time in other non-screen activities, and this gender difference cuts across time in a number of different non-screen activities. They spend significantly more time using devices during time in domestic activities and in other non-screen leisure activities than boys on both school and non-school days. On non-school days, girls spend more time using devices during time spent in homework and reading, and in personal activities and eating.

Sport, screen time and time using devices

A prominent concern around new technology and children's screen time is that it may be having a detrimental impact on their engagement in physical activity. The association between children's monthly engagement in sport and screen time was analysed in Chapter 3. A negative association between engagement in sport and screen time was found but only among boys. Whether this extends to include time using devices such as smartphones and tablets is a question we now consider. Following the method used in Chapter 3, children are split into two roughly equal groups based on the number of times they engage in a sporting activity throughout the month, thus: 1) up to the median number of times; and 2) more than the median number of times. This is done separately for boys and girls, as the former engage in sport to a significantly higher extent.

Children in these two groups are then compared with respect to their average total time in screen-based activities, decomposed into total time in screen-based activities when children are or are not also using a device. The analysis also considers associations between monthly engagement in sport and both children's time using a device during other non-screen activities and their total time using a mobile device. Table 5.5 shows the difference associated with children's monthly engagement in sport and their screen time and time using devices.

The first two rows in Table 5.5 provide a decomposition of total screen time into time when children do not also report using a device (first row) and time when they do report using a device (second row). The results show clearly that the negative association between monthly engagement in sport and screen time is overwhelmingly concentrated in screen time when children do not also report using a device such as a smartphone or tablet. Again, however, the negative association is significant for boys only. No part of children's time using a device was significantly associated with engagement in sport. It is worth noting however that boys, who were relatively more engaged in sport during

Table 5.5: Association between monthly engagement in sport and daily average minutes in screen time with and without devices, other time using devices and total time using devices: boys and girls in 2015

	Boys		Girls	
	School day	Non-school day	School day	Non-school day
Screen time: not using device	−21.0˙	−27.9˙	−13.8	−13.4
Screen time: using device	−3.6	−3.3	1.5	2.6
Other time using device	22.2	16.7	−9.1	11.9
Total time using device	18.6	13.4	−7.6	14.6

Notes: Table shows the difference in the average minutes on school and non-school days between those who report greater than the median number of times engaging in sport during the month and those who report the median or less. *** p < .001; ** p < .01; * p < .05

the month, spend more time using a device during other activities, and in total, but this was not statically significant. It may be that boys use devices like smartphones in activities linked to sports, like travelling to matches or interacting with friends when organising these activities.

The proliferation of mobile devices has added a further dimension to what is commonly understood as 'screen time'. Screen time could be all time when a screen-based activity is the main activity a child is engaged in as shown in Figure 5.1, it could be all time using a device such as a mobile phone or tablet as reported in Table 5.3, or it could be a combination of both these dimensions as shown in Figure 5.3. The results shown here, however, suggest the need to exercise some caution when thinking about combining children's time using different screen-based devices.

Technology and change in the social context of daily life

The second major aspect of children's daily lives influenced by techno-logical change relates to social life and interactions with others, par-ticularly family and friends, throughout the day. On balance, whether this influence has been positive or negative is a subject of much debate. Earlier debates and research on the influence of the internet, covering a period from the 1990s to the early 2000s, centred on whether time spent accessing the internet on home PCs was having a detrimental impact on children's social interactions with family and friends. However, rather than leading to increased social isolation as was feared, research highlights the many ways in which children and adolescents were using the internet to develop and maintain friendships online and in person (Orleans and Laney, 2000; Subrahmanyam and Greenfield, 2008). Some studies, however, have shown that children's time using computers and the internet is negatively associated with the time they spend with their parents (Mesch, 2006; Lee, 2009), and others have found that children's use of the internet was associated with perceptions of declining family time (Lee and Chae, 2007).

The debate took on a renewed force with the emergence of powerful mobile devices from 2007 onwards alongside rapidly improving wireless internet connections. Research shifted toward deepening understanding of how technology is woven into daily life, a shift captured in part by the distinction between 'going online' and 'being online' (Williams and Merten, 2011). Numerous studies demonstrate how families have positively incorporated new technology into their daily lives, using it to facilitate communication and the coordination of family members and activities (Kennedy and Wellman, 2007; Ling, 2012; Raine and Wellman, 2012). Studies also show how children use mobile devices such as smartphones to interact daily with friends and family using instant messaging applications and social media (Bond, 2014; Clark, 2014; Lenhart, 2015; Thompson et al, 2018). Yet there remains concern that technology is eroding the quality of social interactions as we spend more time interacting with people who are not physically co-present and less attention to those we are co-present with, due to being constantly distracted by mobile devices (Turkle, 2011).

In Chapter 4, it was found that, compared with the year 2000, children were spending more time at home when their parents were also at home in 2015, though this was concentrated on non-school days. Here extra information collected about specific locations outside the home in the 2000 and 2015 surveys is used to construct a broader measure of time when children and parents are at the same location; this encompasses time at home as well as time in other locations. Note that in both 2000 and 2015, for most of the time when children and parents are at the same location they are at home (close to 80 per cent), and the remainder of time is when they are travelling (12 per cent), or at other locations (8 per cent).

Table 5.6 shows the average time children aged 8–11 and 12–16 years spent at the same location as their parents (both at home and elsewhere) on school and non-school days in 2000 and 2015. On school days, children aged 8–11 years spent around five hours at the same location as their parents (when awake), and this did not change between 2000 and 2015. Children aged 12–16 years spent around 16 minutes less

Table 5.6: Average minutes at the same location as parents on school and non-school days in 2000 and 2015: children 8–11 and 12–16 years

		2000	2015
		Average mins [95% CI]	
Time at same location as parents: school day	8–11 years	303 [292–313]	300 [285–315]
	12–16 years	287 [276–298]	301 [288–315]
Time at same location as parents: non-school day	8–11 years	505 [488–522]	515 [492–537]
	12–16 years	411 [394–428]	440 [418–462]

time at the same location as their parents than children aged 8–11 in 2000. However, the time children aged 12–16 years spent at the same location as their parents increased between 2000 and 2015 (by around 15 minutes), and there was no longer a difference in 2015 in time at the same location as parents associated with age. Compared with 2000 therefore, older children were spending more time near their parents on school days in 2015 including both time at home and at other locations.

On non-school days, there was a significant increase in time at the same location as parents between 2000 and 2015 for children aged 12–16 years, with a smaller increase for children aged 8–11 years, though at both points in time younger children (8–11 years) spent significantly more time at the same location as their parents than older children (12–16 years). The increase in total time at the same location as parents on non-school days between 2000 and 2015 is lower than the increases for total time at home with parents reported in Chapter 3, highlighting that children's time with parents outside the home decreased over this period. In other words, there has been a clear shift in the family as a whole spending more time at home between 2000 and 2015.

In addition to providing more information about locations outside the home, in the later UK Time Use Surveys (2000 and 2015) children could report who they were co-present with throughout the day, information not collected in the earlier 1975 survey. It is important to bear in mind that children were free to decide for themselves what 'co-present' meant. There may be instances when children are in their bedrooms on their own, which they regard as being 'alone' despite their parents also being home. There may be instances where children are directly interacting with siblings or friends when parents are nearby, but children do not consider themselves as being co-present with their parents. It is possible, using the information children provide about with whom they are co-present, to probe further into time when children are at the same location as their parents to examine with whom they stated they were with during this time.

Figure 5.5 shows the average time children aged 8–11 years and 12–16 years were co-present with parents, others they know, and time when they were alone but at the same location as their parents, in 2000 and 2015 on school and non-school days. Although there was no change in the total time children aged 8–11 years spent at the same location as their parents on school days, there has been some change in who they report being co-present with during this time. They reported spending less time co-present with parents (−27.7 minutes), and more time alone when at the same location as their parents (36.5 minutes). There were similar changes for children aged 12–16 years. Time alone when at the same location increased by around one hour, alongside decreases in time with others known to the child and time with parents. Clearly, children aged 12–16 years report being alone for most of the additional time they are at the same location as their parents between 2000 and 2015.

On non-school days, for children in both age groups, there was an increase between 2000 and 2015 in time alone when at the same location as parents; this mostly accounts for the increase in total time at the same location in this period. Like school days, the time children reported being with others they knew decreased between 2000 and 2015. Unlike school days, however, the time children reported being co-present with parents when they were at the same location did not decrease. In fact, among children aged 8–11 years there was a significant increase in the time they stated they were co-present with their parents. Lastly, as on school days, there was a large and significant increase in the time children in both age groups reported spending alone when at the same location as their parents. Moreover, for almost all of the time they record being alone when at the same location as their parents, children are at home.

Looking beyond time when children are at the same location as their parents, Table 5.7 shows the average time children aged 8–11 years and 12–16 years report being with others they know (for example, siblings, friends) and time when they report being alone when outside school and away from their parents. There has been a substantial drop in the time children spend with others they know, including siblings and friends. This decrease was greater on non-school days than school days and largest among children aged 12–16 years on both school and non-school days. On school days in 2000, children aged 12–16 years

Figure 5.5: Average minutes co-present with parents, others (siblings/ friends) and alone when at the same location as parents on school and non-school days in 2000 and 2015: children 8–11 and 12–16 years

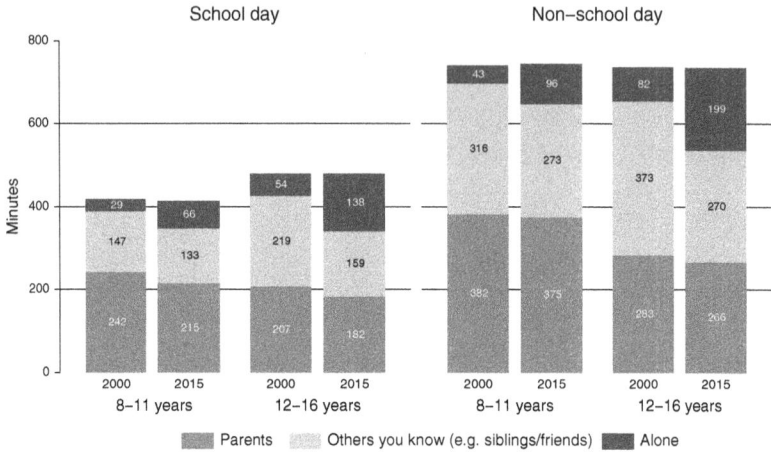

Table 5.7: Average minutes with others (siblings/friends) and alone when not at the same location as parents or at school, on school and non-school days in 2000 and 2015: children 8–11 and 12–16 years

	School day		Non-school day	
	2000	2015	2000	2015
	Average mins [95% CI]		Average mins [95% CI]	
With others (e.g. siblings/friends)				
8–11 years	99 [91–108]	85 [73–97]	203 [187–219]	165 [141–177]
12–16 years	159 [146–171]	110 [98–123]	275 [258–292]	190 [171–208]
Alone				
8–11 years	14 [11–16]	17 [14–21]	18 [14–22]	30 [23–37]
12–16 years	29 [24–33]	55 [48–63]	44 [37–51]	82 [71–94]

spent on average 159 minutes with others they know when not at the same location as their parents and not at school, which decreased by around 50 minutes in 2015. On non-school days, this time decreased from 275 minutes in 2000 to 190 minutes in 2015. Decreases in time with others (when away from parents) for children aged 8–11 years were smaller by comparison, though they were statistically significant on both school and non-school days.

As for time when children are at the same location as their parents, the time children report being alone when not at the same location as their parents increased, particularly on non-school days. On school days, there was no significant change between 2000 and 2015 in the time children aged 8–11 years reported being alone when not near their parents, but this increased by 26 minutes among children aged 12–16 years. On non-school days, there were significant increases in the average time children aged 8–11 and 12–16 years reported being alone when not at the same location as parents (12 minutes and 38 minutes respectively). Note finally that children are at home for much of time they report being alone when not at the same location as their parents, but a substantial portion of this time is when they are at other locations (around 30 per cent of all time alone when not near parents).

The social context of time using devices

This chapter has revealed that children are spending a substantial amount of time using devices, particularly children aged 12–16 years. Whether or not time spent using mobile devices is diminishing the quality and quantity of time children spend with others remains a topic of some debate. Questions about the quality of time are not examined here, but the results given show clearly that there has been an increase in the time children spend alone, most of which is when they are at home at the same time as their parents. Time with parents changed little between 2000 and 2015, but the time children spend with others they know decreased, coinciding with significant increases in the time they spend at home. Many of these changes are most pronounced among children aged 12–16 years. This section brings together information about children's time using devices with information about who they are spending time with. It examines patterns in the social context of children's use of devices to ascertain whether this time is concentrated in time when children are with their parents or others they know, or when they report being alone.

Table 5.8 shows the average time children aged 8–11 and 12–16 years spend using devices in varying social contexts on school and non-school days in 2015. Children aged 8–11 years spent on average 25 minutes using a device when with parents on school days and 46 minutes on non-school days. This is approximately one third of their total time using devices.[3] During around 30 per cent of the total time children aged 12–16 years are using a device they are with their parents (49 minutes on school days and 73 minutes on non-school days). Children spend

Table 5.8: Average minutes using devices with parents, others (friends/ siblings) and alone on school and non-school days in 2015: children age 8–11 and 12–16 years

	School day		Non-school day	
	8–11 years	12–16 years	8–11 years	12–16 years
	Average mins *[95% CI]*		Average mins *[95% CI]*	
Total time using devices when:				
With parents	25 *[19–32]*	49 *[41–58]*	46 *[36–55]*	73 *[61–84]*
With others you know (e.g. friends/siblings)	13 *[8–18]*	41 *[33–50]*	41 *[31–50]*	55 *[45–65]*
Alone	24 *[18–30]*	56 *[45–67]*	34 *[27–41]*	82 *[69–95]*

comparatively less time using devices when with others they know, such as friends or siblings (and not with parents), but the time they spend using devices when alone is very similar to time using devices when with parents. Given that overall children spend less time alone than with parents (even children aged 12–16 years), this suggests that comparatively more of children's time alone is when they are using devices.

Figure 5.6 confirms this, showing the composition of children's time with parents, with others (siblings/friends) and alone, differentiating between time when they are and are not using a device. Children aged 8–11 were on average using a device for 12 per cent of the time they spend with parents on school days, 7 per cent of time with others they know (siblings/friends), and 31 per cent of time when they are alone. The proportions are very similar on non-school days, though the proportion of time with others when using a device increases to 14 per cent, and the average time here increased substantially (see Table 5.7). Children aged 12–16 years spent more time using devices than children aged 8–11 years, and it is therefore not surprising that they are using devices for proportionally more of their time with parents and others they know siblings/friends. However, like younger children (8–11 years), time using devices was relatively more concentrated during time when older children (12–16 years) reported being alone on both school (40 per cent) and non-school days (41 per cent).

Parents' time using devices

The time parents spend using devices forms a major part of the home or family technology environment. The capacity for information and

Figure 5.6: Proportion of time spent with parents, others (siblings/ friends) and alone not using a device and using a device in 2015 on school days and non-school days: children 8–11 and 12–16 years

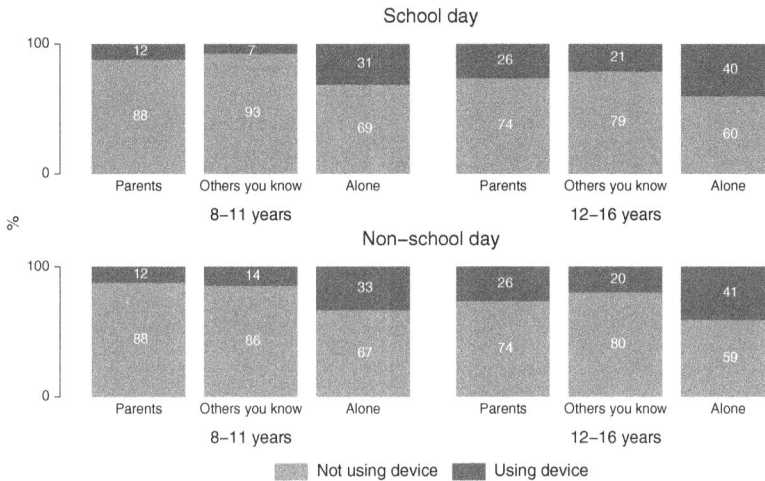

communication technologies to blur boundaries for parents between paid work and family life is long recognised (Daly, 1996; Hughes and Hans, 2001). The emergence and rapid diffusion of smartphones and powerful wireless internet connections further reinvigorated debates about the influence of parents' use of devices on family life. Numerous qualitative studies have drawn attention to the fact that parents often use smartphones when with children in many different locations and not only for work purposes (for a review, see Kildare and Middlemiss 2017). Studies have observed parents using smartphones in various locations with their children, including fast food restaurants (Radesky et al, 2014) and the park (Hiniker et al, 2015), raising questions about the impact of this on family interactions. At home, there is evidence that the increasing use of devices by both parents and children has an adverse effect on the experience of shared family activities (Odour et al, 2016). To mitigate this, parents may set rules to control both their own and their children's time using devices when together, especially during time in shared activities such as eating together (Hiniker et al, 2016).

This final section considers parents' time using devices when they are together with children at the same location. It was shown in the previous sections (and in Chapter 4) that, in 2015, children were spending more time at the same location as their parents (both at home and elsewhere) than in 2000, and that they reported being alone for most of this add-itional time when they were co-located with their parents. Children's

Figure 5.7: Average minutes parents are using devices when they are near their children and children's reports of whom they are co-present with, on school and non-school days in 2015

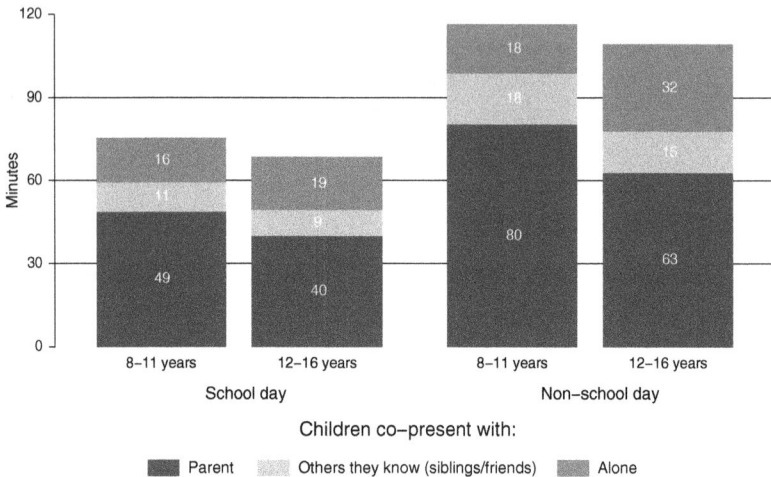

Children co-present with:

■ Parent   ▨ Others they know (siblings/friends)   ▨ Alone

time using devices, moreover, disproportionately occurred during time when they reported being alone. Whether it also coincides with time that parents are using devices is a question to which we now turn.

Figure 5.7 shows the average total time parents spent using devices when near their children (8–11 years and 12–16 years), on school and non-school days, broken down by who children report being co-present with during this time. On school days parents spent around 75 minutes using a device when near children aged 8–11 years and slightly less (68 minutes) when near children aged 12–16 years. Children in both age groups reported being with their parents most during time when parents are using devices, followed by time spent alone. Children aged 8–11 years reported being alone for around 20 per cent of parents' time using devices when near them (16 minutes), whereas children 12–16 years are alone for close to 30 per cent of all time during which parents were using devices when near them (19 minutes).

Like children, parents spent more time using devices on non-school days when near their children. Parents' total time using devices on non-school days was very similar for children aged 8–11 years (116 minutes) and children aged 12–16 years (around 109 minutes). As was the case on school days, for most of the time parents were using devices children in both age groups reported being co-present with their parents, though this was higher among children aged 8–11 years, comprising close to 70 per cent of all the time parents were using a device compared with 57 per cent for children aged 12–16 years. Countering this, children aged 12–16 years spent more time alone when their parents were using devices (32 minutes) than children aged 8–11 years (18 minutes). Average time children spent with others they know when co-located parents were using devices was very similar in both age groups.

It is worth noting briefly at this point that there was comparatively little overlap in the time children and parents spent using devices. On school days, children aged 8–11 years and parents were using devices at the same time for 17 minutes, and this was higher for children aged 12–16 years (27 minutes). Device use by children and parents at the same time was higher on non-school days for children in both age groups (25 minutes for children aged 8–11 years and 40 minutes for children aged 12–16 years).

Most of the time that parents spend using devices occurs when children say that they are with their parents. Some have expressed concern that family activities such as eating together have suffered, in part because of technological developments resulting in children and parents spending excessive amounts of time using devices. Chapter 4 examined time in shared eating and watching TV when children and parents are together at home. Surprisingly, between 2000 and 2015 there was very little change in shared eating (though this increased on non-school days for children aged 8–11 years), with an expected (though modest) decrease in shared time watching TV, but on school days only. However, it may be that parents and children are increasingly using devices during time in shared activities.

Table 5.9 shows the average time children and parents spend in shared activities in 2015 (eating, TV, other leisure activities, and the total time in these shared activities), alongside the average time either a child or parents were using devices during time in these shared activities in 2015.[4] On school days, all children (8–16 years) and their parents spent 14 minutes eating together on average, and a child or parent used a device during this time for three minutes on average. The absolute amount here is small, but this comprises around one fifth of the average time in shared eating. In contrast, children or parents were using devices for a relatively large portion of shared TV time (41 per cent), although again the absolute amount of time using devices is small (8 minutes). Overall, children or parents were using devices for 14 minutes during time in shared activities combined out of 51 minutes in total. Time in shared activities was greater on non-school days, but time using devices during this time did not increase in similar proportions. For example, average time in shared eating almost doubled to 27 minutes on non-school days, but device use

Table 5.9: Average minutes using device during time in parent-child shared activities on school and non-school days in 2015

	Total time shared activity 2015	Child or parent using device 2015
Shared time on a school day		
Eating	14 [12–15]	3 [2–4]
TV	19 [16–22]	8 [6–10]
Other leisure activities	7 [5–9]	2 [1–2]
Total shared activities[1]	51 [47–55]	14 [12–16]
Shared time on a non-school day		
Eating	27 [25–30]	4 [3–5]
TV	36 [32–40]	11 [9–13]
Other leisure activities	39 [34–44]	8 [7–10]
Total shared activities[1]	122 [113–131]	26 [23–30]

Notes: 1 Includes shared time in domestic and personal activities

during this time increased only by 1 minute. Similarly, the proportion of shared TV where a child or parent is using a device decreases to around 30 per cent on non-school days (11 minutes). Overall, the total time a child or parent is using a device comprises around one fifth of all time in shared activities on a non-school day.

Conclusions

Technological change has dramatically altered not only the overall amount of time children spend in screen-based activities, but also the composition of this time. The time children spend watching TV decreased substantially and they are spending more time using computers and playing video games. In addition, children are now spending a substantial amount of time using devices such as smartphones and tablets. Children can use these devices at various locations and during times also spent doing various screen-based and non-screen activities. It may be that children are using these devices to watch TV or play video games, or to engage in other non-screen activities such as communicating with friends or listening to music. Today, therefore it makes less sense to talk of total screen time and to acknowledge that there is an array of different types of screen time. When combining time in screen-based activities (when these are the main activity) and other time using a device there has been an unambiguous increase in 'total screen time'. But it is misleading to constitute this time as a singular block, and doing so risks obscuring understanding of how children have integrated mobile devices into their daily lives and activities.

These changes are highly gendered. Increases in screen-based activities between 2000 and 2015 were concentrated among boys and concentrated in time playing video games, with boys consistently spending more time than girls in screen-based activities between 1975 and 2015. It is important to resist dismissing gender differences in time playing video games as simply reflecting essential gender differences in the leisure preferences of children (in the way we might have previously regarded football as being 'for boys'). The 'Gamergate' controversy brought to public view widespread misogyny in video game culture (Jane, 2017). While not making a direct link to this case, the widening gender differences in time playing video games shown in this chapter, seen in this light, might well reflect the exclusion of, or self-selection by, girls away from a domain where misogyny is seemingly rife.

Gender differences in this area must also be viewed within the social context where men continue to dominate education and employment in the technology sector (ONS, 2017). Although the perceived negative effects of video games, especially violent games, dominate research, some positive effects of playing video games for children's cognitive, social, and emotional outcomes are now receiving attention in the literature (see Granic et al, 2014). Playing video games is one of the ways boys in particular can develop friendships and interact with their friends (Lenhart et al, 2015). Boys' engagement in the world of video games, moreover, introduces them to cultures and networks in the world of technology, and may help foster aspirations for valorised careers in technology, such as software development and game design. Girls may counteract this to an extent through spending more time than boys using devices when engaged in non-screen based activities, and there is no difference between boys and girls in the total time they spend using devices. Girls clearly are not technophobes: they engage with new technology equally but differently than boys and we need to leverage their engagement with technology as children to promote opportunities for them to develop skill and careers in the ever-expanding and evolving technology sector.

Children's time using devices appears to have had little impact on the time they spend in other activities, including physical activities. There has been, however, dramatic change in elements of the social context of children's daily lives that may be connected to the time they spend using mobile devices. Broadly, on both school and non-school days between 2000 and 2015, the amount of time children report spending alone increased significantly, the amount of time they report spending with others they know decreased significantly, and the amount of time they report spending with their parents remained comparatively unchanged. Crucially, children report spending more time alone both when they are at the same location as their parents as well as when they are away from their parents.

These changes clearly align with the view of children spending more time *alone-together* (Turkle, 2011), and less time interacting with the people they are in physical proximity to. The extent to which these changes connect with children's time using devices is a pivotal question and, although not identifying a direct causal link, there is considerable evidence that these changes in the social context of daily life coalesce with children's time using devices. These changes are greatest among children aged 12–16 years, who spend most time using devices, and on non-school days, when time using devices is highest among children irrespective of age. Understanding the implications of this for child well-being requires considerable further investigation. There is little evidence that adolescents' time on social media is linked directly to their well-being (Orben and Przybylski, 2019; Orben et al, 2019), but children's relationships with their friends and family are a major component of their general happiness (The Children's Society, 2017). It may be that spending less time interacting directly with friends and others they know in person (coinciding with increases in time using devices) is having a detrimental impact on children's overall well-being.

The overall picture seen in this chapter is of children spending more time alone (much of which is at home with parents), spending more time using devices when alone, and spending less time in the company of others they know, especially when they are away from their parents. These changes are particularly stark on non-school days among secondary school children aged 12–16 years, and they again raise urgent questions about the extent to which opportunities for children to meet and interact in safe environments away from parents (and the home) have been curtailed dramatically over recent decades. Previous chapters showed children spending less time outdoors and visiting libraries less frequently in 2015 than in 2000, but this is only a tiny part of a larger retrenchment in physical spaces and public resources available for children to meet and interact with each other and engage in a variety of different activities (UNISON, 2016). A singular (negative) focus on a combination of the amount of time children spend in screen-based activities and technological change, carries the risk of missing the critical importance of wider social factors shaping the opportunities children have to spend time away from screens.

The huge increase in the time children spend alone (including when they are near their parents) raises questions also about the extent to which what is commonly understood as being 'alone' has changed, or if the qualitative experience of this time has altered in some way. Mobile devices have become integral to children's interactions and connections with their friends, and for meeting new friends; children see this as one of the key reasons for using mobile devices such as smartphones (Livingstone et al, 2014; Lenhart et al, 2015). Unfortunately, limitations in the time-diary instrument prevent examination of what children are using devices for, such as whether or not they are using them to interact with others. Research elsewhere opens this social space for critical examination, acknowledging the risks but recognising that children often are highly competent managers of risk, unveiling the intricacies of this still comparatively new social space (for example, Lenhart et al, 2015; Berriman and Thompson, 2018). What this study demonstrates, which has not been considered in prior research, is the extent to which children, when asked who they are with, report that they are alone during this time; as a proportion of children's time, this has increased substantially since 2000.

Although children reported 'alone' as the closest appropriate response in answer to the question 'who were you with?', it is possible that making other responses available such as *with others online* might influence the decisions children (and adults) make about whether they are 'alone' or not. Time alone has not only increased, but it has become more differentiated in terms of how it is experienced and interpreted. To examine this further, research on children's time use (and adults' time use) needs to move beyond a single all-encompassing measure of time 'alone'.

This chapter has revealed that parents spend a substantial amount of time using devices when they are near their children, and during most of this time children report being with their parents. It is not, therefore, that parents are using smartphones and tablets when their children say that they are alone, perhaps in other rooms in the house. However, although both children and parents are using devices during time in shared family activities, this is minimal: most of the time either children or parents are using devices is during other time when they are near each other. The overall extent to which parents are using devices when near their children is not in itself especially noteworthy. It serves to underline, however, that the changes observed among children specifically extend across the family more generally. Lastly, it is important to note that we have data here for 2015 only; this does form a baseline from which we can compare future patterns in time use in this continually changing area.

Notes

[1] http://www.digitaldayresearch.co.uk/home/

[2] All estimates from Ofcom's *Digital Day* were obtained using http://www.digitaldayresearch.co.uk/decks/deck-creator/

[3] Note that the total time using devices includes some time when children do not provide any information about who they are co-present with, and time when they are using devices when at school.

[4] Note that the measure of shared activities used here differs from Chapter 4 in that it includes time in shared activities outside the home, but it was restricted to time when children say that they are co-present with a parent. Changes between 2000 and 2015 in these measures of shared eating and TV are substantively equivalent to those found in Chapter 4 (see Mullan and Chatzitheochari, 2019).

6

How Children Feel About How They Spend Time

What children do with their time relates to their well-being in numerous ways. To understand this, we need to appreciate that well-being is a multi-dimensional concept incorporating both objective and subjective components. Objective well-being can be assessed with reference to indicators relating to children's health and education. For example, the proportion of children who are overweight (including obese) and the proportion of children who would like to pursue further or higher education are two headline indicators which the Office for National Statistics (ONS) uses to measure child well-being (relating to health and education respectively) (ONS, 2014a). Aspects of how children spend their time also relate closely to objective indicators of child well-being. For example, children's time in physical activities, and in activities linked to education and culture, are positively associated with objective indicators of well-being (tied respectively to health and education) (ONS, 2014a). Subjective well-being refers broadly to psychological or emotional states or feelings. There are two major components of subjective well-being: 'affective' and 'cognitive' (The Children's Society, 2013). The affective component is measured typically by asking children how *happy* they are[1]; questions about *satisfaction with life* are used to capture the cognitive component. In short, the first relates to how children feel about their lives and the second requires a (subjective) cognitive appraisal or evaluation of life.

This chapter focuses on the affective component of subjective well-being, specifically in connection with how children feel about how they spend their time. How happy children feel about their time use overall has been a core element in efforts to gauge children's subjective well-being. Rees et al (2010) ask children how happy they are across ten life domains, including family, friends, school, appearance and time use. The subjective dimensions of time use – how children feel about how they spend time – are therefore central to evaluations of children's subjective well-being. Although it is helpful to single out overall time use as a distinct area of life, this is comprised of many different activities and there may be considerable variation in children's subjective experience of time in different activities. A Canadian study, for example, found that 73 per cent of adolescents (12–19 years) said that free-time activities were their most enjoyable activity during the day, whereas only 8 per cent considered time at school as the most enjoyable,[2] with 43 per cent of students stating that school was their main source of stress (Zuzanek, 2005).

Furthermore, it is necessary to anchor questions about happiness to a specific temporal period. The ONS measures personal well-being by asking people 'how happy did you feel *yesterday*?' (ONS, 2014a [emphasis added]). Going further, efforts to measure the subjective experience of time use stress that measures capturing the experience of time *in the moment*, when people are engaging in those activities, are superior to asking retrospective questions about how a person felt about time in a particular activity or experience after this time has elapsed (Kahneman, 1999). Responses to so-called retrospective questions about the subjective experience of time in different activities may suffer from systematic biases, as they tend to ignore activity durations, with high or low points during the experience and feelings at the end of the experience having an undue influence on retrospective evaluations of the experience (Kahneman and Krueger, 2006). Therefore, it is preferable to collect information about the subjective experience of time in different activities when those activities are actually occurring.

There are a number of methods for capturing the subjective experience of time use as it occurs in the moment. The experience sampling method (ESM) was the first widely used and validated approach (Csikszentmihalyi and Larson, 1987). In ESM, respondents are prompted at random moments in time (over a day, a week, or longer period) to record their activity at that specific moment and provide information about the subjective experience of this time (for example, how happy, stressed, anxious, or rushed they were). Though yielding valid results, this method is difficult and expensive to implement in large samples because respondents must be supplied with a device, such as a pager, used to collect the data.[3] An alternative to ESM, developed by Daniel Kahneman and colleagues (Kahneman et al, 2004), is called the day reconstruction method (DRM), which combines elements of ESM and time use survey data collection methods. With this method, participants reconstruct the complete sequence of main activity episodes they engaged in during the previous day, including the start and end times for each episode, and then provide information about the subjective experience of time in these episodes. This method brings together information about the total duration of time in different activities with information about the subjective experience of this time.

The latest UK Time Use Survey developed a novel approach to collecting data on the subjective experience of time use that improves upon DRM (Gershuny and Sullivan, 2017). Recall that respondents to this survey completed a time diary, providing information about their daily activities alongside contextual information such as their location and with whom they were co-present. In addition to this information, respondents were asked to indicate how much they 'enjoyed this time' on a scale from 1 ('not at all') to 7 ('very much'). Like DRM, this approach collects information about time use for the whole day alongside information about the subjective experience of time use. However, it provides more detailed information than DRM, as it allows respondents to indicate their enjoyment of time use in ten-minute intervals throughout the day.

To summarise thus far, general measures of affect linked to subjective well-being, such as a global measure of how happy you are overall, may be broken down to focus on specific life domains including time use, as is the case for the child well-being index developed by Rees and colleagues (Rees et al, 2010). It is important, however, to distinguish between the subjective experiences of time in the different activities children engage in throughout the day and the social context of time use, such as who we are co-present with.[4] It is furthermore important to capture the subjective experience of time in different activities during time engaging in those activities. There are a number of approaches to doing this including one adopted in the most recent UK Time Use Survey, where respondents were asked to report how much they enjoyed their time throughout the day in ten-minute intervals.

Subjective experiences of time use must be treated as distinct from global assessments of happiness and those applied to specific life domains. Analyses of the relationship between ratings of the subjective experience of time use and global measures of subjective well-being (such as general happiness) have highlighted some intriguing, seemingly contradictory, results. Paid work, for example, has a low ranking in terms of subjective enjoyment, especially when reported *during* paid work, but unemployed people have lower levels of happiness in general (Robinson and Martin, 2009). Similarly, young people express dislike of time in school-related activities such as homework when they are engaging in these activities, but spending time in school-related activities is positively associated with overall happiness (Csikszentmihalyi and Hunter, 2003). It is important, therefore, to exercise caution when interpreting the results of any analysis of the subjective dimensions of time use.

This chapter explores children's subjective experience of time use in the UK, focusing on their enjoyment of time throughout the day. Although the word 'happy' is not specifically used, in the context of time use 'enjoyment' and 'happiness' may be considered closely interchangeable. It would be preferable also to have a measure of negative affect, such as stress/anxiety, or an indicator capturing the experience of boredom during the activity. It would, moreover, be ideal to analyse general indicators of subjective well-being, such as overall levels of happiness, satisfaction, or anxiety, but the UK Time Use Survey 2015 did not collect this information from children aged 8–15 years. The data available to examine children's subjective well-being are limited, but the available information nevertheless offers an unparalleled opportunity to explore how children feel about the time they spend in different activities and social contexts throughout the day.

To repeat, in the latest UK Time Use Survey (2014–15) children could report their enjoyment of time throughout the day on a scale ranging from 1 ('not at all') to 7 ('very much'). In the initial stage of data collection, not all respondents completed a diary with the enjoyment field and such exclusions were random. Around 16 per cent of children aged 8–16 years did not complete a diary with the enjoyment field (n=162); these children are therefore not included in the analysis in this chapter. The average enjoyment score for each activity across all episodes of time in that activity is computed. For example, if a child reported three episodes of eating and rated their enjoyment of time in these three episodes as 6, 5, 7, their average enjoyment score for eating across the day would be 6. Average enjoyment scores are then collapsed into three categories capturing different levels of relative enjoyment as follows: 1) 'low' enjoyment (1–3); 2) 'moderate' enjoyment (4–5); 3) 'high' enjoyment (6–7).

The chapter begins with an analysis of children's enjoyment of time in eight activities: classes, homework/study, housework and shopping, eating, reading, screen time, sport and exercise, and non-screen leisure. Following this, children's enjoyment of different modes of travel – active travel, car, and public transport – is analysed. The second section moves on to consider enjoyment of the social context of time use, focusing on variation in patterns of enjoyment associated with the time children spend with parents, with others they know, and time spent alone.

This second section also examines the possible influence of the use of devices and the enjoyment of time. The chapter finishes with a study of children's experiences of time pressure. Children's feelings about time pressure in general and their experience of time pressure specifically on the days they completed their time diaries are both examined. The chapter presents data for the first time on the extent to which children in the UK report feeling rushed, factors associated with this, and its relationship with how they spend their time.

Children's enjoyment of daily activities

Figure 6.1 shows the distribution of relative levels of enjoyment (low, moderate and high) for time children spent in eight different activities. Around one third of children at school (classes) on the diary day reported a relatively high average level of enjoyment for this time, and just under half of children who spent time at school reported a moderate level of enjoyment on average (47 per cent). About one in every five children at school on the diary day reported a relatively low level of enjoyment for time at school. Data on enjoyment of time in classes (and all other activities) is for 2015 only, and therefore it is not possible to examine whether children's enjoyment of time in classes changed over the years, perhaps in response to increasing pressures associated with testing. There is limited prior research on this, but it would seem that disliking time at school is not a new phenomenon. Christensen and James (2001: 82) elicited generally negative opinions about school from children aged around 10–12 years. One particularly emphatic response from 'Maxine' was as follows:

> 'BAD BAD BAD BAD BAD BAD BAD BAD BAD BAD!
> I wish they'd never invented it!'

Note though, enjoyment of school here relates the average level of enjoyment of time in classes throughout the day. This covers a large amount of time and there is some variation in reports of enjoyment across the school day. If we look at the maximum level of enjoyment reported at any point during time in classes, 59 per cent report a high level of enjoyment for at least one period during the school day, and one in ten never report anything more than a low level of enjoyment for time at school. Although time at school is comparatively unenjoyable overall, many children do experience some relatively highly enjoyable periods at school, and relatively few find it persistently unenjoyable.

Figure 6.1: Distribution of relative levels of enjoyment for different activities: children 8–16 years in 2015

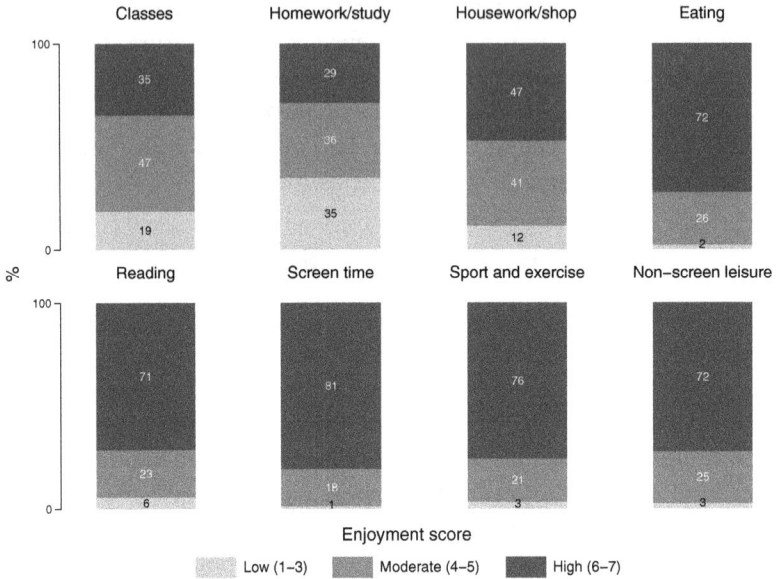

Enjoyment score

Low (1–3)   Moderate (4–5)   High (6–7)

Time doing homework is even less enjoyable than time at school. Around one third of children who spent some time doing homework or study reported relatively low enjoyment for time in this activity (35 per cent). A similar proportion reported moderate levels of enjoyment of time doing homework, and only 28.7 per cent reported relatively high levels of enjoyment for time doing homework or study. This increases to 34 per cent if the focus is the maximum level of enjoyment reported for time in this activity rather than the average. However, the difference here is much smaller than the difference between average and maximum enjoyment for time at school noted in the previous paragraph. Low levels of enjoyment of time doing homework and study, and for school, align with data elsewhere showing that children consistently report comparatively low levels of happiness with school and schoolwork (The Children's Society, 2017).

In stark contrast with time in school and time doing homework and studying, the vast majority of children report relatively high levels of enjoyment on average across a range of different leisure activities. This is highest for screen time (81 per cent) followed by time doing sport and exercise (76 per cent). Most of the remainder of children report moderate levels of enjoyment in different leisure activities, with a small proportion reporting relatively low levels of enjoyment of time in leisure activities.

Children's relative enjoyment of time doing housework and shopping lies between enjoyment of education-related activities and enjoyment of leisure activities. Similar proportions of children report either moderate or high levels of enjoyment of time in housework and shopping, with approximately one in ten children who engaged in these activities reporting a low level of enjoyment. There was very little difference between enjoyment of housework and shopping, though slightly more children reported a low level of enjoyment for the former (13.3 per cent for housework and 9.8 per cent for shopping).

Further exploratory analysis of children's enjoyment of different activities revealed some differences associated with gender, age, and maternal employment. Girls were less likely than boys to report low levels of enjoyment for time doing homework (30 per cent vs 42 per cent), echoing gender differences in children's mean levels of happiness in relation to schoolwork (The Children's Society, 2017). With regards to reading, boys were more likely than girls to report relatively moderate levels of enjoyment for reading (36 per cent vs 15 per cent), but girls were much more likely to report relatively high levels of enjoyment for time reading (81 per cent vs 36 per cent), which aligns with previous research showing girls enjoying reading to a greater extent than boys (Clark and Rumbold, 2006).

These results provide further perspectives on the persistent gender differences in time in these activities favouring girls, showing that the *experience* of time in these activities may well be a component in helping to explain gender differences in time in these activities. With respect to homework, the association is negative, in that girls are less likely to not enjoy time in this activity, whereas for reading the association is directly positive, in that girls are more likely to highly enjoy time in this activity; these factors may be important to consider in relation to promoting children spending time in these activities. It is worth noting in addition here that parental education was not significantly associated with children's relative *enjoyment* of time in these activities, despite the fact that this is strongly associated with children's time in these activities. The extent to which children enjoy time in these activities is not, therefore, likely to be a major factor explaining the influence of parental education.

Age and maternal employment were each significantly associated with enjoyment of a range of different activities. Children aged 12–16 years consistently reported significantly less enjoyment than did children aged 8–11 years across a wide range of different activities. For example, 27 per cent of children aged 12–16 years reported high enjoyment for time in classes compared with 47 per cent of children aged 8–11 years. This result indicates that there is a distinct qualitative difference around the experience of time in primary versus secondary school, perhaps relating to pressures around exams. Children aged 12–16 years were also less likely to report high enjoyment for time doing homework than children aged 8–11 years (26 per cent vs 33 per cent), but this was not a statistically significant difference. Age was significantly associated with time reading, however, and it may be that the time children aged 12–16 years spend reading is more closely tied to education rather than reading solely for pleasure. Older children (12–16 years) were also less likely to report relatively high enjoyment for eating (67 per cent vs 77 per cent), screen time (77 per cent vs 84 per cent) and non-screen leisure (65 per cent vs 78 per cent), but there was no difference in enjoyment of sport. In all cases, differences in the reverse direction in moderate levels of enjoyment for time in these activities offset the significant differences in high enjoyment associated with child age group. These results echo previous research showing that age is negatively associated with feelings of happiness tied to daily activities (Csikszentmihalyi and Hunter, 2003).

Children whose mother is in paid work are significantly less likely to report high levels of enjoyment across a range of activities, with the exception of time in classes, doing homework and reading where there was no significant difference. This factor has not been explicitly considered in previous research on children's subjective experience of time, and these results are noteworthy. Working mothers' experience of time pressure could be an important factor here, but the significant effect of maternal employment remained after controlling for mothers' time pressure and satisfaction with work–family balance. It may be that children with working mothers experience tighter scheduling constraints, which detracts from their enjoyment of time use in general. This chapter considers children's experience of time pressure later.

Enjoyment of different modes of travel

Chapter 3 showed that children spend a substantial amount of time travelling during the day. Most travel occurs in a car, followed by time in active travel (such as walking or cycling to school) though this decreased significantly between 2000 and 2015. Figure 6.2 shows the distribution of relative levels of enjoyment children report for time spent travelling in total and time spent travelling in different modes (active travel, car, public transport). Overall, close to half of children rate travelling as relatively highly enjoyable, close to levels of enjoyment reported for time in housework activities. Enjoyment of active travel is only slightly higher than enjoyment of travel overall. Just over half of children who spent some time in active travel reported a relatively high level of enjoyment for this time, 37 per cent reported moderate enjoyment of this time on average, and around one in ten reported a relatively a low level of enjoyment. Enjoyment of active travel is markedly higher on non-school days, however, where 61 per cent of children report relatively high enjoyment of time in active travel compared with 43 per cent on school days. It is most likely that active travel on non-school days is connected to leisure, whereas on school days it is most likely connected to travel to and from school, which, as we have seen, is one of the least enjoyable periods of a child's day.

Enjoyment of travel by car, which is the most common form of travel, is very similar to enjoyment for travel overall, and does not vary on school or non-school days. Travelling by public transport is comparatively the least enjoyable mode of transport, with around one in five children who travelled on public transport on the diary day reporting relatively low enjoyment for this time. Overall, however, relative to the variation in enjoyment seen for different types of activities, variations tied to modes of travel are small.

There are no gender differences in enjoyment of travel time overall and in different modes, but the negative association between age and enjoyment of time extends to travel, and particularly time in active travel and public transport.

Enjoyment and social context

Enjoyment of time relates not only to the activity, but also to who else might be present during the activity. For example, being with friends or family may enhance our enjoyment of time eating or watching TV, compared with spending time in these activities alone. Indeed, the social dimension of time in many leisure activities is often what makes time in these activities particularly appealing. Alternatively, the solitary nature of some activities might be what makes them particularly enjoyable for some. To examine the possible influence of social context on the enjoyment of time, time in different activities is decomposed according to whether children reported being with their parents, with others they know (for example, friends, siblings), or alone. Although it would be possible to compare the enjoyment of the time children spend in different social contexts overall (for example, time with parents or friends, or time alone), it would be impossible to identify

Figure 6.2: Distribution of relative levels of enjoyment for different modes of travel: children 8–16 years in 2015

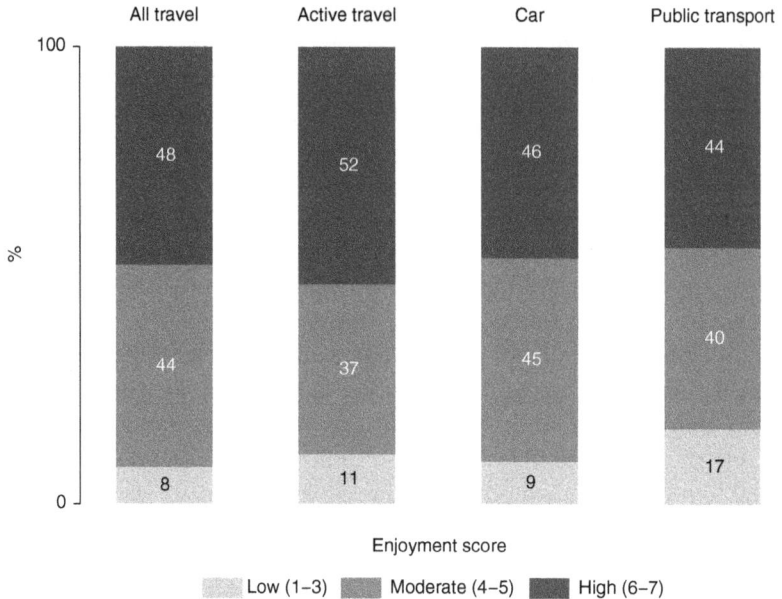

the extent to which enjoyment of this time related to the social context or to the different activities children were engaging in. By comparing different social contexts during the same activity, effectively holding activity constant, we can consider whether enjoyment of time varies depending on who children report being co-present with.

Figure 6.3 shows the distribution of relative levels of enjoyment of time in activities, differentiating between time when children report being co-present with their parents, with others they know, and time when they are alone. As already shown, around 30 per cent of children reported high levels of enjoyment for time in homework (see Figure 6.1). Figure 6.3 shows that this high level of enjoyment is lower when children are alone (18 per cent) than when they are with their parents (32 per cent) or others they know (43 per cent). Homework, therefore, is most enjoyable when children are with others they know. Note, however, that most episodes of homework occur when children are with their parents or alone (84 per cent).

The enjoyment of time doing housework and eating is also lowest when children are alone. Housework (including shopping) is most enjoyable when children are with others they know, and enjoyment of eating is similar when children are with parents and with others

Figure 6.3: Enjoyment of activities in different social contexts

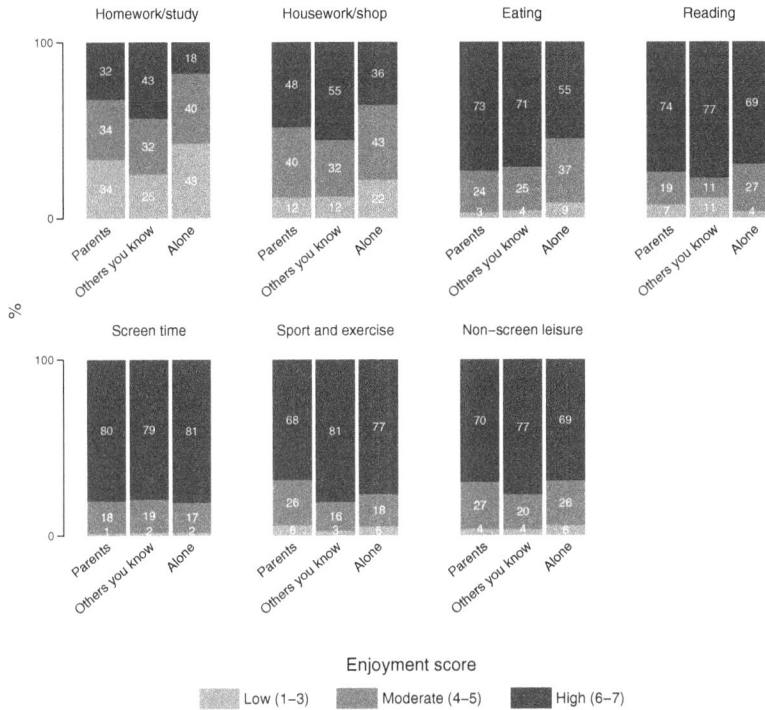

Enjoyment score

Low (1–3)   Moderate (4–5)   High (6–7)

they know. Looking closer at time eating, time during family meals is marginally more enjoyable, with 76 per cent of children reporting this time as highly enjoyable. The difference between this and enjoyment of eating overall (see Figure 6.1) is very small, however.

Turning to leisure activities, children's enjoyment of reading and screen time is very similar, irrespective of with whom they report being co-present. The results for screen time arguably underscore the impression that the social dimension of time use fades to the background when children are engaged in screen-based activities. Children are obviously mindful of the presence of parents and others they know, which comprises 70 per cent of all episodes of screen time, but this has a negligible influence on the enjoyment of time in screen-based activities. It is also worth noting here that enjoyment of time watching TV with parents (that is, when both children and parents are watching TV together) is no different to enjoyment of watching TV overall, with around 81 per cent of children reporting time in shared TV as highly enjoyable.

Enjoyment of time in sport and other non-screen leisure does vary a little depending on who is with children. Specifically, children's enjoyment of sport and other non-screen leisure time is greatest when they report being with others they know, compared with when they report being with their parents. The differences are comparatively small, however, with a vast majority of children reporting high levels of enjoyment for these activities, irrespective of who they are co-present with.

The potential influence of the social context of daily activities on enjoyment of time is comparatively limited, at least in relation to differences in enjoyment observed for different activities. Overall, lower levels of enjoyment associated with being alone when doing homework, housework and shopping, and eating are stronger than the positive influence on enjoyment children report when with others they know during time in active and non-screen leisure.

Enjoyment and time using devices

Chapter 5 showed that children's use of devices nowadays is a major component of their daily lives. Children's use of devices coincides with time when a screen-based activity (watching TV, using computers, playing video games) is their main activity, and clearly this is some of the most enjoyable time children experience. It is interesting to consider whether using devices enhances or diminishes the enjoyment of screen time. Analysis of this shows clearly, however, that enjoyment of screen time is very similar, irrespective of whether or not a child reports using a device. As shown in Figure 6.4, about 82 per cent of children report a high level of enjoyment of screen time when using a device, and 80 per cent report high enjoyment for screen time when not using a device (see Figure 6.4).

Children, as Chapter 5 showed, use devices during time spent in many other activities. Figure 6.4 shows the distribution of enjoyment for time doing homework, housework and shopping, eating, and time in non-screen leisure,[5] differentiating between time in these activities when children are also using a device and time when they are not. As was the case for screen time, enjoyment of time in these activities was very similar, irrespective of whether or not children were using a device at the same time. By a small margin, enjoyment of time doing homework, eating and in non-screen leisure was higher when children were not also using a device. However, Chapter 5 showed that time using a device mostly coincided with time when children were alone, and their enjoyment of time alone tends to be relatively low. In sum, there is no evidence that using a device has any influence, positive or negative, on children's subjective enjoyment of time.

Figure 6.4: Enjoyment of time in different activities when using and not using a device

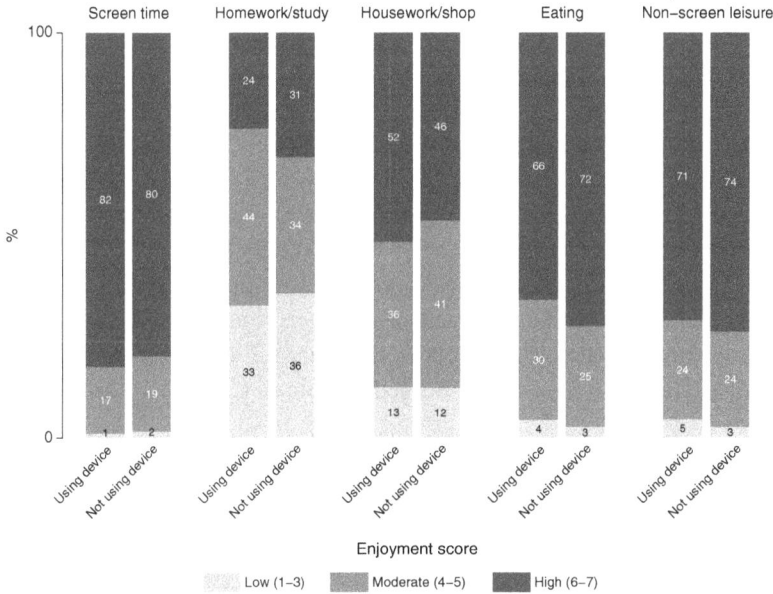

Enjoyment score

Low (1–3)   Moderate (4–5)   High (6–7)

Time pressure among children

Time pressure is another aspect of the subjective experience of time. Time pressure can relate to the experience of feeling that you do not have sufficient time to carry out the activities that you want or need to, or it may arise in situations where multiple tasks jostle for attention to be completed within prescribed timeframes. Among adults, time pressure is associated with increased workloads, especially when time is stretched across commitments to paid work, domestic work and childcare responsibilities, and particularly among women (Craig et al., 2019). Children may experience time pressure due to school-related workloads (Zuzanek, 2005) and from participating in various extra-curricular activities after school (Lareau, 2003).

There are very few studies of time pressure experienced by children and young people. Zuzanek (2005) reported that around two thirds of Canadian adolescents (15–19 years) report, in general, experiencing time pressure. Posel and Grapsa (2017) studied time pressure reported by children aged 10–17 years in South Africa, using a measure of time pressure tied specifically to the day they completed a time diary. They found that around 6 per cent of South African children (10–17 years) described their diary day as 'too busy', around two thirds said it was 'comfortable' and 29 per cent said it was 'not busy enough'. Differences in the age range of children, and country context, in these two studies may account for the differences in the prevalence of time pressure among children. It is also likely, however, that experiences of time pressure in general may be more widespread than experiences of time pressure tied to a specific day.

The UK Time Use Surveys in 2000 and 2015 both included a question about general time pressure, but this was not included in the child questionnaire (for children aged 8–15 years) in the 2015 survey. In 2000, around 52 per cent of children aged 8–16 years reported that in general they 'sometimes feel rushed', and close to 7 per cent said that they 'always feel rushed'. Taken together, therefore, close to 60 per cent of children reported feeling rushed sometimes or always, which is comparable with the prevalence of general time pressure reported by older Canadian adolescents (15–19 years).

In the 2015 survey, but not in the 2000 survey, there was a question in the time-diary instrument asking respondents whether they felt rushed on the diary day, and all children could provide a response to this. Around 14 per cent of children said they were rushed on a school day and slightly fewer (13 per cent) said they were rushed on a non-school day. These proportions are higher than the South African sample, which may reflect a real difference. However, it could be that the difference in the wording of the questions ('rushed' versus 'too busy') is also a factor in explaining this difference.

There are mixed findings with respect to factors associated with children's experience of time pressure, which is unsurprising given the sparse number of studies of children's experience of time pressure. Hilbrecht et al (2008), studying Canadian adolescents (aged 12–19 years), found that a general experience of time pressure was positively associated with age, and was higher among girls than boys (Hilbrecht et al, 2008). However, Posel and Grapsa (2017) did not find any significant association between child age or gender and children's reports of time pressure linked to a specific day.

In the UK in 2000, general time pressure was higher among older children (12–16 years) than children in primary school, and girls were more likely to report experiencing time pressure than boys, echoing the Canadian study. In 2015, children aged 12–16 years were more likely to report time pressure on school days only. Girls were more likely to report time pressure on non-school days, but boys and girls reported similar levels of time pressure on school days. Therefore, in contrast with the South African data, child age and gender are associated with time pressure on the diary day, and there is a degree of congruence between factors associated with both general and specific measures of time pressure in the UK over time.

Further analysis of time pressure among children in the UK revealed some findings not reported elsewhere. To begin with, in the year 2000, children with parents with post-compulsory education were more likely to feel rushed in general than children whose parents do not have post-compulsory education. Socio-economic differences in how children spend time (such as more study and less screen time) might be connected to this result, which is explored further in this chapter. However, time pressure tied to a specific day reported in 2015 was not significantly associated with parental education. Unfortunately, it is impossible to know whether this is a change over time in the influence of parental education, or whether it relates to differences in the measure of time pressure.

Children with a mother in paid work were more likely to report being rushed on a school day only. Maternal employment was not significantly associated with general feelings of time pressure reported by children in 2000 however. In both years, mothers' reports of feeling rushed are significantly associated with children's reports of feeling rushed (both general and specific), and the effect of maternal employment on children's time pressure on school days is no longer significant after controlling for mothers' experience of time pressure. In other words, once mothers' experience of time pressure is taken into account, their employment is no longer a determining factor for children's experience of time pressure. The time pressure experienced by mothers seems, therefore, contagious.

It is difficult to draw out broad conclusions from this brief overview of children's experiences of time pressure. There is a definite need for further research on children's time pressure to build up a better picture, including addressing questions about how to measure children's time pressure, and whether measures designed to capture time pressure for adults are suitable for analysing time pressure among children.

Time pressure and time use

With respect to associations between time pressure and time use patterns, Zuzanek (2005) found that general time pressure among older Canadian adolescents (15–19 years) was positively associated with time doing homework and time in paid work, and negatively associated with free time. For children in the UK in 2000 and 2015, Table 6.1 shows the difference associated with experiencing time pressure in the time children spend in school-related, leisure, and work-related

Table 6.1: Association between feeling rushed and time in homework, screen time, non-screen leisure and work activities in 2000 and 2015

	2000	2015	
Activity	Normally 'sometimes' or 'always' rushed	Rushed on a school day	Rushed on a non-school day
Homework or study	6.2"	6.7	0.9
Screen time	6.6	1.6	−43.7"
Non-screen leisure	−21.8"	−4.4	28.7+
Work (housework/ paid/voluntary)	9.3˙	12.2	18.8+

Notes: Table shows the difference in the average minutes in each activity between those who report being rushed compared with those who do not. *** p < .001; ** p < .01; * p < .05; + p < .1

activities. In 2000, children who reported being 'sometimes' or 'always' rushed averaged significantly more time doing homework and study (6.2 minutes), less time in non-screen leisure, with no difference in screen time, and more time in work-related activities (9.3 minutes). Note, however, that there was no significant association between time pressure and the three separate components of work time. Broadly, therefore, associations between time pressure and time in these activities are similar to those found among Canadian adolescents.

The second and third columns in Table 6.1 show the results from the 2015 survey for being rushed on a school day and non-school day respectively. Children who are rushed on a school day spend more time doing homework and studying; the difference is similar in magnitude to the result for 2000, but it is not statistically significant. This is most likely a consequence of the lower number of children who say they are rushed on a particular day, compared with reporting time pressure in general. Being rushed on a school day is not significantly associated with either screen time or non-screen leisure. Time doing homework and study is not significantly associated with time pressure on a non-school day, but children who are rushed on a non-school day in 2015 spend significantly less time in screen-based activities than those who are not rushed, and more time in non-screen leisure and work activities, though these differences reach only marginal statistical significance (p < .1).

Conclusion

The subjective experience of daily life is an emerging area of research and this chapter provided some initial insight on children's subjective enjoyment of time. The results for children's enjoyment of time in different activities are perhaps unsurprising, showing us that they generally do not enjoy time at school and time doing homework, and they enjoy very much time in screen-based activities and other leisure. Central to our basic understanding of what constitutes a good childhood is that children have the time and space to have fun and enjoy themselves. Based on these results it might well be suggested that in order to maximise child well-being they should be encouraged to spend more time in leisure activities including screen time, and to avoid or minimise time in school and doing homework. One can easily imagine children cheering this proposition on, but prior research demonstrates that there is a degree of mismatch between feelings about time use during activities and indicators of general well-being. Although children tend to find time in education-related activities unenjoyable, and they express comparatively low levels of happiness with this area of their lives (The Children's Society, 2017), some have found these to be positively associated with overall happiness (Csikszentmihalyi and Hunter, 2003).

This does not mean that we cannot or should not consider possible ways to enhance children's experiences of time in these activities, particularly time at school. The emphasis among policymakers in this arena is strongly in favour of increasing attainment, with children placed under increasing pressure to perform well in tests. There remains a deep-seated view that the quality of education relates only to academic rigour and perceived difficulty. Yet there is no reason to suppose that education cannot be both challenging and enjoyable. It is interesting to note in connection with this that there is increasing recognition that happiness in relation to paid work is correlated with productivity (Oswald et al, 2015). Debates in this area would do well to move away from a deeply embedded, arguably simplistic, assumption that if children are enjoying school, then it is somehow too easy or not sufficiently difficult or 'serious', and ultimately not 'good enough'.

Relative to activities, there was less variation in enjoyment of time linked to the social context of activities. Eating alone was relatively less enjoyable than eating with others, and children found a number of activities most enjoyable when carried out with other people they know, including time doing homework, housework and shopping, sport and other non-screen leisure activities. The results for homework are interesting given how unenjoyable children find time in this activity. It is important to acknowledge here that most episodes of homework are carried out when children are alone (the least enjoyable), but it is nonetheless notable that there is some potential for children's engagement in homework to be more enjoyable (or at least less unenjoyable), and that altering the social context of this time might help in this regard. This again calls to mind questions about the availability of social spaces that are safe and appealing for children to meet to do homework and other activities together.

In addition to looking at children's enjoyment of time, the prevalence of children aged 8–16 years in the UK reporting being rushed was examined in this chapter for the first time. There is a sparse literature on children's experiences of feeling rushed or pressed for time, and the findings contained in this chapter add to this. However, it is difficult to make general comparisons and draw firm conclusions about children's experience of time pressure. The results suggest that a substantial proportion of children aged 8–16 years in the UK (60 per cent) at least sometimes feel rushed or pressed for time in general. This figure is from the 2000 survey, however, and recent data are not available. Data from the 2015 survey reveal that close to 15 per cent of children reported that they were rushed on the day they completed their time diary. However, it is not possible to connect these findings across surveys to arrive at any sense of how children's experiences of time pressure may have changed.

Time pressure increased with age, and girls were more likely to report being rushed or pressed for time than boys. This could be linked to pressures associated with education, as these characteristics are positively associated with children's time in homework and study. Children who reported feeling rushed did spend more time in these activities, though this was not consistently significant over time. In connection with this, children with mothers who reported being rushed or pressed for time are themselves more likely to report feeling rushed. It may be that these feelings stem from comparatively more rigid scheduling experienced by children in dual earner families rather than time spent in any particular activity. The data available on this topic are very limited, however, and this chapter has only scratched the surface of questions relating to the subjective experience of time pressure and time use in general. This remains a promising area for future research on the relationship between children's time use and subjective well-being.

Notes

[1] Affect can be both positive and negative, but children have been found to be more readily open to answer questions about positive affect (for example, happiness, excitement) and perceive questions about negative affect (for example, anxious, lonely) as intrusive (The Children's Society, 2013).

[2] Only 1 per cent stated that homework was the most enjoyable activity.

³ There have been efforts to deploy new mobile technology to collect ESM data (for example, the mappiness project: http://v1.mappiness.org.uk/), though these approaches tend not to cover random samples of the population.

⁴ Other domains may be similarly broken down. For example, happiness with school could be broken down into looking at happiness with teachers, different subjects, school facilities, and other pupils.

⁵ The use of devices during time in sport and exercise and reading is marginal and this time is included in time in non-screen-leisure.

7

Conclusion

How children spend time, and whether this may have changed, is routinely the subject of public debates around children's health and well-being. This book has sought to inform these debates by presenting a detailed analysis of change in various aspects of children's time use over four decades between 1975 and 2015, using high quality time use data collected from children directly. Children's daily lives are widely thought to have changed dramatically over the past several decades. Knowledge about change in children's time use is based on extremely limited data, however, with debates struggling to move beyond pointing out in general terms that children are spending either more or less time in whatever activity is of interest. This book set out to deepen understanding of change in children's daily time use, looking at change across a comprehensive range of activities, including time using devices such as smartphones and tablets in recent years. As well as examining children's daily activities, the book foregrounded elements of the social and family context of children's daily activities and studied the influence of parents' time use on children's time use.

The focus of the book is on children's everyday lives. Childhood scholars have drawn attention to this level of analysis as a way to learn more about how children responsively engage with and construct their social worlds as they learn and grow, with the focus very much on understanding children's lives in the present. Children's time use is clearly a step removed from processes of social construction, but it has the potential to offer insights on changes in the action basis of these processes. A second area of research on children's lives in the present revolves around efforts to measure and track child well-being. The measurement of child well-being partially incorporates children's time use, and this study aims to support these efforts further in drawing out more fully than previously a complete picture of change in a child's day in connection with major domains of child well-being. The analysis uses nationally representative time use data and therefore provides both a snapshot of children as a permanent group in our society and a unique perspective on how children's lives are influenced by social change. In this way, children's time use forms a juncture between the study of children as a structural component group in our society and the study of children's everyday lives.

Spanning five major topic areas relating to children's well-being – covering education and culture, health, family, technology, and subjective well-being – this book has presented a detailed analysis of children's time use within these areas, which taken together comprise a child's day. The book addressed three broad sets of questions throughout. First, it investigated whether children's time use changed and the extent to which these changes may be related to changes in society linked to education, technology, and generalised concerns for children's safety. Differences in trends associated with child age, gender and parental education were examined throughout the book. The second set of questions centred on the relationship between different elements of children's time use (such as different activities) and the relationship between the social context of daily life and children's activities (including time using technology). Third, the book examined questions concerning the influence of parents' time use on children's time use. This concluding chapter surveys the key findings and issues raised in these three broad areas of investigation. It ends with some comments on the future for children's time use research.

Social change and changing time use in childhood

Despite persistent change in children's experience of and engagement with education over the past several decades, its impact on their daily lives remained to a great extent unchanged. At the core of this stability lies children's time at school; as a basic structural feature of children's time use, this has changed little throughout the past several decades. Of course, children's time *in* school, and what is required of them, has changed with children being subject to increasing levels of assessment and testing. The data did not provide information about what children do in school or their school workloads, and future research should address children's time use in school. Some evidence of the possible impact on children's daily lives was found through increases in the time they spend doing homework and study outside school. These increases in time doing homework, however, were concentrated in the period between 1975 and 2000, with further small increases between 2000 and 2015 confined to non-school days. There appears, therefore, to be clear limits to the extent to which children are willing, or need, to spend more time doing homework and study. Unlike time doing homework and study, there has been no comparable increase in children's average daily time reading. In fact, on non-school days, as time doing homework and study marginally increased, the time children in secondary school spend reading decreased marginally. Although this is not evidence of a direct transfer of time from one activity to the other, it raises the question about whether increased time in homework might come at the expense of children's time reading.

The analysis of change in children's activities linked to health revealed somewhat diverging trends on school days compared with non-school days. The analysis here studied trends in children's total screen time as a main activity (TV, video games, using computers), and trends in time in sport, out-of-home play and active travel. Surprisingly, on school days children's total screen time remained unchanged for older children (12–16 years) over the four decades between 1975 and 2015 and decreased by half an hour for younger children (8–11 years). Alongside this, there were significant increases in children's time in sport on school days (in both age groups). Countering this, children's time in out-of-home play decreased, but total time in these physical activities on school days increased between 1975 and 2015 (again in both age groups). Viewed together with the results for screen time showing no increase on school days, there is little evidence therefore to support the view that children's daily lives have become markedly less active on school days, at least with respect to time in these activities.

Unlike school days, there was an unambiguous increase on non-school days in the time children spend in screen-based activities when this is their main activity, though with children spending less time watching TV and more time using computers and playing video games. Children's time in sport also increased on non-school days but decreases in time in out-of-home play outweighed this, and children were spending less time in these activities combined in 2015 than in 1975. There were also significant decreases in active travel on non-school days between 2000 and 2015. Taken together, screen time increased as time in these physical activities combined decreased. There is compelling evidence, therefore, that daily life for children on non-school days has become less active and more focused on screen-based activities over the past several decades.

As well as increases in the time children spend in screen-based activities when this is their main activity, children are now spending a substantial amount of time using devices such as smartphones and tablets. For around half of the time children report using a device, they also report a screen-based activity (watching TV, playing video games, using computers) as their main activity. This can include situations where children use these to watch TV or play video games, or they use them for some other purpose (for example, interacting with friends on social media) during time in a screen-based activity. Time using devices in these circumstances is not strictly additional screen-time, though in the latter case it might make sense to talk about a 'deepening' of screen time. Note that it is a limitation of the data used in this book that it is not possible to ascertain the reasons children are using devices. The remainder of children's time using devices extends across time they spend in a wide range of other activities, which could be construed as additional screen time. In this sense, there can be no doubt that children's total screen time was higher in 2015 than in previous years on both school and non-school days.

The analysis of trends in time at home with parents and without parents brought changes in these contextual dimensions of children's time use into view. As with time in health-related activities, trends in time at home with parents diverge on school and non-school days. On school days, children aged 8–11 years spend less time at home with parents in 2015 than was the case in 1975, whereas there was no change for children aged 12–16 years. These trends closely mimic the trends found for screen-based activities on school days, which is unsurprising given the huge overlap shown between time in this activity and time spent at home both with and without parents.

Children's time at home with parents on non-school days decreased between 1975 and 2000, but it increased between 2000 and 2015 such that there was no overall difference between 1975 and 2015. The decrease between 1975 and 2000 was surprising given the substantial increase in screen time over this same period, but this was concentrated in time when children were at other locations outside the home. Around the turn of the millennium, not all children had access to computers and the internet at home, so this change likely reflected children spending more time using computers and the internet at other locations outside the home where they could access these (at the time) new technologies. As well as spending more time in screen-based activities outside the home, children in 2000 were spending significantly more time shopping on non-school days than in 1975.

Children's return to the home between 2000 and 2015 coincides with further increases in screen-based activities (concentrated in time spent at home). In 2015, almost all children had a computer at home and access to the internet, and children were spending substantial amounts of time using mobile devices such as smartphones and tablets when at the same location as their parents in that year. However, between 2000 and 2015 (for which we have comparable data), when children are near their parents (that is, at the same location) they actually report spending more time alone, and less time with their parents and with other people they know (such as friends and siblings). Furthermore, when children aged 12–16 years are away from their parents (that is, at different locations) they also report spending more time alone and less time with other people that they know. Connections between these changes and children's use of mobile devices such as smartphones are discussed further later in this chapter.

Aspects of children's time use linked to health have changed substantially over time, but it is important to bear in mind that there are certain limitations to the measures studied in this book. The data do not provide definitive measures of the time children spend outdoors across all three surveys. Based on what children are doing when not at home it is reasonable to assume that they not outdoors (for example, screen time, homework and study, non-active travel), but a direct measure of time outdoors would be preferable. Information about energy expenditure during activities would provide a stronger basis for concluding that children's daily lives have become less active over time. Another limitation with respect to the measures studied in this book relates to children's engagement in structured or organised activities (although sport was a major exception to this). Unfortunately, there was no specific code to identify children's time in structured activities, particularly relating to arts and creative activities. Children could report time engaging in these activities, however, and this was a minor component of their non-screen leisure time. Also, in connection with homework, it was not possible to identify time when children may be receiving extra tuition or spending time in afterschool homework clubs.

Overall, there was more change over the entire period studied in this book in children's time use on non-school days than on school days. This makes sense, as children have more free time on non-school days and there is thus more scope for change. This is basic to point out, but it is something overlooked in typically doom-laden pronouncements about children's time use, and how this has changed. Clearly, school is a major structuring influence in shaping a child's day, most likely in unison with parental employment, arguably leading to comparatively stable routines on school days over the past several decades. The fact that change in children's time use in areas that are of concern (screen time and time in physical activities) is particularly concentrated on non-school days raises critical questions about opportunities children have to use the additional time available to them on non-school days to best effect with respect to their health, development, and well-being. Leaving this as a problem for individual parents and children to solve for themselves on their own is not sufficient: it touches on areas of public concern with respect to what facilities are available and the steps needed to create a safe environment and culture that is conducive to children leading full and active lives.

Children's time use is often invoked in connection with outcomes relating to health and well-being, and trends found in the book around screen time, time outside the home, and time alone certainly lead to questions about implications for children's well-being. The direct implications are far from clear, however. The analysis of children's subjective enjoyment of time use revealed that their time in leisure activities (including screen time and sporting activities) was most enjoyable, and time associated with education was least enjoyable. Few would suggest though that this should form a basis upon which to formulate proposals for enhancing children's well-being through changes in their time use. Overall, the analysis of trends presented in this book demonstrates how changes in children's time in different activities slot together in place within a child's day. Often debates about children's well-being, in connection with children's time use, focus specifically on single activities, such as screen time, physical activities, or doing homework. What is often missing is any sense of children *juggling* time in wide variety of different activities. The idea of 'balance' is central to our understanding of what constitutes a healthy diet, but it is equally salient in relation to how children spend their time. What might constitute a 'healthy balance' of activities is an open question, but discourse around change in children's time use could be enhanced by more fully acknowledging the benefits of promoting a balanced use of time with a view to enhancing children's well-being.

Change and stability in factors associated with children's time use

Throughout, the book has examined differences in children's time use associated with child age and gender, and with parental education. We have seen at various points that trends in children's time use has varied according to these factors, and, in some instances, the extent to which these characteristics influence children's time use has changed over the past several decades.

Beginning with child age, although increasing for all children, older children (12–16 years) consistently spend more time doing homework and study over the period reviewed. Children aged 12–16 years spent more time reading outside school than children aged 8–11 years in 1975, but there was no difference in later years as reading among older children decreased over time. Age differences in time in sport, particularly on non-school days, also disappeared over time: younger children's time in sport increased, with comparatively less change among children aged 12–16 years. Where time in these activities became less associated with age, age differences in screen-based activities increased over time. In 1975, there was very little difference in children's time in screen-based activities, but children aged 12–16 years were spending significantly more time in screen-based activities than children aged 8–11 years by 2015. The former, moreover, were spending substantially more time using devices than the latter. Screen-based activities and time using devices such as smartphones have therefore emerged as a major site for age-based distinctions in children's leisure time, over a period when technology and the online world (as opposed to the offline outside world) have become increasingly central to children's daily lives.

Turning to gender, the past several decades have witnessed substantial changes in the status of women in society, underpinned by changes in attitudes around men's and women's roles and gender equality. This raises the prospect that gender has become less of a factor in determining how children spend their time. The results presented throughout this book suggest that this is far from being the case. Gender remains a highly significant factor associated with children's time in many different activities. Girls persistently spend more time than boys in domestic activities such as housework and childcare. The gender gap here decreased, but only because girls reduced the amount of time they spend in this activity, arguably reflecting trends in the gender division of domestic work among adults. Girls also persistently spend less time than boys in sport, even though girls' time in sport consistently increased over time. The idea that these activities are *for* girls and boys respectively is one that appears remarkably resistant to any change. Gender differences in screen time have also persisted, with boys spending more time in these activities. Comprised of time watching TV in 1975, gender differences in later years shifted to time playing video games. In contrast, boys and girls spent a similar amount of time using mobile devices such as smartphones and tablets, but gender differences here were concentrated in the way in which this was combined with time in other activities, with girls spending more time using devices during time in non-screen activities.

Change in the influence of age in children's everyday lives and activities may reflect change in social constructions of childhood. Age differences have diminished across many aspects of children's leisure;

this might indicate a blurring of age-related boundaries in terms of social interactions between school-age children of different ages. Gender differences in time use among children normalise – at a young age – socially constructed gender distinctions manifest in everyday life, and gender differences in time use are as prevalent in contemporary society as they were in the mid-1970s. Time use data alone provide little direct insight into changes in the social construction of childhood and processes of social construction in children's everyday lives, and these findings raise questions for further research. There is much scope for mixed-method approaches combining the study of children's time use with qualitative methodologies to investigate processes underlying children's time use, including children's reflections and experiences on how they spend their time, in connection with characteristics such as age and gender.

Socio-economic background continues to have a massive impact on children's outcomes in a number of key areas of their lives. Looking at this in connection with children's everyday lives, this book analysed differences in children's time use associated with parental education. The results confirm well-established patterns where children in families with relatively more formal education spend more time in activities linked to education (homework, study, and reading), and participate more in a range of different cultural activities. Time in physical activities differs little with respect to parental education, but children in families with relatively less formal education spend more time in screen-based activities, though there is no difference in total time using devices such as smartphone and tablets. There was also little difference associated with parental education in the social context of children's daily lives, such as time at home when both with parents and not with parents, and in time in core family time in shared activities. Taken together, therefore, the consistent influence of parental education appears concentrated in a trade-off between screen time and time in activities associated with education at home.

So, what difference does a day make? Inequality marks children in myriad ways and it is certainly the case that this incorporates key areas of their everyday lives. Differences on any given day may be negligible, but accumulating, as they must, they underpin substantial divergences in the lives of children from different socio-economic backgrounds. Time remains one of the key resources at our disposal to effect change in our lives, but differences in time use alone are not enough in explaining socio-economic inequalities in children's lives. The material and social resources available to children and families are essential in *combination* with time to enhancing children's development and well-being throughout society.

Connecting different elements of children's time use

The time children spend in any single activity forms part of a sequence of time in other activities throughout any given day, varying across days in the week, weeks in the month, months in the year, and so on. Activities are also situated within particular social contexts or settings, varying with respect to location and who else is or is not present. Throughout, this book has investigated connections between different elements of children's daily time use, looking at the relationship between time in different activities and at the relationship between changes in activities alongside changes in the social context of daily life.

In the area of education, children's time in homework and study was examined alongside their engagement in cultural activities widely thought to be related to education (such as reading, visiting libraries or art galleries). The results confirmed prior research showing a strong link between children's socio-economic background and time devoted to both education and culture. However, there was limited support for a direct link between activities linked to education (such as time doing homework and study, reading) and children's cultural participation in activities like going to the theatre or an art gallery. This book has not examined educational outcomes, but it has introduced children's time doing homework and study as a new element into research in this area. There are research questions outstanding on the status of children's reading as an activity both directly linked to education (endogenous perhaps) and linked to fostering cultural capital. In future research, it would be preferable to have more information about what children are reading and whether they are reading for pleasure or if this is school-related.

The relationship between screen time and physical activity is another key area of interest and debate, with the view widespread that children's screen time comes at the expense of time in physical activities. Ascertaining whether there is a direct trade-off between screen-based and physical activities is empirically challenging and prior research presents mixed findings. In this book, information about children's monthly engagement in sporting activities was used to identify children who were relatively more or less engaged in sport, and daily time use patterns were compared between children with different levels of engagement in monthly sport. The results showed that, for boys only, time in sport does compete with screen time but only when this was their main activity. There was no association between monthly engagement in sport and children's time (boys or girls) using devices such as smartphones or tablets. These results provide some evidence that, when it is a relatively fixed and substantial part of children's schedules, sport reduces time available for screen-based activities. This suggests that promoting children's engagement in sport would benefit efforts to reduce screen time, among boys at least. However, there may be limits to the extent that this is feasible, given constraints around the availability of sporting activities, family resources, and the organisation and coordination required by family members to facilitate children's engagement in sporting activities. Perhaps reflecting this, children's time in organised sport changed little between 2000 and 2015, whereas screen time and time at home increased significantly during this period alongside decreases in children's time in informal physical activity (out-of-home play and active travel). While it is not possible here to identify a direct link between these changes, this again raises issues in connection with the need to promote safe environments for children to engage in relatively informal physical activities as a viable alternative to home-based screen time and supplement to time in organised sport.

Studying the overlaps between children's time using technology and elements of time use relating to activities and social contexts formed a major part of the analysis of technology in children's everyday lives. It has been shown how children's use of mobile technology arguably has become part of the context of their daily lives, overlapping with time in many different activities and social contexts. While there was little evidence to support the view that children's time using technology detracted from time in other activities, such time use strongly overlaps with major changes in the social context of daily life between 2000 and 2015. As outlined previously, the social composition of time at home, and elsewhere, changed dramatically during this period. There have been substantial increases in the time children spend alone alongside decreases in the time they say they are with others they know, such as friends and siblings. These changes in social context were greatest on non-school days, and children also spent most time using devices on non-school days. This was most pronounced among children aged 12–16 years who spent the most time using devices. Children are using devices across a range of social contexts, but it is particularly concentrated when they report that they are alone. The overlap between time using technology and changes in the social context of children's time use is compelling, but this does not imply a causal link in the sense of technology causing these changes. Nevertheless, bringing information about the social context of daily life together with information about children's time using technology opens up the debate to consider the wider social and environmental factors at play, particularly with respect to opportunities available for children to spend time away from their homes interacting directly in person with their friends.

Further research on the relationship between children's time in different activities is warranted. The approach developed in this book used information about children's monthly engagement in cultural and sporting activities to identify differences in long-term time use patterns or schedules, and then to investigate how these are associated with daily time use. These data were limited, however, and it would be preferable to be able to construct a picture of children's schedules over time and connect this with daily time use patterns to understand more about how specific routines and habits engender different time use patterns on a given day. This shifts attention away from questions about how much time children spend in particular activities on a given day towards thinking about how different routines become established. The influence of parents in this regard is likely to be crucial.

The influence of parents' time use on children's time use

The influence of parents on children's time use is typically gauged in empirical research, including in this book, through associations with parent characteristics such as education or employment. Another critical way in which parents might influence children's time use is through their own time use patterns. Parents can model spending time in particular activities, or parents' time use patterns may reflect interests or preferences that they wish to pass on to their children. Parents' time use may also shape family norms around spending time in particular activities, especially in connection with screen time and time using devices like smartphones and tablets. This book has shown that parents' time use is positively correlated with that of their children, but this is not fixed over time and effects on daily time use were generally limited.

The analysis of parents' daily reading in Chapter 2 (focused on children's education and culture) revealed a broadly positive correlation with children's daily reading, but over time institutionalised cultural capital (for example, parents' level of education) in more educated families become relatively more dominant in comparison with embodied cultural capital (for example, reading practices), as parents' reading time decreased. Parents' reading in families where parents have less education was consistently positively associated with children's reading. While demonstrating the consistent effectiveness of parents' reading in fostering children's reading in lower socio-economic groups, these findings arguably also highlight the depth of advantage children in higher socio-economic groups obtain from having access to parents' cultural capital in multiple forms.

Parents' and children's monthly participation in various cultural activities was also strongly correlated, but parents' monthly participation in cultural activities had no significant association with children's daily time use in activities linked to their education. In the case of homework and study, this may stem in part from the fact that time in this activity follows from the amount of homework set by teachers, and again cultural capital in its institutionalised form (parental education) was dominant here. Like cultural activities, there was a significant positive association between parents' and children's monthly engagement in sporting activities. However, parents' monthly engagement in sport had no impact on children's daily time in sport and other key activities. In both cases (cultural and sports activities), these results suggest that the influence of parents' time use is structural in terms of shaping children's longer-term schedules but with considerable day-to-day variation inbuilt. This analysis has been exploratory and there is need for more research on the influence parents' time use may play in shaping children's time use.

The future of children's time use

The last time point for which there is data is 2014–15, which raises immediate questions about whether there has been any change in children's time use between this point and the years leading up to 2020. In the years since 2015, are children spending even more time at home with their parents? Are they spending even more time alone and less time with their friends? Has children's time doing homework on non-school days increased further, and has it remained unchanged on school days? Has the amount of time that children spend in active travel continued to decrease or has this stabilised? Answers to these and many other questions will have to wait until suitable data become available. Although the UK is exceptional in having collected time use data from children over many decades, it is collected relatively infrequently. It is most useful therefore to think forward to studying change in children's time use in the intervening period up to 2025, with the potential to examine fifty years of change in children's daily lives in the UK.

There is little to gain by attempting to predict how children's time use might change in coming years. Change in children's time use rarely follows a straightforward linear path (upwards or downwards), and patterns of change are often not consistent across different groups of children. It is especially tempting, given the changes highlighted in this book, to suggest that children's time using devices will have increased further since 2015, as access to these devices continues to expand. Yet parents might counter this by seeking to limit children's time using devices, and it is critical to not discount the possibility that children themselves might simply get bored or reach some kind of limit in terms of how much of their time they wish to spend using these devices. We simply will not know whether, and how, children's time here, and in other areas, has changed until new data become available.

This study of a child's day provides the most extensive picture currently available in the UK, and elsewhere in the world, into how children's time use has changed over the past several decades. It identifies areas of expected change as well as other areas of surprising stability. It reveals how change and stability in children's time use blend together to comprise a child's day, uncovering also the multi-layered contexts of a child's day. Aspects of children's time use, and how this may have changed, will no doubt continue to surface in public debate in connection with their well-being. While welcoming this, it is necessary to always question and seek to understand how supposed changes actually fit within a child's day, the types of days where these changes are concentrated, among whom, and to seek out evidence on how such changes relate to other activities and the social contexts of daily life. Each day, more of the same and something new, provides a glimpse on a child's world and, through time, their lives. This time warrants our careful ongoing attention.

References

Adam, B. (1994) *Time and social theory*. Cambridge: Polity Press.

Alanen, L. (2001) 'Childhood as a generational condition: children's daily lives in a central Finland town' in L. Alanen and B. Mayall (eds) *Conceptualizing child-adult relations*. London: RoutledgeFalmer.

Altintas, E. (2016) 'The widening education gap in developmental child care activities in the United States 1965–2013', *Journal of Marriage and Family*, vol 78, no 1, pp 26–42.

Aronsson, K. (2012) 'Family life activities and everyday time politics' in M. Hedegaard, K. Aronsson, C. Hojholt and O.S. Ulvik (eds) *Children, childhood and everyday life*. Charlotte, NC: Information Age Publishing.

Becker, G. (1993) *Human capital: A theoretical and empirical analysis, with special reference to education*. Chicago: University of Chicago Press.

Ben-Arieh, A. and Frønes, I. (2011) 'Taxonomy for child well-being indicators: A framework for the analysis of the well-being of children', *Childhood*, vol 18, no 4, pp 460–76.

Bennett, T., Savage, M., Silva, E., Warde, A., Gayo-Cal, M. and Wright, D. (2009) *Class, culture, distinction*. London: Routledge.

Berriman, L. and Thompson, R. (2018) 'Spectacles of intimacy: The moral landscape of teenage social media' in R. Thompson, L. Berriman, and S. Bragg (eds) *Researching everyday childhoods: Time, technology and documentation in a digital age*. London: Bloomsbury Academic.

Bianchi, S.M. (2000) 'Maternal employment and time with children: Dramatic decline or surprising continuity', *Demography*, vol 37, no 4, pp 401–14.

Bianchi, S.M. and Robinson, J. (1997) 'What did you do today? Children's use of time, family composition, and the acquisition of social capital', *Journal of Marriage and Family*, vol 59, no 2, pp 332–44.

Biddle, S.J.H., Atkin, A.J., Cavill, N. and Foster, C. (2011) 'Correlates of physical activity in youth: A review of quantitative systematic reviews', *International Review of Sport and Exercise Psychology*, vol 4, no 1, pp 25–49.

Bond, E. (2014) *Childhood, mobile technologies and everyday experiences: Changing technologies = changing childhoods?* Basingstoke: Palgrave Macmillan.

Bourdieu, P. (2010 [1984]) *Distinction*. London: Routledge.

Bradshaw, J., Dale, V. and Bloor, K. (2016) 'Physical health' in J. Bradshaw (ed) *The well-being of children in the UK*. Bristol: Policy Press.

Brannen, J. (1995) 'Young people and their contribution to household work', *Sociology*, vol 29, no 2, pp 317–38.

Buckingham, D. (2011) *The material child: Growing up in consumer culture*. Cambridge: Polity Press.

Bucksch, J. Sigmundova, D., Hamrick, Z., Troped, P.J., Melkevik, O., Ahluwalia, N., Borraccino, A., Tynjala, J., Kalman, M. and Inchley, J. (2016) 'International trends in adolescents screen-time behaviors from 2002 to 2010', *Journal of Adolescent Health*, vol 58, no 4, pp 417–25.

Cain, N. and Gradisar, M. (2010) 'Electronic media use and sleep in school-aged children and adolescents: A review', *Sleep Medicine*, vol 11(2010), pp 735–42.

Carson, V., Hunter, S., Kuzik, N., Gray, C.E., Poitras, V.J., Chaput, J-P., Saunders, T.J., Katzmarzyk, P.T., Okely, A.D., Gorber, S.C., Kho, M.E., Sampson, M., Lee, H. and Tremblay, M. (2016) 'Systematic review of sedentary behaviour and health indicators in school-age children and youth: an update', *Applied Physiology, Nutrition, and Metabolism*, vol 41, no 6, pp S240-S265.

Cassidy, R., Cattan, S., Crawford, C. and Dytham, S (2018) *How can we increase girls' uptake of maths and physics at A-level?* London: Institute for Fiscal Studies.

Cheng, L.A., Mendonca, G. and deFarias Junior, J.C. (2014) 'Physical activity in adolescents: Analysis of the social influence of parents and friends', *Jornal de Pediatria*, vol 90, no 1, pp 35–41.

Cheng, S.L., Olsen, W., Southerton, D. and Warde, A. (2007) 'The changing practice of eating: Evidence from UK time diaries, 1975 and 2000', *British Journal of Sociology*, vol 58, no 1, pp 39–61.

Chinn, S. and Rona, R.J. (2001) 'Prevalence and trends in overweight and obesity in three cross sectional studies of British children, 1974–94', *BMJ: British Medical Journal*, vol 322, no 7277, pp 24–6.

Chitty, C. (2009) *Education policy in Britain* (2nd edition). Houndmills: Palgrave Macmillan.

Christensen, P. and James, A. (2000) 'Childhood diversity and commonality: Some methodological insights' in P. Christensen and A. James (eds) *Research with children: Perspectives and practices.* London: RoutledgeFalmer.

Christensen, P. and James, A. (2001) 'What are schools for? The temporal experience of parental education practices in Northern England' in L. Alanen and B. Mayall (eds) *Conceptualizing child-adult relations.* London: RoutledgeFalmer.

Christensen, P., James, A. and Jenks, C. (2000) 'Home and movement: Children constructing "family time"' in S.L. Holloway and G. Valentine (eds) *Children's geographies: Playing, living, learning.* London: Routledge.

Clark, C. (2011) *Setting the baseline: The National Literacy Trust's first annual survey into young people's reading – 2010.* London: National Literacy Trust.

Clark, C. and Rumbold, K. (2006). *Reading for pleasure: A research overview.* London: National Literacy Trust.

Clark, L.S. (2014) *The parent app: Understanding families in the digital age,* Oxford: Oxford University Press.

Cooper, H., Robinson, J.C. and Patall, E.A. (2006) 'Does homework improve academic achievement? A synthesis of research, 1987–2003', *Review of Educational Research*, vol 76, no 1, pp 1–62.

Cooper, K. and Stewart, K. (2017) 'Does money affect children's outcomes? An update.' CASE Paper 203. London School of Economics and Political Science.

Coyne, S.M., Padilla-Walker, L.M., Fraser, A.M., Fellows, K. and Day, R.D. (2014) ' "Media time = Family Time": Positive media use in families with adolescents', *Journal of Adolescent Research*, vol 29, no 5, pp 663–88.

Craig, L. (2006) 'Does father care mean fathers share? A comparison of how mothers and fathers in intact families spend time with children', *Gender and Society*, vol 20, no 2, pp 259–81.

Craig, L. (2007) 'How employed mothers in Australia find time for market work and childcare', *Journal of Family and Economic Issues*, vol 28, no 1, pp 69–87.

Craig, L. and Bittman, M. (2008) 'The incremental time costs of children: An analysis of children's impact on adult time use in Australia', *Feminist Economics*, vol 14, no 2, pp 59–88.

Craig, L. and Mullan, K. (2011) 'How fathers and mothers share childcare: A cross-national time-use comparison', *American Sociological Review*, vol 76, no 6, pp 834–61.

Craig, L. and Mullan, K. (2013) 'Parental leisure time: a gender comparison in five countries', *Social Politics: International Studies in Gender, State & Society*, vol 20, no 3, pp 329–57.

Craig, L., Brown, J.E. and Jun, J. (2019) 'Fatherhood, motherhood and time pressure in Australia, Korea, and Finland', *Social Politics: International Studies in Gender, State & Society*. Published online: https://doi.org/10.1093/sp/jxz006

Cribb, J., Keiller, A.N. and Waters, T. (2018) 'Living standards, poverty and inequality in the UK: 2018'. London: Institute for Fiscal Studies.

Csikszentmihalyi, M. and Hunter, J. (2003) 'Happiness in everyday life: The uses of experience sampling', *Journal of Happiness Studies*, vol 4, no 2, pp 185–99.

Csikszentmihalyi, M. and Larson, R. (1987) 'Validity and reliability of the experience-sampling method', *Journal of Nervous and Mental Disease*, vol 175, no 9, pp 526–36.

Dallacker, M., Hertwig, R. and Mata, J. (2018) 'The frequency of family meals and nutritional health in children: A meta-analysis', *Obesity Reviews*, vol 19, pp 638–53.

Dallman, J., Norton, K. and Norton, L. (2005) 'Evidence for secular trends in children's physical activity behaviour', *British Journal of Sports Medicine*, vol 39, no 12, pp 892–7.

Daly, K.J. (1996) *Families & time: Keeping pace in a hurried culture*, Thousand Oaks: Sage.

Daly, K.J. (2001) 'Deconstructing family time: From ideology to lived experience', *Journal of Marriage and Family*, vol 63, no 2, pp 283–94.

DCMS [Department for Culture, Media, and Sport] (2015) *Taking Part 2014/15 Annual Child Report*. London: Department for Culture Media and Sport.

De Graaf, N.D., De Graaf, P.M. and Kraaykamp G. (2000) 'Parental cultural capital and educational attainment in the Netherlands: A refinement of the cultural capital perspective', *Sociology of Education*, vol 73, no 2, pp 92–111.

Devine, F. (2004) *Class Practices: How parents help their children get good jobs*, Cambridge: Cambridge University Press.

DfEE [Department for Education and Employment] (1998) *Homework: Guidelines for primary and secondary schools*. London: Department for Education and Employment: Standards and Effectiveness Unit.

DfES [Department for Education and Skills] (2007) *Gender and education: The evidence on pupils in England*. London: Department for Education and Skills.

DHSC [Department of Heath and Social Care] (2015) *Future in mind: Promoting, protecting and improving our children and young people's mental health and wellbeing.* https://assets.publishing.service.gov.uk/government/uploads/system/uploads/attachment_data/file/414024/Childrens_Mental_Health.pdf

DiMaggio, P. (1982) 'Cultural capital and school success: The impact of status culture participation on the grades of U.S. high school students', *American Sociological Review*, vol 47, no 2, pp 189–201.

Durkheim, E. (1961) *Moral education: A study in the theory and application of the sociology of education.* New York: Free Press.

Ebbeling, C.B., Pawlak, D.B. and Ludwig, D.S. (2002) 'Childhood obesity: Public-health crisis, common sense cure', *The Lancet*, vol 360, pp 473–82.

Edwardson, C.L. and Gorely, T. (2010) 'Parental influences on different types and intensities of physical activity in youth: A systematic review', *Psychology of Sport and Exercise*, vol 11(2010), pp 522–35.

El-Sayed, A.M., Scarborough, P. and Galea, S. (2016) 'Socioeconomic inequalities in childhood obesity in the United Kingdom: A systematic review of the literature', *Obesity Facts*, vol 5, no 5, pp 671–92.

England, P. (2010) 'The gender revolution: Uneven and stalled', *Gender and Society*, vol 24, no 2, pp 149–66.

Ennew, J. (1994) 'Time for children or time for adults' in J. Qvortrup, M. Bardy, G. Sgritta and H. Wintersberger (eds) *Childhood matters: Social theory, practice and politics*, Aldershot: Avebury.

Eurostat (2009) 'Harmonised European time use surveys: 2008 guidelines'. Luxembourg: Office for Official Publications of the European Communities.

Fardouly, J. and Vartanian, L.R. (2016) 'Social media and body image concerns: Current research and future directions', *Current Opinion in Psychology*, vol 9, pp 1–5.

Faulkner, G., Mitra, R., Buliung, R., Fusco, C. and Stone, M. (2015) 'Children's outdoor playtime, physical activity, and parental perceptions of the neighbourhood environment', *International Journal of Play*, vol 4, no 1, pp 84–97.

Finch, N. (2002) 'Physical activity: Structured sport vs active play' in J. Bradshaw (ed) *The well-being of children in the UK* (1st edition). London: Save the Children.

Furedi, F. (2002) *Paranoid parenting: Why ignoring the experts may be the best for your child.* Chicago: Chicago Review Press.

Furedi, F. (2005) *Culture of fear: Risk-taking and the morality of low expectation.* London: Continuum.

Gauthier, A.H., Smeeding, T.M. and Furstenberg, F.F. (2004) 'Are parents investing less time in children? Trends in selected industrialized countries', *Population and Development Review*, vol 30, no 4, pp 647–71.

Genadek, K.R., Flood, S.M. and Roman, J.G. (2016) 'Trends in spouses' shared time in the United States, 1965–2012', *Demography*, vol 53, no 6, pp 1801–20.

Gershenson, S. and Holt, S.B. (2015) 'Gender gaps in high school students' homework time', *Educational Researcher*, vol 44, no 8, pp 432–441.

Gershuny, J. (2000) *Changing times: Work and leisure in postindustrial society*. Oxford: Oxford University Press.

Gershuny, J. and Sullivan, O. (2017) United Kingdom Time Use Survey 2014–2015. [data collection]. UK Data Service SN: 8128.

Gill, T. (2007) *No fear: Growing up in a risk averse society*, London: Calouste Gulbenkian Foundation.

Golding, A. (2008) 'Libraries and cultural capital', *Journal of Librarianship and Information Science*, vol 40, no 4, pp 235–7.

Gracia, P. and García-Román, J. (2018) 'Child and adolescent developmental activities and time use in Spain: The gendered role of parents' work schedules and education levels', *European Sociological Review*, vol 34, no 5, pp 518–38.

Granic, I., Lobel, A. and Engels, R.C.M.E. (2014) 'The benefits of playing video games', *American Psychologist*, vol 69, no 1, pp 66–78.

Hale, L. and Guan, S. (2015) 'Screen time and sleep among school-age children and adolescents: A systematic literature review', *Sleep Medicine Reviews*, vol 21, pp 50–8.

Han, J.C., Lawlor, D.A. and Kimm, S.Y.S. (2010) 'Childhood obesity – 2010: Progress and challenges', *The Lancet*, vol 375, no 9727, pp 1737–48.

Hand, M., Shove, E. and Southerton, D. (2005) 'Explaining showering: A discussion of the material, conventional, and temporal dimensions of practice', *Sociological Research Online*, vol 10, no 2, pp 1–13.

Harrison, M.E., Norris, M.L., Obeid, N., Fu, M., Weistangel, H. and Sampson, M. (2015) 'Systematic review of the effects of family meal frequency on psychosocial outcomes in youth', *Canadian Family Physician*, vol 61, no 2, pp e96-e106.

Hedegaard, M. (2012) 'Children's creative modelling of conflict resolutions in everyday life as central in their learning and development in families' in *Children, childhood and everyday life*, Hedegaard, M., Aronsson, K., Højholt, C. and Ulvik, O.S. (eds). Charlotte, NC: Information Age Publishing.

Hilbrecht, M., Zuzanek, J. and Mannell, R.C. (2008) 'Time use, time pressure and gendered behaviour in early and late adolescence', *Sex Roles*, vol 58, no 5, pp 342–57.

Hillman, M., Adams, J. and Whitelegg, J. (1990) *One false move: A study of children's independent mobility*, London: Policy Studies Institute.

Hills, A.P., Andersen, L.B. and Byrne, N.M. (2011) 'Physical activity and obesity in children', *British Journal of Sports Medicine*, vol 45, no 11, pp 866–70.

Hills, A.P., King, N.A. and Armstrong, T.P. (2007) 'The contribution of physical activity and sedentary behaviours to the growth and development of children and adolescents: Implications for overweight and obesity', *Sports Medicine*, vol 37, no 6, pp 533–45.

Hiniker, A., Schoenebeck, S.Y. and Kientz, J.A. (2016) 'Not at the dinner table: Parents' and children's perspectives on family technology rules' in *Proceedings of the 19th ACM conference on computer-supported cooperative work & social computing*, pp 1376–89.

Hiniker, A., Sobel, K., Suh, H., Sung, Y-C., Lee, C.P. and Kientz, J.A. (2015) 'Texting while parenting: How adults use mobile phones while caring for children at the playground' in *Proceedings of the 33rd annual ACM conference on human factors in computing systems*, pp. 727–36.

Hofferth, S.L. (2010) 'Home media and children's achievement and behaviour', *Child Development*, vol 81, no 5, pp 1598–1619.

Hofferth, S.L. and Sandberg, J.F. (2001) 'How American children spend their time', *Journal of Marriage and Family*, vol 63, no 2, pp 295–308.

Holloway, S.L. and Valentine, G. (2000) *Children's geographies: Playing, living, learning.* London: Routledge.

Hughes, R. and Hans, J.D. (2001) 'Computers, the Internet and families: A review of the role new technology plays in family life', *Journal of Family Issues*, vol 22, no 6, pp 776–90.

Jæger, M.M. (2011) 'Does cultural capital really affect academic achievement? New evidence from combined sibling and panel data', *Sociology of Education*, vol 84, no 4, pp 281–98.

Jæger, M.M. and Breen, R. (2016) 'A dynamic model of cultural reproduction', *American Journal of Sociology*, vol 121, no 4, pp 1079–115.

James, A. and Prout, A. (1997) 'Re-presenting childhood: time and transition in the study of childhood' in A. James and A. Prout (eds) *Constructing and reconstructing childhood.* Abingdon: RoutledgeFalmer.

James, A., Jenks, J. and Prout, A. (1998) *Theorizing childhood.* Cambridge: Polity Press.

Jane, E. (2017) *Misogyny online: A short (and brutish) history.* London: Sage.

Janssen, I. and LeBlanc, A.G. (2010) 'Systematic review of the health benefits of physical activity and fitness in school-aged children and youth', *International Journal of Behavioral Nutrition and Physical Activity*, vol 7, no 40, pp 1–16.

Jarosz, E. (2017) 'Class and eating: Family meals in Britain', *Appetite*, vol 116 (September 2017), pp 527–35.

Jimenez-Pavon, D., Kelly, J. and Reilly, J.J. (2010) 'Associations between objectively measured habitual physical activity and adiposity in children and adolescents: Systematic review', *International Journal of Pediatric Obesity*, vol 5, no 1, pp 3–18.

Jones, A. 2002 'Child labour' in J. Bradshaw (ed) *The well-being of children in the UK* (1st edition), London: Save the Children.

Kahneman, D. (1999) 'Objective happiness' in *Well-being: The foundations of hedonic psychology*, D. Kahneman, E. Diener, and N. Schwartz (eds). New York: Russell Sage Foundation.

Kahneman, D. and Krueger, A.B. (2006) 'Developments in the measurement of subjective well-being', *Journal of Economic Perspectives*, vol 20, no 1, pp 3–24.

Kahneman, D., Krueger, A.B., Schkade, D.A., Schwarz, N. and Stone, A.A. (2004) 'A survey method for characterizing daily life experience: The Day Reconstruction Method', *Science*, vol 306, pp 1776–80.

Karsten, L. (2005) 'It all used to be better? Different generations on continuity and change in urban children's daily use of space', *Children's Geographies*, vol 3, no 3, pp 275–90.

Katz, C. (2004) *Growing up global: Economic restructuring and children's everyday lives*. Minneapolis: University of Minnesota Press.

Kelly, P., Hood, S. and Mayall, B. (1998) 'Children, parents and risk', *Health and Social Care in the Community*, vol 6, no 1, pp 16–24.

Kennedy, T.L. and Wellman, B. (2007) 'The networked household', *Information, Communication & Society*, vol 10, no 5, pp 645–70.

Kildare, C.A. and Middlemiss, W. (2017) 'Impact of parents' mobile device use on parent-child interaction: A literature review', *Computers in Human Behaviour*, vol 75 (October 2017), pp 579–93.

Kingston, P.W. (2001) 'The unfulfilled promise of cultural capital theory', *Sociology of Education*, vol 74(Supp), pp 88–99.

Kubey, R. (1990) 'Television and the quality of family life', *Communication Quarterly*, vol 38, no 4, pp 312–24.

Keung, A. (2016) 'Children's time and space' in J. Bradshaw (ed) *The well-being of children in the UK* (4th edition). Bristol: Policy Press.

Lam, C.B., McHale, S.M. and Crouter, A.C. (2012) 'Parent–child shared time from middle childhood to late adolescence: Developmental course and adjustment correlates', *Child Development*, vol 83, no 6, pp 2089–103.

Lamont, M. and Lareau, A. (1988) 'Cultural capital: Allusions, gaps, and glissandos in recent theoretical developments', *Sociological Theory*, vol 6, no 2, pp 153–68.

Lamote de Grignon Pérez, J., Geshuny, J., Foster, R. and De Vos, M. (2018) 'Sleep differences in the UK between 1974 and 2015: Insights from detailed time diaries', *Journal of Sleep Research*, https://doi.org/10.1111/jsr.12753

Lareau, A. (2003) *Unequal childhoods: Class, race, and family life*, Berkeley: University of California Press.

Larson, R. and Richards, M. H. (1991) 'Daily companionship in late childhood and early adolescence: Changing developmental contexts', *Child Development*, vol 62, no 2, pp 284–300.

Lauricella, A.R., Cingel, D.P., Beaudoin-Ryan, L., Robb, M.B., Saphir, M. and Wartella, E.A. (2016) 'The common sense census: Plugged-in parents of tweens and teens'. Retrieved from www.commonsense.org.

Layard, R. and Dunn, J. (2009) *A good childhood: Searching for values in a competitive edge*. London: Penguin.

Lee, S. J. (2009) 'Online communication and adolescent social ties: Who benefits more from Internet use?', *Journal of Computer-Mediated Communication*, vol 14, no 3, pp 509–31.

Lee, S.J. and Chae, Y.-G. (2007) 'Children's Internet use in a family context: Influence on family relationships and parental mediation', *CyberPsychology & Behavior*, vol 10, no 5, pp 640–4.

Lenhart, A. [Pew Research Center] (2015) *Teen, Social Media and Technology Overview,* Washington DC: Pew Research Center.

Lenhart, A., Smith, A., Anderson, M., Duggan, M. and Perrin, A. (2015) *Teens, Technology and Friendships*. Pew Research Center, August, 2015. http://www.pewinternet.org/2015/08/06/teens-technology-and-friendships/

Lindqvist, A-K., Kostenius, C., Gard, G. and Rutberg, S. (2015) 'Parent participation plays an important part in promoting physical activity', *International Journal of Qualitative Studies on Health and Well-being*, vol 10, no 1, pp 1–9.

Ling, R. (2012) *Taken for grantedness: The embedding of mobile communication into society*, Cambridge, MA: MIT Press.

Livingstone, S. (2002) *Young people and new media: Childhood and the changing media environment*, London: Sage.

Livingstone, S. (2009a) 'Half a century of television in the lives of our children', *The Annals of the American Academy of Political and Social Science*, vol 625, pp 151–63.

Livingstone, S. (2009b) *Children and the internet: Changing expectations, challenging realities*. Cambridge: Polity Press.

Livingstone, S., Haddon, L., Vincent, J., Mascheroni, G. and Ólafsson, K. (2014) *Net children go mobile: The UK report*. London: London School of Economics and Political Science.

Lobstein, T.J., James, W.P.T. and Cole, T.J. (2003) 'Increasing levels of excess weight among children in England', *International Journal of Obesity*, vol 27, no 9, pp 1136–38.

Machin, S. and Vignoles, A. (2006) 'Education policy in the UK', Centre for the Economics of Education Discussion Paper no. 0057. London: Centre for the Economics of Education, London School of Economics.

Marshall, S.J., Gorely, T. and Biddle, S.J.H. (2006) 'A descriptive epidemiology of screen-based media use in youth: A review and critique', *Journal of Adolescence*, vol 29, no 3, pp 333–49.

Marshall, S.J., Biddle, S.J.H., Gorely, T. and Murdey, I. (2004) 'Relationships between media use, body fatness and physical activity in children and youth: A meta-analysis', *International Journal of Obesity*, vol 28, no 10, pp 1238–46.

Mascheroni, G. and Ólafsson, K. (2016) 'The mobile internet: Access, use, opportunities and divides among European Children', *New Media and Society*, vol 18, no 8, pp 1657–79.

Maudlin, T. and Meeks, C.B. (1990) 'Sex differences in children's time use', *Sex Roles*, vol 22, no 9/10, pp 537–54.

Mayall, B. (1994) 'Children in action at home and school' in B. Mayell (ed) *Children's childhoods: Observed and experienced*, London: The Falmer Press.

Mayall, B. (2002) *Towards a sociology for children: Thinking from children's lives*. Buckingham: Open University Press.

McDonald, A.S. (2001) 'The prevalence and effects of test anxiety in school children', *Educational Psychology*, vol 21, no 1, pp 89–101.

McGuinness, F. (2018) *Poverty in the UK: Statistics*. House of Commons Library Briefing Paper No 7096.

McLanahan, S. (2004) 'Diverging destinies: How children are faring under the second demographic transition', *Demography*, vol 41, no 4, pp 607–27.

McNeish, D. and Roberts, H. (1995) *Playing it safe: Today's children at play*. Ilford: Barnardo's.

Melkevik, O., Torsheim, T., Iann, R.J. and Wold, B. (2010) 'Is spending time in screen-based sedentary behaviors associated with less physical activity? A cross-national investigation', *International Journal of Behavioral Nutrition and Physical Activity*, vol 7, no 46, pp 1–10.

Mesch, G. S. (2006) 'Family relations and the Internet: Exploring a family boundaries approach', *Journal of Family Communication*, vol 6, no 2, pp 119–38.

Mestdag, I. and Vandeweyer, J. (2005) 'Where has family time gone? In search of joint family activities and the role of the family meal in 1966 and 1999', *Journal of Family History*, vol 30, no 3, pp 304–23.

Morley, D. (1988) *Family television: Cultural power and domestic leisure.* London: Routledge.

Morrow, V. (1994) 'Responsible children? Aspects of children's work and employment outside school in contemporary UK' in B. Mayell (ed) *Children's childhoods: Observed and experienced.* London: The Falmer Press.

Mullan, K. (2009) 'Young people's time use and maternal employment in the UK', *British Journal of Sociology*, vol 60, no 4, pp 741–62.

Mullan, K. (2010) 'Families that read: A time-diary analysis of young people's and parents' reading', *Journal of Research in Reading*, vol 33, no 4, pp 414–30.

Mullan, K. (2018) 'Technology and children's screen-based activities in the UK: The story of the Millennium so far', *Child Indicators Research*, vol 11, no 6, pp 1781–800.

Mullan, K. (2019) 'A child's day: Trends in time use between 1975 and 2015', *British Journal of Sociology,* vol 70, no 3, pp 997–1024.

Mullan, K. and Chatzitheochari, S. (2019) 'Changing times together? A time-diary analysis of family time in the digital age in the UK', *Journal of Marriage and Family*, vol 81, no 4, pp 795-811.

Mullis, I.V.S., Martin, M.O., Foy, P. and Hooper, M. (2015) *TIMSS 2015 International Mathematics Report.* Boston: TIMSS & PIRLS International Study Center, Lynch School of Education, Boston College.

Mullis, I.V.S., Martin, M.O., Gonzalez, E.J. and Chrostowski, S.J. (2004) *TIMSS 2003 International Mathematics Report.* Boston: TIMSS & PIRLS International Study Center, Lynch School of Education, Boston College.

Murcott, A. (1997) 'Family meals – a thing of the past?' in P. Caplan (ed) *Food, health, and identity*, (pp. 32–49). London: Routledge.

Neilson, J. and Stanfors, M. (2017) 'Time alone or together? Trends and trade-offs among dual-earner couples, Sweden 1990–2010', *Journal of Marriage and Family*, vol 80, no 1, pp 80–98.

Oakley, A. (2015) *Sex, gender and society*. Farnham: Ashgate.

Odour, E., Neustaedter, C., Odum, W., Tang, A., Moallem, N., Tory, M. and Irani, P. (2016) 'The frustrations and benefits of mobile device usage in the home when co-present with family members' in *Proceedings of the annual designing interactive systems conference*, pp 1–13.

Ofcom. (2015) *Children and parents: Media use and attitudes report*. London: Ofcom.

Ofcom. (2017) *Communications market report 2017*. London: Ofcom.

Offer, S. (2018). 'Time Use and Childcare', *Oxford Bibliographies Online in Sociology*. doi: 10.1093/obo/9780199756384-0152.

ONS [Office for National Statistics] (2002) *Family spending: A report on the 2000–01 Family Expenditure Survey*. London: The Stationery Office.

ONS [Office for National Statistics] (2009) *Social trends 39*. Basingstoke: Palgrave Macmillan.

ONS [Office for National Statistics] (2014a) *Measuring national well-being: Children's well-being, 2014*.

ONS [Office for National Statistics] (2014b) *Family spending: A report on the living costs and food survey 2013*. London: The Stationery Office.

ONS [Office for National Statistics] (2015) *Participation rates in the UK labour market*. Newport: The Office for National Statistics.

ONS [Office for National Statistics] (2016) *Families and households in the UK: 2016*. Newport: The Office for National Statistics.

ONS [Office for National Statistics] (2017) *EMP13. Employment by industry*. https://www.ons.gov.uk/employmentandlabourmarket/peopleinwork/employmentandemployeetypes/datasets/employmentbyindustryemp13

Orben, A. and Przybylski, A.K. (2019) 'Screen, teens, and psychological well-being: Evidence from three time-use-diary studies', *Psychological Science*, vol 30, no 5, pp 682–96.

Orben, A. Dienlin, T., and Przybylski, A.K. (2019) 'Social media's enduring effect on adolescent's life satisfaction', *Proceedings of the National Academy of Sciences of the United States of America*, vol 116, no 21, pp 10226–8.

Orleans, M. and Laney, M.C. (2000) 'Children's computer use in the home', *Social Science Computer Review*, vol 18, no 1, pp 56–72.

Oswald, A.J., Proto, E. and Sgroi, D. (2015) 'Happiness and productivity', *Journal of Labor Economics*, vol 33, no 4, pp 789–822.

Palmer, S. (2007) *Toxic childhood: How the modern world is damaging our children and what we can do about it*. London: Orion.

PHE [Public Health England] (2013) *How heathy behaviour supports children's wellbeing*. London: Public Health England.

Plowman, L. and Stevenson, O. (2012) 'Using mobile phone diaries to explore children's everyday lives', *Childhood*, vol 19, no 4, pp 539–53.

Pooley, C.G., Turnbull, J. and Adams, M. (2005) 'The journey to school in Britain since the 1940s: Continuity and change', *Area*, vol 37, no 1, pp 43–53.

Posel, D. and Grapsa, E. (2017) 'Time to learn? Time allocations among children in South Africa', *International Journal of Education Development*, vol 56, pp 1–10.

Presser, H.B. (1989) 'Can we make time for children? The economy, work schedules, and child care', *Demography*, vol 26, no 4, pp 523–43.

Prout, A. (2005) *The future of childhood*. London: RoutledgeFalmer.

Putnam, R.D. (2015) *Our kids: The American Dream in crisis*. New York: Simon and Schuster.

Qvortrup, J. (1997) 'A voice for children in statistical and social accounting: A plea for children's right to be heard' in A. James and A. Prout (eds) *Constructing and reconstructing childhood*. Abingdon: RoutledgeFalmer.

Qvortrup, J. (2011) 'Childhood as a structural form' in J. Qvortrup, W.A. Corsaroand M-S Honig (eds) *Palgrave handbook of childhood studies*. Basingstoke: Palgrave Macmillan.

Qvortrup, J. (2012) 'The development of childhood: Change and continuity in generational relations', *Sociological Studies of Children and Youth*, vol 12, pp 1–26.

Radesky, J.S., Kistin, C.J., Zuckerman, B., Nitzberg, K., Gross, J., Kaplan-Sanoff, M., Augustyn, M. and Silverstein, M. (2014) 'Patterns of mobile device use by caregivers and children during meals in fast food restaurants', *Pediatrics*, vol 133, no 4, pp e843-e850.

Raine, L. and Wellman, B. (2012) *Networked: The new social operating system*. Cambridge, MA: MIT Press.

Ramey, G. and Ramey, V. (2009) 'The rug rat race', *National Bureau of Economic Research Working Paper 15284*. Cambridge: NBER.

Rees, G. and Main, G. (2016) 'Subjective well-being and mental health', in J. Bradshaw (ed) *The well-being of children in the UK*. Bristol: Policy Press.

Rees, G., Goswami, H. and Bradshaw, J. (2010) *Developing an index of children's subjective well-being in England*. London: The Children's Society.

Richards, L., Garratt, E. and Health, A.F. with Anderson, L. and Altintas, E. (2016) 'The childhood origins of social mobility: socio-economic inequalities and changing opportunities'. London: Social Mobility Commission.

Roberts, A. (1980) *Out to play: The middle years of childhood.* Aberdeen: Aberdeen University Press.

Robinson, J.P. (1985) 'The validity and reliability of diaries versus alternative time use measures' in *Time, goods and wellbeing*, F.T. Juster, and F.P. Stafford (eds). Ann Arbor: University of Michigan.

Robinson, J.P. and Martin, S. (2009) 'Comments on Krueger presentation and article', *Social Indicators Research*, vol 93, no 1, pp 27–30.

Sandberg, J.F. and Hofferth, S.L. (2001) 'Changes in children's time with parents: United States, 1981–1997', *Demography*, vol 38, no 3, pp 423–36.

Sayer, L. C., Bianchi, S. M. and Robinson, J. P. (2004) 'Are parents investing less in children? Trends in mothers' and fathers' time with children', *American Journal of Sociology*, vol 110, no 1, pp 1–43.

Sharp, C., Keys, W. and Benefield, P. (2001) *Homework: A review of recent research.* National Foundation for Educational Research.

Shaw, B., Watson, B., Frauendienst, B., Redecker, A. and Jones, T. with Hillman, M. (2013) *Children's independent mobility: A comparative study in England and German (1971–2010)*, London: Policy Studies Institute.

Shove, E. (2003) 'Converging conventions of comfort, cleanliness and comfort', *Journal of Consumer Policy*, vol 26, no 4, pp 395–418.

Shrewsbury, V. and Wardle, J. (2008) 'Socioeconomic status and adiposity in childhood: A systemic review of cross-sectional studies 1990–2005', *Obesity*, vol 16, no 2, pp 275–84.

Silva, S.K., da Silva Lopes, A., Dumith, S.C., Garcia, L.M.T., Bezerra, J. and Nahus, M.V. (2014) 'Change in television viewing and computers/videogames use among high school students in Southern Brazil between 2001 and 2011', *International Journal of Public Health*, vol 59, no 1, pp 77–86.

Skenazy, L. (2009) *Free-range kids: How to raise safe, self-reliant children (without going nuts with worry)*. San Francisco: Jossey-Bass.

Smith, G. (2000) 'Schools' in A.H. Halsey (ed) *Twentieth-century British Social Trends*. Basingstoke: Macmillan.

Steinberg, L. (2002) 'We know some things: Parent-adolescent relationships in retrospect and prospect', *Journal of Research in Adolescence*, vol 11, no 1, pp 1–19.

Subrahmanyam, K. and Greenfield, P. (2008) 'Online communication and adolescent relationships', *The Future of Children*, vol 18, no 1, pp 119–46.

Suchert, V., Hanewinkel, R. and Isensee, B. (2015) 'Sedentary behaviour and indicators of mental health in school-age children and adolescents: A systemic review', *Preventive Medicine*, vol 76, pp 48–57.

Sullivan, A. (2001) 'Cultural capital and educational attainment', *Sociology*, vol 35, no 4, pp 898–912.

Sullivan, A. (2007) 'Cultural capital, cultural knowledge and ability', *Sociological Research Online*, vol 12, no 6, pp 1–14.

Sullivan, O. (2010) 'Changing differences by educational attainment in fathers' domestic labour and childcare', *Sociology*, vol 44, no 4, pp 716–33.

Taylor, E.A. and Scott, J. (2018) 'Gender: New consensus or continuing battleground?' in D. Phillips, J. Curtice, M. Phillips and J. Perry (eds) *British Social Attitudes: The 35th Report*. London: The National Centre for Social Research.

The Children's Society (2013) *The Good Childhood Report 2013*, London: The Children's Society.

The Children's Society (2017) *The Good Childhood Report 2017*. London: The Children's Society.

Thompson, R., Berriman, L. and Bragg, S. (2018) *Researching everyday childhoods: Time, technology and documentation in a digital age.* London: Bloomsbury.

Tremblay, M.S., LeBlanc, A.G., Kho, M.E., Saunders, T.J., Larouche, R., Colley, R.C., Goldfield, G. and Gorber, S.C. (2011) 'Systematic review of sedentary behaviour and health indicators in school-aged children and youth', *International Journal of Behavioural Nutrition and Physical Activity*, vol 8, no 98, pp 1–22.

Turkle, S. (2011) *Alone together: Why we expect more from technology and less from each other.* New York: Basic Books.

UNICEF (2007) 'Child poverty in perspective: An overview of child well-being in rich countries.' Innocenti Report Card 7, 2007. Florence: UNICEF Innocenti Research Centre.

UNISON (2016) *The Damage: A future at risk, cuts in youth services.* London: Unison.

Vagni, G. and Cornwell, B. (2018) 'Patterns of everyday activities across social contexts', *Proceedings of the National Academy of Sciences of the United States of America*, vol 115, no 24, pp 6183–8.

Valentine, G. 1997 ' "Oh yes I can." "Oh no you can't.": Children and parents' understandings of kids' competence to negotiate public space safely', *Antipode,* vol 29, no 1, pp 65–89.

Valentine, G. (2004) *Public space and the culture of childhood.* Aldershot: Ashgate.

Valentine, G. and McKendrick, J. (1997) 'Children's outdoor play: Exploring parental concerns about children's safety and the changing nature of childhood', *GeoForum*, vol 28, no 2, pp 219–35.

Waldfogel, J. (2006) *What children need.* London: Harvard University Press.

Weston, P. (1999) *Homework: Learning from practice.* London: The Stationery Office.

Williams, A. L. and Merten, M. J. (2011) 'iFamily: Internet and social media technology in the family context', *Family and Consumer Sciences Research Journal*, vol 40, no 2, pp 150–70.

Wyness, M.G. (2006) *Childhood and society: An introduction to the sociology of childhood.* Basingstoke: Palgrave Macmillan.

Zuzanek, J. (2005) 'Adolescent time use and well-being from a comparative perspective', *Society and Leisure*, vol 28, no 2, pp 379–423.

Index

Note: *Italic* page numbers indicate figures and tables

A

active travel time
  decrease in 22, 61, 72–4, 75, 78
  enjoyment of 152–3, *154*
  links to sport and screen time *78*
  and parental engagement in sport *82*
affective component of subjective
    well-being 145–6
age differences
  change in influence of 171–2
  in enjoyment of activities 151–2
  and time use 170–1
Alanen, L., Finnish study 8
alone time 132–5
  enjoyment of 154–5
  increase in 142, 143
  and time using devices 135–6, *137*
  while parents use devices 138
art galleries, visits to 21–2, 31–3,
    45–6, 56
assessment in primary schools 28, 29
attainment gap, socio-economic 29–30
  and cultural capital 30–2
attainment pressures 27–9, 33

B

BBC survey (1974–75) 14, 15, 18
  Family Occupational Status
    (FOC) 16–17
Bourdieu, Pierre, cultural capital 21,
    30–1, 32, 42, 49, 51, 56

C

Canadian adolescents, time pressure
    experiences 157–8, 159–60
Cheng, L.A., time spent eating
    together 106–107
Children's Commissioner for England,
    role of 9

Christensen, P.
  negative views of school 149
  study of children's time use 8
cinema visits 45–6, 47–9, *50*
classes *see* school time
computers 117–18
  increase in ownership 60–1
  times spent using 120–3
cultural activities
  children's participation in 45–9
  and daily time use 51–3
  and parent engagement in 48–51
cultural capital 30–1
  and educational outcomes 30–1, 56
  institutionalised 30–1, 42, 44, 175–6
  link between parent and child
    reading 42, *44*
  role of libraries in developing 45
  transmission from parent to child 31–2
  see also parental education
cycling *see* active travel time

D

data from time use surveys 14–16
day reconstruction method
    (DRM) 146–7
device use 122–4
  and children's time alone 133–6, 138,
    142, 143
  concerns over 120, 123, 126
    negative link to sport time 129–30
  during time in other activities 126–9
  enjoyment of time 156–7
  by parents 133–7
    during parent-child shared
      time 137–40
  screen time measure 125–6
  social context 135–6
DiMaggio, P., cultural activities 32
domestic activities, trends in 103–105

E

eating time *19*
  enjoyment of *150, 157*
    and device use 139, 156, *157*
    and social context 154–5
  shared with family 106–10, 115,
    139, *140*
education 27–33
  key indicator of socio-economic
    background 17
  social science perspectives 7–8
  see also cultural capital
education-related activities
  children's reading time 37–42
    link between parent and child
      reading 42–5
  school, homework and study time 33–7
  time spent in *19*
  see also cultural activities
enjoyment of time use 148
  for different activities 149–52
    modes of travel 152–3, *154*
  in different social contexts 153–6
    shared TV watching 155
    sport and other non-screen
      leisure 155–6
    when using and not using a
      device 156–7
  eating *150*, 154–5, *157*
  measurement issues 147–8
exercise *see* sport
experience sampling method (ESM) 146
experience of time, subjective 25,
    146–9, 151–2
  time pressure 157–9

F

face-to-face interactions, influence of
    mobile devices on 120
family meals 115
  decrease in duration of 110
  enjoyment of time during 155
  participation in 106, 108, *109*
Family Occupational Status (FOC),
    BBC 1975 survey 16–17
family time 87–8
  children's activities in context 97–105
    domestic activities 103–104
    homework, study and
      reading 101–103
    non-screen leisure 104–105
    screen time 98–101
  children's time at home with and
    without parents 88–97
  shared activities 105–13
    device use disrupting 137, 139–40
    eating together 106–10

    TV watching 110–13
feelings *see* subjective well-being
free-time activities 21
  teenagers' enjoyment of 146
  time spent in *19*

G

'Gamergate' controversy 141
games
  out-of-home play 69–72
  see also video games
gender differences 5–6
  in cultural activities 46–7
  device use 125, 129
  happiness levels relating to
    schoolwork 151
  homework time 30, 35, 151
  in mental health problems 62
  reading time 38, 40, 54
  in school attainment 21, 30, 32
  in screen time 66, 83, 99, 122, 171
  shared time watching TV 111
  sporting activities 69, 76, 83
  time pressures 162
  time spent in domestic activities 103–104
  video game playing 141, 171
Gershuny, J., time use survey
    (2014–15) 14
Grapsa, E., children's reports of time
    pressure 157–8

H

happiness 145–8
Harmonised European Time Use Survey
    (HETUS) guidelines 15
health 59–63, 80–5
  link between sport and screen
    time 75–9
  parental influence 79–80
  physical activities 66–74
    active travel 72–4
    out-of-door play 69–72
    sport and exercise 66–9
  screen-time trends 63–6
  see also mental health issues; well-being
    of children
higher education
  expansion in 17
  parental 35, 42–3, *48*, 55, 99–101,
    118, 119–20
  qualifications for 29, 30
Hilbrecht, M., time pressure in
    adolescents 158
Hillman, Mayer, children's independent
    mobility 1–2, 61
Hofferth, S.L., changes in children's time
    with parents 89

homework time 28–9
 and cultural activities 51–3
 enjoyment of 150
 gender differences 30, 35, *41*, 151
 and maternal employment *103*
 and parental education 35, *36*, 37, 55,
  98, *102*
 socio-economic disparities 30
 and time pressure 159–60
 trends in 33–7
 and use of devices 127–9
housework
 gender differences 171
 link to feeling rushed *160*
 relative enjoyment of *150*, 151
  and device use *157*
  when with others 154, *155*
 time children spend doing *19*, 20

I

independent mobility of children,
  reduction in 2, 61
internet access 60–1, 117–19, 123, 124,
  130–1, 168–9

J

James, A
 children's views of school 149
 study of children's time use 8
 'time of childhood' 9

K

Kahneman, Daniel, day reconstruction
  method 146–7

L

leisure time 21
 context-dependent enjoyment
  of 97
 enjoyment of non-screen *150*
 and parental engagement in sport *82*
 see also screen time
libraries 45
 children's visits to 46
 as cultural intermediaries 45
 fall in visits to 46, 48, 49, 50, 53, 54
 gender differences in use of 46–7
 links to reading and homework/study
  times 52
 parent and child participation 49, *50*
 and parental education *48*, 50–1
 parental visits to 49, *50*
Livingstone, Sonia 60, 64, 117, 143

M

Main, G., mental health problems 59–60

Marshall, S.J., time watching TV 121
maternal employment
 and children's enjoyment of different
  activities 151–2
 and decrease in shared eating
  107–108
 and education-related activities
  102–103
 and feelings of time pressure in
  children 159
 increased time in 90
 and screen time 101
 and shared TV time 111–13
 and time children spend at
  home 96–7, 115
meeting places (physical) for children,
  reduction in 142–3
mental health issues 59–62
Mestdag, I, family meal times 106–107
misogyny in video game culture 141
mobile phone ownership 118–19, 124
 and time using devices on school
  days 124
 see also smartphones
Mullis, I.V.S., homework time 29
multivariate regression analysis 16, 18
museum visits 31, 45–6, 54

N

negative affect, need for measure of 148
negative trends in health
  outcomes 60, 61–2
non-screen leisure time 103–105
 and engagement in sport *78*
 enjoyment of 155–6
 and parental engagement in sport *82*
 and time pressure *160*

O

obesity concerns 59, 62, 80–1, 83
objective well-being 145
occupation-based measure of social
  class 17
Ofcom
 device use by children 123
 TV watching alone 110
Office for National Statistics (ONS)
 children's well being report
  (2014) 145, 146
 time use survey (2000–01) 14
One False Move (Hillman) 61
organised sporting activities 61, 67, 72
outcomes of children's time use 7–12
outdoor physical activity/play, less time
  spent in 1–2, 60, 61, 70
overview of child's day 18–21

P

parental education
  and active travel time 74
  and children's device access 119
  and children's homework time 35, *36*, 37, 55, *102*
  and children's time at home with parents 92, *93–4*
  and internet and computer access *118*, 119
  and mobile phone ownership 119–20
  and 'out-of-home' play time 70–2
  and participation in cultural activities 47–51, 53
  and screen time trends 64–6, 83, 99–100
  and shared eating time 108, *109*
  and shared TV time 111, *112*, 113
  and sport time 67–9
  and time parents devote to children 89–90
  and time pressure among children 159
  and time spent reading *38–9*, 40, *41*, 42–3, *44*, 55, *102*
parents' time use
  on devices 136–40
  influence on children's time use 175–6
  see also family time
personal care activities, time spent in 19–20
physical activities
  active travel 72–4
  gender differences in 62
  link to improved health outcomes 60
  out-of-door play 69–72
  vs sedentary activities 61–2
  see also sport
playing outside, less time spent in 1–2, 60, 61, 70
Posel, D., children's reports of time pressure 157–8
post-compulsory education *see* higher education
Prout, A., 'time of childhood' 9

Q

qualifications
  children's increased grades 27
  of parents 18, 22, 31
  socio-economic disparities 29

R

reading time 37–42
  and device use 127, *128*
  in different contexts 101–103
  and educational outcome 32
  and engagement in cultural activities 31–2, 51–3
  enjoyment of *150*
  gender difference in 54, 151
  gender differences *39*, *41*
  link between parent and child reading 42–5, 175–6
  and maternal employment *103*
  and parental education *39*, *41*, *44*, 55, 98, *102*
  reading for pleasure 30, 37
  role of library visits in promoting 52–3
  school and non-school days *38*
  versus homework and study time 54, 167
recall-based measures of time use 12–13
Rees, G
  mental health problems 59–60
  subjective well-being 145–6, 147
Register General Social Class (RGSC) 16–17
retrospective questions about happiness, bias in responses to 146
rights of children 9

S

safety concerns 4
  effect on children's independent mobility 61
  and increase in screen-based activities 23, 62
  and increase in time spent at home with parents 88, 114
  limiting active travel/time spent outdoors 22, 83
  and reduction in outdoor physical activities 61
  and time spent playing outside 71, 72
Sandberg, J.F., changes in children's time with parents 89
'scholarisation' of childhood 6
school time 33–4
  enjoyment of 149, *150*, 151–2
screen time 22–3, 63–6, 120–6, 167–8
  in context 98–101
  enjoyment of 150
  extended measure of 125–6
  gender differences 66, 83, 99, 122, 171
  link to mental health issues 60
  and parental education 64–6, 83, 99–100
  and physical activity 84, 173–4
  sedentary activity 61–2
  and sport 75–80, *82*, 84, 129–30
  see also device use
sedentary activities

increase in vs physical activity
    outdoors 60–1
see also screen time
shared family activities *see* family time
    television viewing 110–13
Shaw, B., children's independent
    mobility 61
shopping by children
    in 2000, more time spent on 104,
        114, 168
    during 2000–2015, less time
        spent on 104
    enjoyment of *150*, 151, *156*
    see also housework
Skenazy, Lenore, safe raising of children 4
sleep time, changes in 18–19
smartphones
    ownership 117, 118–19
    and internet access 118, 119
    parental use of when with
        children 137, 143–4
    time children spend using 120,
        123, *124*
    to interact with friends and
        family 131, 143
social change and time use
    change 166–73
social class, measures of 16–17
social construction
    of the ageing process 9
    of childhood 3, 171–2
    of gender differences 172
social context of children's time use 23
    influence on enjoyment of time 153–7
    influence of technology 130–40, 174–5
social interactions, technology eroding
    quality of 130–1
social media
    eroding social interaction time 131
    increasing pressure on appearance 20
socio-economic background 16, 172–3
    and children's health outcomes 83
    overweight and obesity risk 62
    education as a key indicator of 17
    in school attainment 29–30
    and cultural capital 30–1
    and screen time 64, 83
    and time spent on educational
        activities 55
    see also parental education
sport
    enjoyment of *150*
    gender differences 76–7, 83
    influence of parents' engagement
        in 79–80, *81*
    organised vs informal out-of-home
        play 72, *73*

and screen time 75–80, *82*, 84
    time children spend playing 66–9
sports events
    children's attendance of 45–8
    parents' attendance 48–9, *50*
statistical analysis 16–18
'structural' perspective on children 3
study time *see* homework time;
    reading time
subjective experience of time use 146
    methods of capturing 146–7
    time pressure 157–60
    vs global assessments of happiness 147–8
subjective well-being 145–9
    enjoyment of daily activities 149–53
    enjoyment and social context 153–7
Sullivan, A., cultural capital
    and educational attainment 31–2
    and reading 44–5
Sullivan, Oriel, time use survey
    (2014–15) 14

T

tablets
    for internet access at home 118,
        119, *124*
    ownership by children 117
    time spent using 120, 122–4
technological change 4
    and increase in children's time at
        home 88
    and increase in sedentary activities 60–1
        vs time physical activities 75
    and shared TV viewing time 110–11
    see also screen time
technology 117–20
    and change in social context of daily
        life 130–5
        children's increased 'alone' time 135–6
        parents' time using devices 136–40
    device use by children versus other
        activities 126–9
        impact on physical activity 129–30
    trends in screen time 120–2
        device use 122–4
        extended screen time measure 125–6
testing in primary schools 27–8, 29
theatre visits 31–2, 45
time pressure among children 157–9
    and time use patterns 159–60
time use measures 12–14
time use surveys 13, 14
    see also UK Time Use Surveys
travel modes
    enjoyment of different 152–3
    time spent in different 73, *74*
    see also active travel time

TV watching, decrease in shared 110–13

U

UK Time Use Surveys 15, 24, 25
  access to home computers and
      internet 117–18
  device use 123, 125
  engagement in sport 75–6
  general time pressure 158
  subjective experience of time 147
  subjective well-being 148
  time spent with 'co-present' others 132
United Nations Convention on the
    Rights of the Child (1991) 9

V

Vandeweyer, J., family meal
    times 106–107
video games

gender differences 141
time spent playing 121–2, 125

W

walking *see* active travel time
weight concerns 59, 60, 62
well-being of children
  measurement of 165–6
  subjective well-being 145–9
    enjoyment of daily activities 149–53
    enjoyment and social context 153–7
  see also health
work
  time children spend in paid work *19*, 20
  see also maternal employment

Z

Zuzanek, J., time pressure in Canadian
    adolescents 157, 159

www.ingramcontent.com/pod-product-compliance
Lightning Source LLC
Chambersburg PA
CBHW070926030426
42336CB00014BA/2559